Global Chicago

Global Chicago

Edited by Charles Madigan

PUBLISHED WITH THE CHICAGO COUNCIL ON FOREIGN RELATIONS

UNIVERSITY OF ILLINOIS PRESS

URBANA AND CHICAGO

Frontispiece: Noted for its innovative architecture, Chicago has
transformed itself many times since its incorporation in 1837.
Here, workers place a beam on a building under construction
near I-55 and Damen Avenue. Chicago construction rates have
boomed over the past two decades. Photograph by Robert
Davis. Copyright 2003 by Davis Designs Enterprises, Inc.
Courtesy of the Comer Archive of Chicago in the Year 2000,
Richard J. Daley Library, University of Illinois at Chicago.

Library of Congress Cataloging-in-Publication Data
Global Chicago / edited by Charles Madigan.
    p.   cm.
"Published with the Chicago Council on Foreign Relations."
Includes bibliographical references and index.
ISBN 0-252-02941-0 (cloth : alk. paper)
ISBN 0-252-07196-4 (pbk. : alk. paper)
1. Chicago (Ill.)—Civilization.
2. Chicago (Ill.)—Relations—Foreign countries.
I. Madigan, Charles.
F548.52.G56   2004
977.3'11—dc22   2004002532

CONTENTS

Illustrations follow page 142

⊕

THE STORY OF CHICAGO has always been the story of a city that thrived against the odds.

In the nineteenth century Chicago transformed itself from a swampy trading post to a great industrial city in seven decades. It put meat on the American table. It opened the door to mail-order abundance for a growing nation. It became the home address for countless thousands of people from around the world who settled in the Midwest in the quest for a better life.

In the twentieth century, as capital of the Rust Belt, it should have foundered when the nation's industrial base collapsed and manufacturing started its steep decline. Instead, Chicago reinvented itself as a capital of services of all kinds.

It is in the process of reinventing itself once again.

This is what I discovered upon my return to Chicago in 2001. I first came here as a graduate student studying South Asia. I returned twenty-five years later to become president of the Chicago Council on Foreign Relations, and I found a city with ever more extensive connections to the world, a city made stronger by immigrants from around the globe, and a city made more vital and attractive to live in by a mayor with vision and energy. In short, Chicago is a city on the move.

To my mind, there have been only two truly global cities in the world, New York and London, and they have held their titles for years. But I believe Chicago is well along the pathway to joining them. To be sure, there are those who argue (and argue the case strongly in this volume) that Chicago has already won its "global city" status, and that now its job is to work that much harder to make certain its connections to the world grow.

I have my concerns. Where will Chicago find the economic growth that it will need to thrive in the future? How will it raise its value and visibility as a dynamic, innovative center for global commerce, communication, and culture? How will it keep from becoming "Global-Lite," a city that has what it needs to play a strong role on the world stage—that even looks global— but just can't compete with London and New York because it doesn't know how to leverage and project its own considerable strengths?

Looking at it objectively, the city certainly has the rich array of skills and capacities it needs to meet the challenge, in its businesses and its universities, in its people and neighborhoods, and in governmental and nongovernmental leaders. Its rich cultural and arts scene and its quality of life are powerful assets in a fierce global competition to attract investment and talented individuals. But subjectively, Chicago sometimes doesn't seem to recognize and make the best of these. It remains in some respects a fragmented community, but its principal problem is often its hesitancy to tap fully its diversity and use it to connect globally.

For the truly global city, diversity is an asset to be constantly celebrated and nurtured, so integral that it defines a place more than it describes it.

· · ·

This book has grown from an initiative of the John D. and Catherine T. MacArthur Foundation. The MacArthur Foundation has a deep commitment to Chicago. It also works in eighty-five countries and wanted to learn more about the ways in which its hometown, Chicago, was connected to the world. Two reports, one by Richard Longworth (an author of a chapter in this book), then of the *Chicago Tribune,* and the other by Sharon Morris of the MacArthur Foundation staff, documented what some knew already: Chicago's global assets were tremendous but often unknown and more often underutilized.

The city's leading global players from universities, business, labor, and civil society who came together to discuss the reports were meeting for the first time. It was not long before they had established an organization, Global Chicago, and a Web site. A book to give some visibility to Chicago's global resources and connections was an obvious next step.

Global Chicago's mission was simple: to enhance Chicago's strengths as a global city and to raise awareness, both here and abroad, of its global connections by:

1. identifying Chicago's local-global assets and its economic, social, intellectual, and cultural links to the rest of the world;

2. facilitating communication and collaboration among internationally minded groups; and

3. helping Chicagoans understand the challenges and opportunities of globalization.

Henry H. Perritt Jr., then dean of the Chicago-Kent College of Law at the Illinois Institute of Technology, helped to establish the organization by creating the Web site and housing the program. Then in February 2002, in order to bring the concept to an even wider audience inside and outside Chicago, Global Chicago merged with the Chicago Council on Foreign Relations.

The Chicago Council on Foreign Relations presents in this book a variety of perspectives on Chicago's character and role as a global city, and on the connections between Chicago and the world. The authors recognize that the impact of globalization on Chicago and the way the city is responding is a complex story that has to be seen from multiple perspectives. Assembling these essays into a cohesive whole was not an easy task, and my thanks go to Charles Madigan who persuaded many of the authors to contribute to the project, edited the volume, and brought it to completion.

This book is not meant to be a comprehensive examination of all the ways in which Chicago is (or is not) a global city. Here we attempt only to introduce some of the global connections and convey the complexity of the issues. There are gaps. Each reader will certainly know of examples, perspectives, or connections that have not been included. It is our hope that you will share them with us and with others at <www.globalchicago.org>.

While Chicagoans should celebrate our globalizing city, we cannot be complacent. To keep up with the world, to remain a draw for people and businesses, we need to be intentional about addressing the gaps in Chicago's capacity to connect in multifaceted and highly adaptive ways to the rest of the globe. The following pages explore aspects of a city that is both thriving and suffering from the impact of forces outside its borders. We hope that readers will be encouraged to learn more.

My own hope is that the analyses and viewpoints presented here will help to raise awareness of Chicago's great accomplishments and of what must be done to ensure its future. That is an ambitious goal, I know, but one that is not at all beyond the reach of a city that has always found a way to beat even the toughest odds.

> Marshall Bouton
> President
> The Chicago Council on Foreign Relations

ACKNOWLEDGMENTS

FOR ONE PERSON, it is never easy to write a book. Adding many people to the task doesn't make it any easier, and thus abundant thanks must go to the authors of these chapters, whose names are, of course, attached. Global Chicago thanks them for their diligence and their patience with a long and sometimes arduous process. Now there is a book, and it stands as a tribute to those who wrote it.

In the course of events, the works of some contributors fell by the wayside, for no reason other than the fact that producing such a book is always a question of what to cut more than a question of what to allow. Initial proposals change over time; subjects are dropped and others are added. An endless number of chapters would have allowed them all to appear here. It also would have made the book too big to carry and, however interesting, broad beyond its mission. Thanks go to Maria de los Angeles Torres and Theodoric Manley Jr., both of DePaul University, to business writer Bob Yovovich, and especially to Sapna Gupta for their assistance in shaping this volume.

Global Chicago got a great deal of support from the outside on this book project. It would have gone nowhere without the John D. and Catherine T. MacArthur Foundation, the Chicago Community Trust, Chicago-Kent College of Law at the Illinois Institute of Technology, the Chicago Council on Foreign Relations, and the McCormick Tribune Foundation.

Insiders were crucial, too, in getting the project under way and seeing it through. Among them, Michael H. Moskow, president and chief executive officer of the Federal Reserve Bank of Chicago (and a contributor to the book), lent his support, enthusiasm, and encouragement as chairman of

Global Chicago. Adele Simmons, vice president and senior executive of Chicago Metropolis 2020 (and a contributor), provided the vision and the patience; Marshall Bouton, president and chief executive officer of the Chicago Council on Foreign Relations, provided financial and moral support; William A. Testa (a contributor), vice president and senior economist at the Federal Reserve Bank of Chicago, shared his economic brilliance and deep historical knowledge; Michael Diamond, then executive director of the Global Chicago Center of the Chicago Council on Foreign Relations, provided light and heat during the effort's darkest, coldest moments; Willis Regier, director of the University of Illinois Press, read the manuscript and gently proclaimed what simply did not work; Henry Perritt Jr., vice provost, professor of law, and director of the Center for Law and Financial Markets at Illinois Institute of Technology, counseled author, editor, and contributors alike; and Richard C. Longworth, formerly a senior correspondent of the *Chicago Tribune* and now executive director of the Global Chicago Center, wrote a visionary essay on Global Chicago that was at the heart of the process.

In its earliest stages, Global Chicago created a book project advisory committee, which was fueled by the thoughts and contributions of Eileen Mackevich, president and chief executive officer of the Chicago Humanities Festival; Maria de los Angeles Torres, mentioned earlier, an associate professor at DePaul University and one of the earliest proponents of this effort; Saskia Sassen, a professor at the University of Chicago and a chapter contributor; Paul O'Connor, executive director of World Business Chicago; Marti Rabinowitch, the first executive director of Global Chicago, who initiated the book project and guided it through its earliest days; Sandra Bozis, administrative assistant at the Global Chicago Center (who, amazingly, kept all the files, all the essay versions, and all the correspondence in perfect order); and Robert Cordes, vice president of the Chicago Council on Foreign Relations, who provided legal help.

Global Chicago

Chicago Region

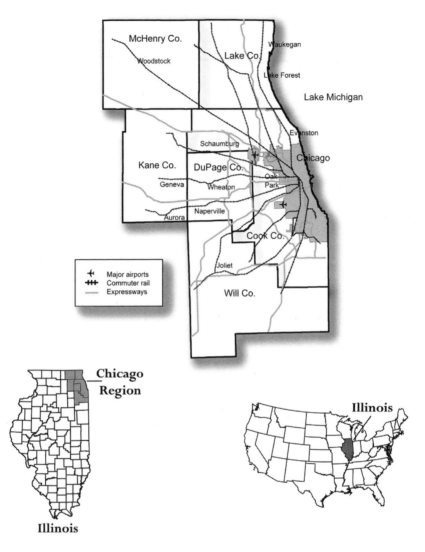

Map 1. Chicago Region

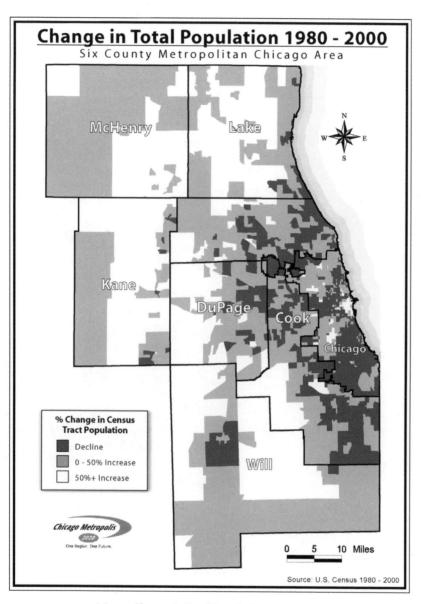

Change in Total Population 1980 - 2000
Six County Metropolitan Chicago Area

McHenry

Lake

N
W   E
S

Kane

DuPage

Cook

Chicago

% Change in Census Tract Population
- Decline
- 0 - 50% Increase
- 50%+ Increase

Chicago Metropolis
2020
One Region. One Future.

Will

0   5   10 Miles

Source: U.S. Census 1980 - 2000

Map 2. Change in Total Population, 1980–2000

Research maps immigrant population

A new study showing immigrant population by state House district suggests that suburban legislators need to be more aware of foreign-born residents' needs.

NUMBER OF FOREIGN-BORN RESIDENTS
By state House district

KEY:
- 0 to 3,200
- 3,201 to 9,000
- 9,001 to 18,500
- More than 18,500

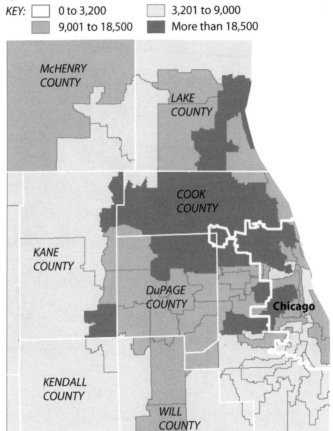

McHENRY COUNTY

LAKE COUNTY

COOK COUNTY

KANE COUNTY

DuPAGE COUNTY

Chicago

KENDALL COUNTY

WILL COUNTY

Source: Roosevelt University Institute for Metropolitan Affairs, National Center on Poverty Law

Chicago Tribune

Map 3. Immigrant Population

2000 Hispanic Percentage Population by Cities and Towns in the Chicago Metro Area

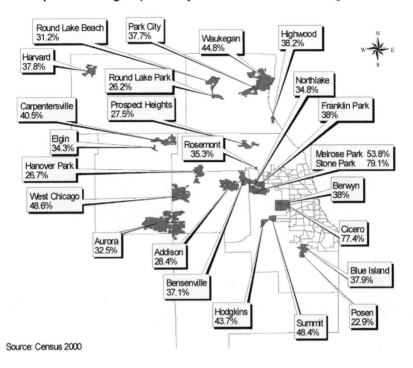

Round Lake Beach
31.2%

Park City
37.7%

Waukegan
44.8%

Highwood
38.2%

Harvard
37.8%

Round Lake Park
26.2%

Northlake
34.8%

Carpentersville
40.5%

Prospect Heights
27.5%

Franklin Park
38%

Elgin
34.3%

Rosemont
35.3%

Melrose Park 53.8%
Stone Park 79.1%

Hanover Park
26.7%

West Chicago
48.6%

Berwyn
38%

Cicero
77.4%

Aurora
32.5%

Addison
28.4%

Blue Island
37.9%

Bensenville
37.1%

Hodgkins
43.7%

Summit
48.4%

Posen
22.9%

Source: Census 2000

Map 4. 2000 Hispanic Percentage of Population by Cities and Towns in the Chicago Metro Area

INTRODUCTION

Adele Simmons

IN CHICAGO, my hometown, the local florist's lilies may come from Holland, the grocer's grapes from Chile, the computer assembler's chips from Taiwan, the bicyclist's brakes from Japan. While those goods are flying in, Chicago academics are flying out—to advise the governments of Chile, Indonesia, and Nigeria, to name a few. Scientists from all over the world gather to conduct experiments at our laboratories—particularly Argonne National and Fermi Laboratory—and human rights activists from every continent doff their hats to their comrades here, without whom the new International Criminal Court might not exist. Chicagoans import and export goods, ideas, and people hourly. To us, this is no big deal.

The fact that Chicago has become one of the world's great global cities has yet to impress most Chicagoans, in part because the global fabric is so thickly woven here. In a city with 130 non-English newspapers, where an emergency call to 911 can be responded to in 150 languages, a foreign tongue turns few heads. Similarly, no face seems out of place—each one seems legitimate for a Chicagoan. (We concede native status without much regard for nativity. If you're here, not living in a hotel, and not wearing any Green Bay Packers paraphernalia, we assume you're one of us.) Immigrants make up 22 percent of the city's population and they send an estimated $1.8 billion annually to the families they've left behind. Entire villages depend on that Chicago money. To us, this is old news. People have always come. Money has always gone back.

A Chicagoan who favors a local Korean dry cleaner, the Thai restaurant down at the corner, and an Eastern European tradesman recommended by a neighbor is unlikely to pay much notice to the Loop offices of foreign multi-nationals like Société Générale, Sumitomo Bank, and ABN Amro. Similarly, the consular offices of seventy nations, clustered mostly around the Loop, make few Chicagoans ponder the city's place in the world. We expect those diplomats to be here. And city residents traveling abroad don't think twice anymore when they see the logo of some hometown corporation—McDonald's, Motorola, Boeing, and the Bulls, to name a few. We expect them to be there too.

The curiosity of the native Chicagoan might have been aroused recently when two candidates for the office of governor of the Mexican state of Michoacán campaigned for votes here. Then again, Chicagoans are accustomed to candidates trolling far and wide for votes, sometimes even into the afterlife, and thus the Mexican campaign may have appeared more like Cook County politics than anything particularly foreign. Similarly, the globalization of crime seems not so new here. Yes, we have ethnically varied criminal networks, but we've had those before. We have immigrants exploited in the workplace, but that too is not new. The exploiters may have changed and the number of exploited may have increased, but the act is an old one.

We're a tough crowd. We don't impress ourselves. We've become an economic and cultural powerhouse, a commercial and artistic center of growing international importance. Mayor Richard M. Daley created World Business Chicago to promote the city to business investors from all over the world and to ensure that foreign trade delegations connect with the right partners in Chicago. Foreign delegations routinely stop by city hall for a chat, where they may board elevators with German architects filing their drawings, Irish contractors applying for building permits, or Italian restaurateurs petitioning for liquor licenses. Globalization touches all of our lives daily, sometimes hourly. Most of us take no notice at all.

The goal of *Global Chicago* is to make us see ourselves and our place in the world, to help us understand how we have absorbed global influences, how we have come to play myriad roles on the international stage, and how we are daily making a difference in lives all over the planet.

Global before "Globalization"

Chicago's interaction with the world began long before "globalization" became a buzzword, embraced by some and reviled by others. From its inception in the 1770s as a fur-trading post founded by Jean-Baptiste Point du

Sable, an immigrant from Sainte-Domingue (Haiti), Chicago has been a place where cultures, languages, and traditions have mixed.

Here, Native Americans intermingled with settlers from France, Great Britain, and Germany. Rather than being hurt by being situated in what was then the western part of the American territories, the outpost profited from its location at the mouth of a river flowing into the largest body of water in the region. It was this fortuitous location that helped transform a fur-trading outpost into a national hub for transportation. Transportation brought immigrants, and those immigrants brought skills, and those skills have built a metropolitan area that is home to more than eight million residents.

The 1893 World's Columbian Exposition in Chicago set in motion the city's transformation into the gleaming, bustling metropolis it is today. The exposition's Chicago organizers staged the grandest and most memorable world's fair ever held. They broke new ground in showcasing each country— the exhibits were designed by the members of each exhibiting country and not by Americans. As a result, each exhibit represented its country's particular sensibility and how its people saw themselves—rather than how Americans saw them. Chicagoans were thus infected with new ideas and perspectives. The Ho Ho Den building in the Japanese Village, for example, profoundly influenced Frank Lloyd Wright, and he incorporated elements of the building's design in his renowned Prairie style of architecture. Nearly three decades later, the Japanese hired Wright to design the Imperial Hotel in Tokyo, completed in 1922—a neatly closed loop of Chicagoans influenced by the world and the world influenced by Chicagoans.

That pattern repeated itself in industry, science, religion, and the arts in the decades that followed. Fifty years after the exposition, within a mile of the site where Wright had been inspired, a team of physicists led by the Italian refugee physicist Enrico Fermi created the world's first self-sustaining nuclear reaction. The experiment, staged under the football stadium at the University of Chicago, redefined energy development, altered the terms of international conflict, and changed the course of diplomacy around the world.

A hundred years after the exposition, the World's Parliament of Religions, one of the enduring legacies of the Chicago fair, marked its centennial by forging a consensual document entitled "Towards a Global Ethic." Commonly referred to as "The Chicago Declaration," the document is a pledge to work for a just social and economic order, for mutual understanding among peoples and nations, and for a recognition of the interdependence of all living things.

Global Chicago at Work

A glimpse into the life of Chicago and its citizens during one spring month in 2002 shows the international dimension of everyday activities of individuals from all walks of life.

Business

On a typical day in May, Robert Langlois, director of international relations at Motorola, walks into his office in Schaumburg at seven in the morning. "I get in early so that I have a few hours of overlap with my colleagues working in Europe, Africa, and the Middle East," he says.

On this particular morning, Langlois checks his e-mail and responds to a message from a colleague at the company's production facility in Israel. He calls the Moscow office to talk about the sale of Motorola pagers. He then calls Cairo and talks with the country manager for Egypt. At 10:30 A.M., he leaves his office for downtown Chicago, where he attends a luncheon for the vice president of Botswana. After lunch, he calls on the South African consulate to discuss that government's order of Motorola walkie-talkies. He ends the day by giving a talk on the international business climate to a group of young professionals.

In the Loop offices of Perkins and Will, one of Chicago's most respected architectural, interior design, and planning firms, William Doerge and Ralph Johnson have spent a good portion of the same day negotiating the timeline for construction of a university in Luanda, Angola. Eighteen of their colleagues in the Chicago office work on the project, while five others are in Mumbai, India, where they are retrofitting an existing concrete structure to accommodate a hospital. A dozen other international projects are in various stages of planning and completion. The firm, which is accustomed to exporting expertise, has no hesitation to import it as well. Consultants from Britain advised Perkins and Will on the design of two green "sustainable" projects— a middle school in Bloomington, Indiana, and a courthouse in Los Angeles.

While Perkins and Will is planning for the Angolan university, Flying Food Group is dispatching meals all over the globe. FFG was founded in Chicago by Sue Ling Gin in 1983, and it now caters meals for twenty-eight international airlines that fly out of Chicago's airports. During the month of May, the O'Hare kitchen alone made 183,598 meals. Says Gin, "Flying Food Group is a global company not only in its sales, but in its people. The 1,800 people who work for us come from all over the world, so we are truly global from production to sales to end users."

Minority-owned Blackwell Consulting Services, Inc., has a similarly international workforce. Blackwell employs natives of Cuba, Russia, India, Ireland, and Venezuela to advise clients on management and information technology, and this May they are laboring on a project for a local client, Waste Management. "Our clients call us the League of Nations," says Bob Blackwell, founder and CEO of the Chicago-based firm. "Our employees come from around the world and each person brings something different to the team. We do better work because of our diversity."

Medicine and Science

In early May, Dr. Robert Murphy, who works in the infectious diseases lab at Northwestern University, is preparing to leave for the 2002 HIV/AIDS conference in Barcelona. One of the world's leading HIV/AIDS treatment researchers, Murphy is the only non–French citizen to serve on France's Conseil d'Administration, Objectif Recherche Vaccin SIDA, a committee for the discovery of a therapeutic AIDS vaccine. Working with Dr. Toyin Falusi, a Nigerian who directs HIV/AIDS clinical research at Cook County Hospital, Murphy recently established the Nigerian Adult Clinical Trials Group (NACTG) in Ibadan, a city sixty miles north of Lagos, Nigeria. The goal of the Nigerian project is to set up an AIDS treatment infrastructure to be run by Nigerians for Nigerians. To that end, AIDS specialists from Chicago will spend two weeks in Nigeria and their Nigerian colleagues will spend three weeks at three Chicago hospitals. Murphy will head to Masai country in Kenya where he is helping a local doctor upgrade a general clinic so it can treat HIV/AIDS patients.

While that AIDS treatment infrastructure is being planned on the city's north and west sides, Dr. Olufunmilayo Olopade, another native of Nigeria, is working on the South Side. Olopade directs a clinical and laboratory research program in cancer genetics at the University of Chicago's School of Medicine. She is investigating why black women develop breast cancer at younger ages and why they suffer higher mortality rates from cancer than other population groups. Her research in Chicago and Nigeria will eventually examine the genetic material of 100,000 women who developed breast cancer before the age of forty-five.

At the Field Museum in May 2002, Debbie Moskovitz, director of the museum's Environment and Conservation Program, is talking on the phone with Alaka Wali, curator of the museum's Center for Cultural Understanding and Change. Wali is in Peru meeting with residents of Tocache, a town in the Huallaga Valley, and with staff from local nongovernmental organizations (NGOs). To ensure the protection of the Parque Corillera Azul, created through the collaboration of the museum, the government of Peru, and Peruvian conservationists, Wali and her team want to help Tocache residents find ways of sustaining their livelihoods while minimizing ecological damage to the buffer zone that surrounds the park. Wali tells Moskovitz that she began to make real progress in Tocache after the mayor realized that his cousin was a volunteer for the Field Museum.

Art

At the Cultural Center of Chicago, Mike Lash, the director for the City of Chicago's Office of Public Art, is on the phone with Sylvie Fleury, an artist in Geneva, Switzerland. Fleury is a Swiss national who has agreed to do a project sponsored by the city, Tiffany's, and Sears, where she will explore consumerism in a series of photographs and paintings.

For Millennium Park, Chicago's ambitious scheme to turn its lakefront park into a major cultural attraction, Lash's department has recently approved two other major pieces from European artists. A metal sculpture by Anish Kapoor, a London-based artist, will measure forty-seven feet by thirty-three feet by sixty-six feet and will be the largest noncommemorative piece of art in the world, weighing more than a hundred tons. The new park will also feature a fountain designed by the Spanish artist Jaume Plensa with LCD screens that will project images of Chicagoans.

The city's willingness to embrace the unorthodox in art is not new. "In the nineteenth century and the beginning of the twentieth century, Chicago art patrons had an appreciation for European artists, such as the impressionists," says the cultural historian Tim Samuelson. "Chicago art patrons were not constrained by the East Coast and European orthodoxy, and so they collected impressionist paintings before the rest of the East Coast and European art collectors came to value it. This was a reflection of the pioneering, open-minded attitude that characterized Chicagoans from the start. It was because of this openness that there are so many famous impressionist paintings at the Art Institute."

This pioneering spirit and the willingness to embrace new ideas is alive and well, as evidenced by Art Chicago, one of America's largest international contemporary art expositions. Two hundred six galleries from twenty countries exhibited work at the five-day festival in May 2002, the tenth anniversary of the event.

May is also a busy month for Carlos Tortolero, the founder and executive director of the Mexican Fine Arts Center Museum in Pilsen, a neighborhood in Chicago where many Mexican immigrants have settled. He spends a week in Mexico finalizing which pieces would appear in an upcoming exhibition of artwork from the Museo de Arte Carillo Gil, meeting with officials from the Instituto Nacional de Antropología y Historia (INA) regarding an exhibition of clothing from the pre-Columbian period to the present, and planning for an exhibition of art from the Gelman Collection planned for January through April.

"Much of my work is creating bridges between Mexico and the U.S.," he says. "While I was in Mexico City, I also met with the director of INA and discussed a possible collaboration over an amnesty program which would allow historical artifacts trafficked into the U.S. to be returned anonymously, displayed in the museum, and then repatriated to Mexico."

Music and Dance

The Chicago Symphony Orchestra (CSO) has its home in Symphony Center, located across Michigan Avenue from the Art Institute. Considered an orchestra with few peers, the CSO is an unofficial ambassador of Chicago to the world, while also bringing the world to Chicago. Daniel Barenboim, the CSO's artistic director, hails from Argentina, was educated in Europe, and has lived in Israel.

In May 2002, Barenboim is preparing for the Fourth Annual West-Eastern Divan Workshop, a program he created to bring together seventy gifted young musicians from Israel and Arab countries for three weeks of intensive musical training. The program is unique in its format and makeup. The participants would otherwise never interact. Held on the campus of Northwestern University in 2001, the workshop will be in Seville, Spain, in 2002.

Chicago's vibrant jazz scene also draws world-class performers to the city. The Empty Bottle's Annual International Festival, held every April, brings internationally known musicians to play alongside local jazz artists. The festival is directed by John Corbett, a Chicago producer, writer, and musician, who has created numerous collaborations between European and Chicago-based musicians. While the CSO's Barenboim prepares for his Divan, Corbett is in Europe organizing the program for the 2002 Berlin Jazz Festival, for which he is artistic director. He is a good example of the large number of musicians who call Chicago home while collaborating with artists all over the world.

Dance in Chicago is also a global importer and exporter of ideas and personnel. In May, while dancers from Burkina Faso are performing at Columbia College in Chicago, the Hubbard Street Dance Company is touring the United Kingdom. Twenty-five percent of Hubbard's world-renowned company members are from outside the United States.

Why the Fuss?

At this point, the true Chicagoan might say, "Yeah, so what's the big deal?" Paul O'Connor, executive director of World Business Chicago, puts it like this:

> We invented the skyscraper, split the atom, made our river flow backwards, created a lakefront from scratch, figured out the transistor, drew all the railroads to us, pioneered and continuously dominated commercial air travel, broadcast the world's first all-color TV station, built the number-one manufacturing city of America, invented risk management markets, won more Nobel Prizes than any city on earth, communicate more data on a daily basis than any other city on earth, threw away more basic industries than most other cities ever had, you know, like, hog butcher, stacker of wheat, steel capital of America. Should we tell anyone?

Well, the answer is yes, we should. Being known as a global city is an economic and cultural asset. It helps attract corporations of Boeing's magnitude. It reminds us and our friends around the world that we are no longer a city defined by a manufacturing and industrial base, that we have a history of transformation, that we welcome new ideas, new markets, and new kinds of business opportunities. Being a beautiful city with twenty-nine miles of lakefront is not enough to guarantee our future. We must continue reinventing ourselves and keeping pace with global opportunities. The chapters in this book help us understand what we are today, outline the directions we are going, and identify the challenges ahead.

⊕

1   A Global City

SASKIA SASSEN

CITIES ARE where the world's business is done. For millennia they have grown where men and women came together to trade goods, money, and ideas. On city streets and in city neighborhoods, artisans from tinsmiths to hatmakers gathered to compete and to cooperate. With the Industrial Revolution, vast mills grew in cities, drawing workers from surrounding farms and from far countries to make goods to be shipped around the world. The economies of cities shaped the world, and the world economy shaped cities. In this sense, there have always been global cities.

But beginning in the 1970s, the world economy began a profound transformation, from the industrial age to the global age. One result is that the requirements for being a global city have expanded. It is no longer sufficient to be a producer of goods and products. The great industrial cities—Detroit, Manchester, Liverpool, and, yes, Chicago—lost their role as leaders in manufacturing.

The major firms may have kept their offices in these cities, but they exported their manufacturing jobs to developing countries with cheap labor and few regulations. As instant communications enabled trillions of dollars to move across the globe in a worldwide network of transactions, the same technology created the global corporation. With many departments and functions, the global corporation is no longer located in one central headquarters but is literally scattered across the globe.

The transformation has utterly changed the role and life of great cities. A new type of global city has appeared for a global era. Like the cities of antiquity, this global city is a place where work gets done. But this work now guides, serves, and coordinates the global economy. Money can be mobile, moving around the globe. So can jobs, workers, goods, and services. But all this mobility has to be managed, serviced, and coordinated, and this work takes place in cities. As corporations spread across the globe and the world becomes ever more integrated, there is a need for highly concentrated command points. These relatively lean headquarters, in turn, need a multitude of services—legal, advertising, accounting, consulting, and financial.

A New Business

Theoretically, modern technology could scatter the provision of these services as widely as it has the manufacturing of goods: global managers could work wherever they have a modem and a satellite dish. But in fact, these services are concentrated in great cities, and the cities are being transformed by this process as they were by the Industrial Revolution a century or more before. These cities, then, are still in the manufacturing business. But what the global city makes are not industrial goods but financial goods, not things but highly specialized services.

Does Chicago belong to this new hierarchy of global cities? The answer is a definite yes. Without doubt, Chicago has the combination of resources to service the global operations for corporations and of markets. It has a highly internationalized professional class, which is crucial for these services. It has world-class cultural institutions and events. And by virtue of its waves of immigration it has a historically internationalized social environment—a global culture and global worldview that is common to all global cities and gives them many advantages in today's world.

But if Chicago is a global city, it is not a typical one. Its impact is felt around the world, but its globalization is often invisible, unrecognized by most of its citizens. If Chicago virtually defined the industrial era and thrived mightily in that time, its role in the global era is ambiguous and still evolving. In some areas it is strong, in some, weaker and needing support. In still other areas it is weak and not worth supporting. In some services, it competes with other cities. In others it complements them and fits into a cooperative network.

Like other global cities, Chicago is seeing its central core—the Loop and the neighborhoods next to it—revitalized and remade by globalization. But more than most global cities, it serves and draws strength from the region beyond its borders.

The top tier of the forty global cities is small. We know which places they are—New York, London, Tokyo, Frankfurt, and Paris. But there is a powerful second tier of some twenty cities that command many of the resources and services that define global hubs. These include Hong Kong, Zurich, Amsterdam, Milan, Toronto, Sydney—and Chicago. And then there is a third tier, which includes São Paulo, Shanghai, Johannesburg, Mexico City, and Mumbai. In the United States, there are only three indisputably global cities—New York, Chicago, and Los Angeles.

Defining the Global City

Global cities can be defined, and Chicago fits the definition. I use seven basic hypotheses about what makes a city global to support this conclusion.

1. The scattering of markets and corporations across the world raises the importance of central corporate command and control. The more dispersed a firm's operations, the more important its central functions to manage, coordinate, service, and finance the work of a global corporation.

2. These central functions become so complex that global corporate headquarters can't or don't want to handle them alone. Instead, they buy them from highly specialized service firms dealing with accounting, law, public relations, programming, telecommunications, and other such services.

3. These service firms like to be near each other, to locate in the same neighborhood, because of the complexity of interactions required in their work, the uncertainty of the markets in which they operate, and the rapid changes taking place as more and more countries deregulate their economies.

4. This mix of firms, talents, and expertise makes a certain type of urban environment work best as a center. A global city is one where these elements meet and work together. Being in this kind of city means being inside an extremely intense and dense information loop. This loop can't be replicated online. It feeds on face-to-face exchange of information—not just raw facts, but analysis, judgment, and plain old gossip.

5. The more firms outsource these high-level functions, the freer they are to move their headquarters to other locations, because the work that remains to be done in the corporate offices doesn't need such an intense information environment. So although the departure of a corporate headquarters from a city center may be a civic catastrophe, it is not necessarily an economic one. The true sign of a city's strength is what's left behind. For global cities, it is the high-level agglomeration of state-of-the-art specialists—the global law firms, accounting firms, and the like—that create the core.

6. Because these service firms need to provide global service, they have created global networks of alliances and partnerships that are strengthening cross-border city-to-city ties. We may be seeing the beginning of new global urban systems, a sort of transnational super-city, locking cities together beyond the borders of their traditional national settings. This can be seen in the growth of global markets for finance and other services, the need for networks to serve increasing international investment, and the reduced role of national governments. The trend could lead to an increasing disconnection of global cities from their regions or nations.

7. This process leads to a new inequality within cities that may well be the seed of future political and social stress. The industrial economy created a broad working class that was relatively well paid, protected, and politically potent. The global economy creates large numbers of high-paid expert employees at the top—traders, lawyers, accountants—many of whom choose to live in the city centers where they work. In a true global city, the downtown is rapidly becoming residential as well as commercial, with expensive townhouses and lofts and an infrastructure of fine restaurants, shops, and personal services. At the same time, the global economy runs on large numbers of poorly paid employees at the bottom—store clerks, dishwashers, dog walkers, parking valets—to serve this new global class. The importance of expert talent to the global economy's demand for services means this inequality is likely to increase.

Until now, most discussions about globalization have focused on the frantic motion it causes—the hypermobility of money, the flight of jobs, the global reach of corporations, the tidal flows of trade. But, in fact, many of the functions needed to make all this work are not mobile at all but happen in certain set places. Indeed, they are dependent on these certain places, which we call global cities.

These cities are the launching pad, the home base, the roots that feed the growth of the global economy. If the global economy is all about motion, these cities are the prime movers.

Chicago as a Global City

In few cities is the global transformation more dramatic than in Chicago. For more than a century, the city lay at the heart of an enormous agro-industrial complex and boasted a vibrant, manufacturing-based urban economy. Chicago's financial markets sprang from this complex and were centered on it. But in recent decades, both the city and its regional economy experienced enormous declines. From an exemplar of industrialization, Chicago became the very symbol of the Rust Belt. The city's major financial markets also faced potentially radical transformation and the loss of their former majority share in the global futures market.

In her masterly book *America's Global Cities* (1999), the urbanist Janet Abu-Lughod recited this litany of loss. From 1967 to 1982, one-quarter of Chicago's factories closed and 46 percent of its manufacturing jobs disappeared. This deindustrialization continued through the 1990s and was accompanied by a widespread loss of service jobs as well—thirty-one thousand of them disappeared in 1991–92 alone. Of this loss, almost half were in advanced corporate services. By disturbing contrast, New York managed to increase employment in this area even while it, like Chicago, was losing its factory jobs.

Worse, employment fell in the financial markets of Chicago. Office vacancy rates in the city center were over 20 percent (New York's vacancy rate never passed 18.8 percent). Nonresidential construction fell.

Abu-Lughod looked at this urban catastrophe and concluded that although Chicago's financial markets might hold onto some important niches in specialized financial sectors, the city itself lacked the critical mass to be a global city. In the growing global competition, she concluded, Chicago was a has-been, an also-ran, a left-behind.

My own research shows something quite different. By the late 1990s, Chicago had entered a new phase. You couldn't see it yet in the official statistics, but you could sense that it was happening. You can see it now by walking through the Loop, or by driving through the near west and near south sides or through the many gentrifying neighborhoods of the city.

Yes, unemployment is high for the less educated and poorly trained, and poverty remains rampant in some neighborhoods. The departure of leading headquarters hasn't stopped; since Abu-Lughod wrote, takeovers have changed the ownership and headquarters of such major Chicago firms as Amoco, Ameritech, First Chicago, Waste Management, Morton International, and Inland Steel.

But Chicago today reminds me of New York when I was doing research there in the late 1970s and early 1980s. The consensus then was that New York was finished, done in by manufacturing losses, headquarters flight, the city's fiscal crisis, and a decaying infrastructure. But the areas I was researching—producer services, both advanced services and industrial-service jobs—showed the growth and vitality that signal the birth of a global city from a disintegrating industrial city. Chicago today shows the same pattern.

The period studied by Abu-Lughod does not necessarily represent the end of the decline—which actually continues to afflict much of the old industrial-era city—but rather a time when an entirely new set of basic economic activities is emerging. To use only the old statistics is to miss this transformation. The old figures—on manufacturing jobs and factories or certain kinds of service jobs—have nothing to do with this new era. This holds true even for some parts of the global economy, such as the financial markets or headquarters location.

For instance, Chicago's share of the global futures market is falling, but this is not a sign of decline. Because this market is becoming much more networked, with many more centers of activity, a leading center like Chicago can actually gain strength as new centers are added. The overall volume increases, and networking becomes more complex. Even as Chicago's physical exchanges have lost market share to electronic exchanges founded in other cities, its substantial base of human capital in trading, risk management, financial engineering, and information technology ensures the city's future as a center of financial-market innovation. Indeed, both the actual number and the value of futures transactions in Chicago have increased sharply over the last decade in tandem with the growth in the global market. If the number is increasing, then this means more work in Chicago, more jobs and employment, and more need for Chicago's skills in specialized parts of the market. The crisis that has affected financial centers and whole economies everywhere in the world has reversed some of these trends. But history suggests that this crisis will last at most a few years.

Similarly, the departure of major corporate headquarters is a fact, but it is also misleading if taken as an omen of decline. Chicago's growth today comes more from advanced corporate services than from Fortune 500 headquarters. These services have kept growing even as some of their large corporate clients like Amoco have moved out. Chicago is rich in global law firms, global accounting firms, global consultants, and other specialized service companies, and these entities keep serving their old customers, even when these customers leave town. Local doesn't necessarily mean local anymore. Increasingly, it means networked.

For instance, in 1999, when the city was focused on corporate headquarters departures, one information technology consultant firm, Whittman-Hart, saw a 68 percent growth in revenues as its services to major corporations increased. Mayer, Brown, Rowe, and Maw was the leading law firm for several departed corporations, but its business grew by a third in the decade after most of them moved. This is a new trend, and it's a crucial one.

Global Trends in Chicago

The spearpoint of Chicago business is changing from major corporate head-quarters to a network of specialized corporate service firms. The departure of corporate headquarters does have a big impact, from the loss of charitable giving to the loss of the medium-level and clerical jobs at headquarters. But these jobs are increasingly being outsourced anyway. Even headquarters that stay put are cutting these in-house jobs and setting up back offices in suburbs or small towns. Advanced corporate services are thriving and creating jobs and, in the process, raising the demand for professional workers with the kind of talent that commands high salaries.

In every global city where this has been the pattern, one result has been a boom in high-priced housing in and near the central city. These advanced corporate service companies demand lots of workers who are well educated, highly skilled, and highly paid. Many of these younger workers are the children and grandchildren of the postwar generation that moved to the suburbs, and they're returning to the city in droves. They prefer to eliminate the long commute and live downtown where the action is, and they can afford to do it. As manufacturing companies move out, their buildings are turned into loft apartments or are torn down and replaced by townhouses for this new generation of city dwellers.

You can see this trend in New York and in London—and you can see it in Chicago. Local employment by Chicago's top ten advertising agencies, investment banks, law firms, benefits consultants, accountants, and management consultants jumped to about 60,000 jobs in 1998, from fewer than 17,000 in 1986. Many of these people want to live downtown. This is what the boom in Loop apartments, lofts on the Near West Side, and townhouses on the Near South Side is all about.

This trend produces an opposite effect, which is the growth in demand for low-wage workers to serve this high-salaried professional class. The professional citizens of a global city require lots of restaurants, boutiques, and specialized services, and they want someone to walk the dog, park the car, do the dry cleaning.

A walk through the Loop makes this mix of trends visible, much of it based on an immigrant workforce. In short, a global city lives on a specialized, state-of-the-art urban economy that is based on a highly networked, highly specialized and globalized service sector. Most cities do not meet this description, and many never will. But the few dozen that do are key cities of the future. Acting individually and together, they will be the centers that run the world.

Worldwide Networks, Central Command

There is a peculiar geography of globalization. It both scatters and concentrates, disperses and centralizes. It has uprooted most economic functions—not only manufacturing but also sales, accounting, research and development, communications, and many other jobs—from their old local and national clusters and has strewn them across the world.

Not so long ago most companies made things in a central factory with the corporate offices and functions upstairs or at least in the same town. If the general public in the United States is aware of globalization at all, it is for the way it has exported manufacturing, services, and jobs from their home cities to developing countries around the world. This dispersal is transforming economies everywhere.

What is less recognized is the fact that this dispersal requires control, a tight central command structure to ride herd on these far-flung corporate empires, and this centralization of top-level management and control has tended to take place in cities.

A wealth of statistics illustrates the dispersals of the global economy. America and other developed nations have gone on a spree of foreign direct investment that has given them affiliates in countries around the world. By 1999, more than a half million of these affiliates existed, with total sales of $11 trillion. This is an astounding figure when we consider that total world trade is $8 trillion. In other words, this foreign investment is as powerful economically as trade.

Another example lies in the global financial markets. Global money markets trade no less than $1.5 trillion every day. Internationally traded derivatives reached $192 trillion at the end of 2002. Stock markets, which remain largely national, are a growing component of the global capital market. Most business financing used to take place through banks, with equity markets playing only a secondary role.

A few big stock markets, such as the New York Stock Exchange, have always been powerful, but many countries didn't even have a stock exchange. Those that existed, including the NYSE, were almost completely national. But the late 1980s and early 1990s saw deregulation and incorporation of a growing number of markets into a global network of stock exchanges. In the 1980s,

New York, London, Paris, and even Tokyo, among others, deregulated and opened up to listings of foreign firms. In the 1990s, others—including Buenos Aires, São Paulo, Mexico City, Bangkok, Taipei, Moscow—became integrated into the global financial market. By 2000, worldwide capitalization of these markets surpassed $30 trillion.

These statistics suggest a picture of decentralized decisionmaking, free-flowing funds, and anarchic financial conditions, but this image is untrue. When firms disperse their activities around the globe through foreign direct investment and affiliates, they need central coordination and servicing. Global financial flows may circle the globe, but the markets themselves are located in cities (in Chicago, LaSalle Street is the financial headquarters).

Even though more cities are joining the global trading network and aggregate value has grown, there has been no real reduction in the disproportionate concentration of assets in first-world cities. Exchanges are physical places where many traders interact, even when much of the work gets done electronically. A core presence of trust can develop there, and trust is a key factor when trading large amounts of high value at high speed. It is not easy to decentralize this kind of mix of trust and trading.

Central control cannot take place without a myriad of specialized services. By this I mean all the top-level financial, legal, accounting, managerial, executive, and planning functions necessary to run a corporate organization operating in multiple countries. Once upon a time, corporations had all this expertise under their own roofs and on their own payrolls.

But global business is immensely complicated, too complicated to be controlled by one set of managers. Many global corporations now operate in dozens of different countries. These countries have different legal systems, accounting systems, and advertising cultures. Their systems are changing to meet global needs, but there is also a level at which they remain entrenched, shaped to fit local political demands. Global law firms, global accounting firms, and global advertising agencies can help sort out these national differences, so companies are outsourcing these functions to these specialized agencies. These agencies themselves have affiliates around the globe to provide services to their customers no matter where the need may be: indeed, the globalization of these specialized agencies makes it possible for their large corporate customers to locate virtually anywhere.

Nonetheless, corporations operating in global markets tend to keep or move particular top headquarters functions, such as financial and new development functions, into global cities. Boeing's move to Chicago from Seattle is one clear example of this. The existence of tight command headquarters for global corporations acts as a magnet, drawing in specialized agencies, which themselves need a variety of services. In this way, global cities become the focal points of the global economy. As this economy grows, so will these cities. Much of the urban economy has little to do with this world of global operations. Indeed, many of the operations of individual corporations are national, not global. Chicago still does more business with the Midwest than it does with other countries. This fact can order our priorities without denying the growing role of global operations and global corporations.

Whether national or global, both markets and organizations need central places where work gets done. Cities are the preferred place for this work, particularly for the most innovative or speculative or internationalized services. Money can be mobile, moving around the globe. So can jobs, workers, goods, and services. But all this mobility has to be managed, serviced, and coordinated, and this work takes place in cities.

The Geography of Money

Globalization is global only in a manner of speaking. When we look at the global cities and their networks, we can see that there is a definite geography of globalization, and though it may be widespread, it is not all-encompassing. Patterns of foreign investment and global finance show that it is focused on certain areas of the world.

The center of gravity is the North Atlantic region. For all the talk about export of jobs to developing countries, the trans-Atlantic world—the United States, Canada, and the European Union—represents the most significant concentration of cross-border transactions. The North Atlantic accounts for two-thirds of worldwide stock market capitalization. Sixty percent of foreign investment is in the developed countries of the North Atlantic region, and 76 percent of all foreign investment comes from this area.

Other major regions, such as Southeast Asia and Latin America, receive foreign investment and other important countries, like Japan, send it. But these are dwarfed by the weight of the Northern Atlantic system. Even outside this area, most investment goes to specific places rather than to regions as a whole. Investment in Latin America, for instance, grew rapidly in the 1990s, but most of it was in Brazil, Argentina, and Mexico.

Patterns are also evident when we consider the purpose of foreign investment. Most foreign direct investment—89 percent—is for cross-border mergers and acquisitions rather than for financing or starting new companies or factories. In 1996, for example, 90 percent of all investment made in the United States by non-U.S. firms went for mergers and acquisitions.

A so-called "average transnationality index" reveals the share of foreign sales, assets, and employment in a corporation's operations. The average transnationality index for the United States is 38.5 percent, but in Europe it's more than half—56.7 percent. Since the index was first used in 1990, it has risen for the one hundred largest global corporations. For instance, it stands at 51 percent for IBM, 55 percent for Volkswagen Group, 91 percent for Nestlé, and 96 percent for Asea Brown Boveri. Thus, we are seeing the consolidation of a transnational economy that is focused on the North Atlantic. Corporations and governments of these nations dominate the deals, sales, and, not surprisingly, emerging rules and standards. Globalization does indeed involve dispersal, but it also intensifies concentration.

Communications

For as long as cities have existed they have had centers, the places where economies, governments, and societies come together. Anyone who wanted a web of economic functions, a mass of information, and a marketplace had to go to the city center to find it.

In London, this central place is known, quite simply, as The City. In New York it is Wall Street—and, increasingly now, Midtown. Elsewhere it is "downtown" or "the business district" or, in Chicago, the Loop. The importance of the city center waned when mass manufacturing dominated the economy and surburbanization drove growth. It is a great irony that globalization, with its far-flung operations and markets, is reviving the importance of city centers. But special features of the global economy have changed the meaning—even the actual location—of the center. There is no longer a straightforward relationship between "the center" and "downtown." Instead, modern communications give the center several new forms.

First, the downtown itself is being transformed. Many large headquarters are moving out, while there is a boom in the number of small firms that specialize in foreign-oriented services. Office buildings are being turned into apartments, and warehouses into lofts. Restaurants, theaters, and boutiques spring up to cater to the new, affluent downtown dwellers. Downtown itself swells and grows, gobbling up once-seedy districts on its fringe, converting old factories into luxury apartments. All this describes what is happening in the Loop, but it is being replicated in global cities everywhere.

Second, "the center" now can have many centers, as the business activities normally associated with downtown spread into the suburbs. This creates a grid of small but intense business centers. Of course, this process has been going on in Chicago for years, but it has been thought of as a "suburbanization" of business, a departure of commercial power and sophistication from the Loop that has sapped the vitality of the old downtown by moving its functions to new homes in the lands beyond O'Hare. This misses the point.

What's happening is a new definition of the center, a downtown with several nodes, perhaps miles apart but in instant cyber-touch—and close enough geographically for its residents to meet regularly. Indeed, in a world of commuters, they may live next door to each other. Usually, there is a major city at the center of these nodes providing a center of gravity for the new far-flung grid.

If this redefines the downtown, it also redefines the region. If a region is to work, it must be connected not only by digital highways, but by real ones. By keeping business people in physical contact with each other, the old conventional infrastructure of rapid rail and highways, in tandem with the new infrastructure of telecommunications, leverages the effectiveness of the region and its economy.

Third, there is a new networked "center" of global cities. This network connects multiple global cities through electronic markets and the growing intercity movement of goods, information, companies, and especially people. For an individual city to be part of this new global center, it must have both the expertise and the physical capability. Once these exist, key players in distant cities can create a new "center," a unity of functions and markets that is as central to the economy as though it were all in the same office. Some cities have the power and resources to become such centers, others don't. In the Midwest, once-powerful cities like Detroit or St. Louis that soared in the early industrial era seem doomed to be left behind by the global era. Globalization thus creates new inequalities between cities, just as it creates new class inequalities within cities.

Traditionally, a great city is the hub of its region, as Chicago is of the Midwest, and is intimately tied into the economy of that region. Globalization is changing that. Cities that are strategic sites in the global economy tend to disconnect from their regions, to leave their traditional homes and make their fortune in the wide world. But interestingly, Chicago seems to be an exception. It remains far more intertwined with its regional economy than are most global cities. Greater Chicago trades more with its midwestern hinterland than it does with the wider world. New York, by contrast, thrives disproportionately on exports, especially of services.

The reasons for this Chicago exception are just beginning to be studied. One cause may be the kinds of industries which dominate a city and its region. New York is more dominated than Chicago by specialty services, including finance. Chicago still owns a lot of manufacturing, warehousing, and transport, which provides a link to the traditional agro-industrial past. We know that a prosperous city needs a mixed economy with many strong sectors. A thriving trade with the surrounding region can feed a diverse economic base, with the modern service industries of the global era interacting and supporting the more old-fashioned sectors.

The evidence seems to show that many smaller industrial cities in the Midwest are still strong exporters of machinery, machine tools, auto parts, and other industrial goods. If New York's links to the wider world are more direct, Chicago's may be routed through this complex, dense, diverse midwestern economy. Having lost much of its own manufacturing, Chicago can use this midwestern manufacturing complex as a new base, keeping one foot in its old industrial past as it lunges forward into the global future. It seems reasonable to assume that this past will shape the future, with Chicago developing expertise in the global services, such as law and accounting, that serve these older sectors.

Global Regions

In the industrial era, regions specialized. Some grew wheat, some mined coal. Later, regions became industrially specialized—autos near Detroit, steel near Chicago, and, later, computer chips near San Francisco. With the advent of globalization, it has been suggested that the whole notion of the region and of regional specialization may become obsolete. A region that has become home to certain companies or certain kinds of manufacturing may wake up one morning to find that the company and its functions have picked up and moved far away.

The truth, though, is more complicated. A global services complex in a global city creates an infrastructure comprised of a vast network of communications that can be used by other economic nodes in that region. These nodes can and do connect with the central city and then through it to a worldwide net of firms and markets. This regional grid means that the benefits of globalization are no longer confined only to firms within those cities. If a city specializes in certain activities, as Chicago and other global cities do, their regions can specialize, too.

But these regions have geographic limits. All the telecommunications miracles in the world have not eliminated the need for face-to-face transactions. Business travel, even across oceans, is necessary for some economic work to be done. For everyday activity, everyday togetherness is necessary.

I want to emphasize that this is more than just the human need for contact with other humans. Beyond this, there is the actual work process in many of these specialized services that requires interactions among many specialized and talented professionals and managers. A functioning regional network of firms needs a conventional communications infrastructure of highways or rail. This means that an effective region will probably include locations not more than two hours apart.

Many people think that modern communications remove the need for this conventional infrastructure. But the "production" process in modern industries requires face-to-face contact. Business travel and electronic links have grown together, and neither replaces the other. The virtual office sounds more complete than it is. Certain types of work can indeed be done from a virtual office located anywhere. But work that requires specialized knowledge, considerable innovation, and risk-taking needs direct meetings and environments that bring together many diverse, highly specialized professionals with experience in different parts of the world.

This means that companies that are deciding where to locate their offices have to think about where other companies and their specialists are located. Companies that sink roots into soil that is more than a reasonable commute from a center of global expertise may be cutting themselves out of the global loop. Standard work, whether manufacturing or services, can be located anywhere, but not management and specialized services.

And here is another irony of globalization: in today's electronic era, the older notion of the region and the older forms of travel, including the humble train, reappear as critical components of the global center. This center is different, as we have noted. The people who live and work in the old downtown are different, and they may be creating a new downtown that links several centers in their region. But in the process, the new thing they are creating looks and behaves in many ways like the old, pre-global region.

The Local Part of Global

To understand what global cities do, we need to look at two major changes and how they affect each other. The first is the sharp growth in the global economy since the mid-1980s that has increased both the size and the complexity of economic transactions. As we have seen, this has created the need for top-level control and command at the headquarters of global companies and the need for a wide range of corporate services nearby.

The second is the growth in these services and their increasing depth and complexity. All firms in all parts of the economy—from mining and manufacturing to finance and retail—need these services. Some never needed these services before, so they go out and hire them. Others used to have them in house, but as the economy becomes more complex, these companies are outsourcing the work, looking to independent and highly specialized firms to provide the expertise.

We are seeing the formation of a new urban economy. Many of these cities have been centers for business and finance for a century or more, but since the 1980s these business and finance centers have transformed themselves into global powers. Interestingly, this management and finance sector may not dominate a global city's economy in sheer numbers. In many cities, manufacturing employment outnumbers the global employees downtown. But manufacturing is now a larger tail on a smaller dog. Through its sheer vitality and profit potential, it is the global sector that imposes itself on the overall urban economy. The possibility for superprofits in finance is devaluing manufacturing, where profits are lower.

This profit potential makes itself felt in other ways. Everything has a price, especially economic activities themselves, and the highest bidder wins. The prices are higher and the profits greater in some activities—business hotels, gourmet restaurants, chains of coffee shops, offices rented to global lawyers or global accountants. This makes it ever harder for other businesses to compete for space and investments. Neighborhood shops tailored to local needs find themselves priced out by upscale boutiques and stylish restaurants catering to the new high-income global elites. Mom-and-pop stores vanish; Starbucks and Office Depots thrive.

It is important to remember that manufacturing remains crucial to the economy of the global city even when it has left town for some distant land. Many global companies make things around the world, and as we have noted, their headquarters in the city center exist to control and service this manufacturing. In this sense, manufacturing supports the global city, just as it did the industrial city that preceded it.

But today, it no longer makes much difference to the city's specialized services sector whether this manufacturing takes place locally or across the globe. All that's necessary is a multinational corporation, headquartered anywhere, that needs the expertise of global experts clustered together in the new global downtowns. In fact, the dispersal of factories around the world actually raises the demand for services and so adds to the power of global cities. The growth of service firms in New York or Chicago, London or Paris can be fed by manufacturing located anywhere in the world, as long as it is part of a global corporate network. Managing a dispersed manufacturing component is complex. It involves the laws on labor, taxation, and trade of dozens of countries, and so needs the services of highly skilled global experts.

The export of manufacturing jobs may be a cause for concern, but the loss of these jobs in the factory actually creates jobs in the global offices—better-paying jobs but, alas, so far not so many of them. There is, however, a kind of manufacturing that is part of the modern global city, one that is often overlooked by urban policy-makers and researchers. Once, service industries existed to service mass manufacturing. Today, new small manufacturers exist to service the needs of the service firms that drive the global city. These small, often specialized manufacturers make customized products. They include specialized construction companies, makers of furniture and lighting, and creators of clothing.

I call this "urban manufacturing" because it is part of dense networks of contractors and subcontractors and it needs to be in the city to do this work. With its rich manufacturing history, Chicago might well try to understand and nurture this significant sector.

Cities and Global Business

The revival of city centers like the Loop as the cockpit of the global economy should not have happened, according to conventional wisdom about the information economy. All these global businesses—the major corporations and the accountants, lawyers, and financiers that serve them—are thoroughly linked through the most advanced information technology. With this technology they could set up shop anywhere—somewhere remote and isolated, say, where the rentals are low and the air clean. But as we have seen, the central city is where the action is, and this is increasingly the case. No matter what the information theorists say, there are good reasons for this.

It may help to think of all these professional service firms as so many factories. The industrial economy and the service economy are not totally different. Both produce things. Even in law and consulting offices, there is a product, a service that is bought and sold. Just as factories need easy access to raw materials and railroad lines, so do these service firms benefit from proximity to other specialized services. The more complex and innovative the service, the more this is true, because these services need many highly specialized inputs. Take a financial instrument like innovative bonds. To produce such a financial instrument, help is needed from accountants, advertising firms, lawyers, economic consultants, public relations people, designers, and printers.

Theoretically, all this consultation and cooperation could be done by a widely dispersed array of specialized firms, and this does happen when the product is relatively routine or when time is not of the essence. But when time is important and advice is needed fast, it helps to have all these services near at hand. In short, it helps to have your advisers together in one room where you can all talk together. And it helps to have them moving together through a dense, complex environment populated by the experts of many different firms.

This is why cities have become home to complexes of producer services. Headquarters can and do move out of town, but they still need a producer services complex where they can get specialized and complementary services and financing.

Even so, it is mostly the headquarters of national or more traditional industries with standardized work processes that move to the suburbs. Headquarters of firms with global or complex lines of business tend to stay downtown or move there, or sometimes just relocate their back offices. This shines a new light on the familiar civic hand-wringing over the loss of corporation headquarters. When a company like Amoco leaves, it is seen as a civic disaster, just as when a company like Boeing arrives, it is a civic triumph. But it's not that clear-cut.

Some of the world's largest firms are still manufacturers and are likely to have their main headquarters near their major factory complex. Because of space and cost constraints, this is unlikely to be in a large city. But such firms are likely to have a secondary or subheadquarters in the city center to deal with the highly specialized functions required by the global market. To repeat, manufacturers oriented to the national market do not need to be in a global city. Many of the much-publicized departures from New York City in the 1960s and 1970s involved this type of firm. The firms that stayed in Manhattan are those that get more than half their revenue from international sales.

There are other, more personal reasons why the global city is the place to be. These can be boiled down to the fact that, even in this day and age of teleconferencing, people still like to eat lunch with each other. Social contacts count.

As we have seen, the dispersal of corporations has led directly to the importance of central coordination and control. Innovation is important; complexity is extreme; speed is essential; and new ideas are paramount. A network has to span many different specializations. For all this, there is nothing like day-to-day contact, face-to-face schmoozing, the swapping of ideas over lunch, the unexpected encounter.

The global economy needs access to top talent. This kind of talent likes to be close to other talent, to socialize and work with interesting people. It likes to be in a place with cultural sophistication and urban excitement. And it loves the massive concentration of state-of-the-art resources that lets them maximize the benefits of new communication technology—not only fiber optic cables, but the best office buildings, too.

A second fact that is emerging deals with the meaning of "information." There are two kinds of information. One is the datum, the stark fact, which may be complex but is standard knowledge—the closing quote on a stock market, the privatization of a public utility, the bankruptcy of a bank. Such information is available anywhere, on a beach or a mountain top—or in a suburban office park.

But there is another kind of information, which deals in interpretation or evaluation or judgment. In the processing of this kind of information, raw fact is taken and run through the kind of brains and experience that a global city attracts to produce information of a higher order. The second type of information requires a complicated mixture of elements, not least a social setting where minds work together.

There is a third kind of information, of course, which is gossip or guesswork. The generation, spreading, and evaluation of gossip drives markets and corporate decisions. Most often, it moves from mouth to mouth, face-to-face. In a world where gossip counts, anyone who is out of the Loop is definitely out of the loop. Singapore, for example, has technical connectivity to match Hong Kong's, but it doesn't have Hong Kong's social connectivity. The same can be said of Frankfurt, which is rich in banks and markets and technology but cannot match the sheer human mix of London.

When the more complex forms of information needed to execute major international deals can't be found on existing databases, then companies need the social information loop that comes with bouncing information among talented, informed people.

Mergers and the City

Global financial firms need enormous resources, a fact which is leading to mergers and acquisitions among major firms and strategic alliances among markets in different countries. The financial pages report growing numbers of mergers among financial service firms, accounting firms, law firms, insurance brokers—in short, firms that provide global services.

In addition, several financial exchanges are trying to form highly integrated alliances. The most important and visible of these was the attempted alliance between the London Stock Exchange and Frankfurt's Deutsche Borse—and indeed, these mergers are so complex that most have failed. But the will to merge continues and it is quite possible that future mergers will succeed. Already, an alliance between the Paris, Amsterdam, and Brussels bourses has led to the creation of a multinational exchange, Euronext, which acquired London's London International Financial Futures and Options Exchange (LIFFE) in 2001 and the Portuguese exchange in 2002. Other looser networks are appearing, such as the moves by NASDAQ, the second-largest U.S. stock market, to set up Nasdaq Japan and Nasdaq Canada, giving investors in Japan and Canada direct access to the U.S. market. The development of these networks is likely to strengthen intercity links in the worldwide network of about forty cities, including Chicago, through which the global financial industry operates. A major financial center needs to have a significant share of global operations to be a global center.

At the end of 1999, twenty-five cities—again including Chicago—accounted for about 80 percent of the world's equities under management. These centers don't just compete with each other, they also collaborate and divide labor into specialities. Competition exists, of course, but the mere fact of competing in this limited league of global cities makes a city even stronger.

All this may strengthen global cities, but it weakens national ties for global firms and their customers and weakens the need for national financial centers. Global financial products are available in national markets, and national investors can operate in global markets. For instance, some major Brazilian firms now list on the New York Stock Exchange, bypassing the São Paulo exchange. A city that thinks it has a lock on its own country's business is likely to find that the global economy thinks otherwise.

As this process moves forward, important parts of a national economy can become denationalized or globalized, while leaving other parts of a national economy basically unaltered. China is a good example of this. It adopted international accounting rules in 1993, long before the United States or Japan did, in order to engage in international economic operations, but it didn't change much of its noninternational, domestic economy—or its domestic politics. And Japanese firms operating overseas adopted international accounting standards long before Japan's government considered requiring them.

Chicago Earned Its Global Title

If globalization is here to stay, so are global cities. But if globalization is still a half-formed process, so too are global cities. Globalization is a trillion puppets dancing on very long strings, and global cities are where the puppeteers live and work. As the puppets and their dances change, so will the puppeteers.

Global cities do not spring fresh from virgin soil. Instead, the global cities of today and tomorrow are mostly the great cities of the past. Cities are organic things, with life cycles, constantly changing. Many, like Paris or London, have reinvented themselves many times over the centuries in response to historical and economic challenges. Others, like Chicago, are relatively young, products of the Industrial Revolution, manufacturing giants that grew from raw labor pools to places of power and sophistication in little more than a century. These cities are reinventing themselves now for the first time.

Some cities, like New York or London, are accustomed to life at the center of the universe. Others, like Frankfurt, are probably headed for more power than they have ever known. Some once-mighty cities, like Detroit, seem destined to be global backwaters. Others flirted with this danger in a postindustrial slump but have managed to join the relatively small number of urban centers that can be called global cities. Chicago has earned its place in that group.

2 A City Reinvents Itself

WILLIAM A. TESTA

THE CHICAGO REGION, nerve center of a rich and mature manufacturing and agricultural economy in the American Midwest, is locked in a determined struggle to reinvent itself as a global city—that is, as an international business-service and meeting place for the world's most ambitious and talented businesses and people.

Troubled economic times may slow this process but will not stop it. The region has always changed as it has grown, spinning off the products of its creative endeavors to other places while they were still successful, but had become routine. An early Chicago-area example of such regional transition is the meat-packing industry. Once, owing to the innovation of refrigerated railroad cars and assembly-line processing of carcasses, Chicago was the meat-packing capital of the world. Then refrigeration of trucks pulled this industry westward to Iowa, Nebraska, and beyond.

So, too, Chicago was once the retail goods mail-order capital of the world, yet this innovative profit center eventually skipped to cheaper areas, where sprawling warehouses could be built and operated less expensively.

Chicago has been a center of innovation in so-called "electronic trading" of contracts. The Chicago Mercantile Exchange developed one of the most significant electronically traded products: E-mini Stock Index Futures. Chicago-based Archipelago is the first totally open, electronic exchange to trade all NYSE, AMEX, PCX, and OTC listed securities. Yet, because of changes emanating from electronic trading, Chicago is struggling to keep key parts of its financial futures industry from slipping away. Electronic trading has apparently doomed much of the "open outcry" trading-floor activity that generated jobs and income for generations of Chicagoans. Today's trading from and through computer terminals may require less labor, and those who execute trades electronically may choose to do so remotely from many possible locations, including one of the financial centers of the world such as London, Frankfurt, Paris, or New York City.

Technological change and business competition have always triggered competitive upheaval and the need for reinvention, even without help from globalization. But beginning in the latter part of the twentieth century, globalization has magnified the challenges—and, let us not forget, the opportunities—for Chicago.

Winds of Change

Toward the end of the twentieth century, transportation costs of tradable goods such as steel and machinery fell worldwide at the same time that many artificial barriers to trade such as tariffs and quotas were lowered through governmental agreements. Between 1975 and 2000, average nominal freight and insurance costs for U.S. imports fell by about 50 percent. In the same period, average tariffs on industrial goods in developed countries fell from 40 to 50 percent of product price to around 4 percent.

Accordingly, traded goods—exports and imports—have risen to 26 percent of the U.S. economy today, from 12 percent in 1975. Chicago's steel and machinery now compete with products made around the world, and such competition has helped to move Chicago manufacturing production abroad as well as to more remote and even rural regions of the United States.

Leapfrogging advances in communication; information retrieval, processing, and storage; and travel have accompanied and spurred the growth in international commerce. Communication advances assist the transit of goods (and services) and have also fueled the movement of capital across the world. Since 1990, the flow of estimated gross private-sector capital into and out of advanced economies has quadrupled, to over $6.5 trillion per year. More abundant, timely, and accurate information has provided transparency for operations of distant investments, which has in turn enticed investors to move capital and invest on a global scale.

Chicago-based corporations and individual investors can now more easily scour the globe for investment opportunities or scout out potential sites for expanding their own company operations. Similarly, companies around the world can quickly and cheaply compare Chicago with many other cities in Asia, South America, or Europe.

People are moving, too. Immigration into the United States has recently accelerated, although its rate remains lower than in the early twentieth century. Foreign-born residents made up 10.4 percent of the U.S. population in 2000 versus 13.6 percent in 1900. But immigration has rebounded smartly in recent decades, as a result of both less-restrictive legal immigration and the entrance of undocumented workers, mainly along the U.S.-Mexico border. Compared to other developed nations, such as Japan and some of the Western European countries, which are staring gloomily at the prospect of declining and aging populations as the midcentury approaches, the United States will experience growth of its workforce and a less pronounced shift in age distribution.

Risks for Chicago

The forces of globalization tend to confer benefits and opportunities on cities and regions experiencing them, especially those that act strategically in response. As with other changes in technology and cultural transition, however, not every individual, industry, or subregion prospers, nor do positions in the hierarchy remain stable. Dislocation and transition will be experienced by some people and corporations, sometimes quite agonizingly, and income disparities may widen.

National governments are not particularly adept at compensating the losers when the pot of wealth creation is forcibly enlarged. Thus, workers often bristle and resist the upheavals resulting from national trade initiatives. In fact, globalization is not, overall, the most powerful phenomenon dislocating the lives of working people today, but it is certainly one of the least popular. Given that central governments can accede to it, or not, through trade and investment agreements, there is often ample room for industries and people to resist such changes and voice their discontent.

But dislocations will be far worse if individuals and regions do not adapt to inevitable changes of globalization strategically and in a timely fashion. The worry for Chicago is that, because the world is globalizing rapidly and because technology seems to be changing business and industry even faster, without planning the city may miss out on emerging opportunities or fail to adapt rapidly enough to the changing marketplace.

Might the now great "Second City" fail to move up the proverbial food chain or, worse, even to maintain its position? Failure to find a high-value niche or two would mean that wages, incomes, and job opportunities of Chicagoans would lag. Growth would stagnate, as would local businesses and real estate values, and the continuity of funds to support the culture, parks, great public monuments, and sports teams of Chicago would suffer, too.

Chicago has not always looked outward in self-doubt and struggle. In earlier times, there was little or no preoccupation with the city's status or function: there is no need to worry much about your place in the world when your economy is doubling and tripling in size every ten years. So it was with Chicago, the "City of the Century," in the nineteenth century. During this time, the globalization of North America was represented by the often-violent displacement of the continent's indigenous people by another. In the Chicago region, much like the remainder of the continent, the displacements were overwhelmingly beneficial for the European settlers—yielding bountiful agriculture and other natural resources.

Later, Chicago's emergence as the premier gateway city to the American frontier and as the midcontinent's transportation hub easily carried it though the early twentieth century, the age of mass industrialization. Most of Chicago's roles did not change greatly during that century, though the torrid pace of growth associated with settlement and expansion cooled down sharply. Over the past fifty to sixty years, as the region matured and growth spilled westward, two general changes pulled Chicago's growth back to earth. First, midwestern growth slowed dramatically as the natural-resource base of its economy—coal, timber, and agriculture—dwindled in importance. Competition came from regions to the west that had filled in through continental expansion and from the South, finally recovered from the slavery and Civil War disaster. Second, manufacturing activity began to leave the central cities and spread out to other regions of the country. Large, densely populated central cities such as Chicago—and New York, Philadelphia, Baltimore, and Detroit—were no longer well suited to the changing nature and technology of manufacturing. During the course of its evolution, manufacturing production substituted machinery in place of hordes of neighborhood workers, low-slung countryside or suburban buildings in place of multifloored urban structures, and truck transportation in favor of railway lines that converged in a central urban terminus. Consequently, Chicago lost manufacturing even faster than did its hinterland.

That international trade and investment played a secondary role to technological change and geographic preference in the loss of manufacturing jobs is evident from the timing of the phenomenon. The number of manufacturing jobs in large central cities like Chicago was falling rapidly during the decades after World War II, the time at which the Midwest stood alone in the world as having the capacity to manufacture durable goods. At the same time, manufacturing plants in traditional industries were deconcentrating from the Northeast-Midwest region to the South and West. Indeed, today's drama of "well-paying manufacturing jobs going overseas to foreigners" has been played out before in a domestic context, as many northern workers and communities found that their industrial base had shifted to southern states.

As the resource- and manufacturing-based midwestern region dwindled, Chicago also lost many of its customers for business and financial services. Nonetheless, it is these sectors that ultimately became the foundations of the city's revival and reinvention.

Life after Industry

Chicago has reinvented itself in many ways, but the most prominent one is its ongoing evolution toward a national and international center of business services, a more global city in shape and occupation. The city is now an international leader in the trading of commodities, stock options, currency, and interest rate futures. In this niche, there are an officially reported fifty thousand "direct" jobs in Chicago.

The city's early beginnings were as an arena for forward and "futures" markets in "butter and eggs." Its major exchanges—the Chicago Board of Trade, Chicago Mercantile Exchange, and Chicago Board Options Exchange—still lead the world in market share for derivatives contracts. Of course, along the way much has changed within this industry.

> Chicago is the birthplace of financial derivatives. When President Nixon abandoned fixed exchange rates, Leo Melamud, then chairman of the Chicago Mercantile Exchange, recognized that the same risk management techniques that had stimulated agriculture by organizing the trading of commodity futures could be adapted to manage the new risks associated with exchange rate fluctuations. Melamud got on the phone with Milton Friedman, the Nobel Prize–winning University of Chicago economist. Friedman wrote a short white-paper endorsing the idea of exchange rate derivatives. Melamud took the paper to Washington, and before long he had the U.S. government's support. Twenty-five years later, trillions of dollars in financial derivatives are traded globally every year.

From its beginnings, Chicago was the business-service capital of the region, but it took an enormous expansion and reinvention of this role to compensate for the inevitable decline of once-dominant manufacturing. The magnitude of the transformation of the Chicago economy from its goods orientation to a business-service center is easy to see from job numbers. From 1970 to 1997, the six-county Chicago area lost over one-third—300,000—of its original jobs in the manufacturing sector. Over that same period, the region gained over 600,000 jobs in business service and finance–insurance–real estate. (See Saskia Sassen's discussion, chapter 1.)

Transportation's Key Role

Chicago's sharp growth in business services and finance facilitated its growth as a hub for personal air travel. The links between these two industries—business services and air travel—may not seem evident at first, but the connection is strong. Increasingly, workers and business people must communicate in person, whether at the office, at a convention, on a jetliner making its way overseas, over lunch, or during the course of a casual conversation. Information that is impressionistic and agreements based on personal relationships and trust continue to grow in economic importance. For this rea-

Figure 1. Employment by Sector, 1970–97

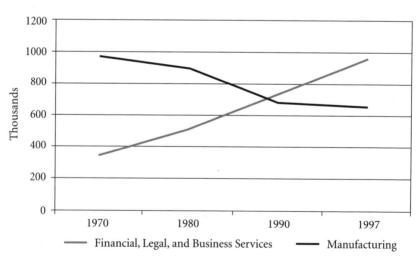

Source: U.S. Department of Commerce, County Business Patterns, author's calculations

son, far-flung global business activity demands frequent, fast, and wide-ranging air transport.

As the information age began to unfold and business-service industries were growing, Chicago had a compelling need for a new personal travel industry and airfield infrastructure. The city developed a mighty presence in the business travel arena, and early and deep investment in both convention and trade show facilities has been one part of its success.

Another element was the construction in 1962 of what has become the world's busiest jetport, O'Hare Field. In the course of its development, O'Hare Airport became the home hub of two of the world's most extensive domestic airline networks—those of American Airlines and the hometown airline, United. Chicago serves many domestic and international destinations, with frequent flights to business-center cities. Chicago's other airport, Midway, is smaller (and older) and handles local traffic and short-haul international flights. By 2002, Chicago's two airports handled 83.6 million passengers a year, leading the world.

It is impossible to predict the impact that the coming structural changes in the airline industry will have on the Chicago region over the long term. As the writing of this book was being completed, United had already filed for bankruptcy and American Airlines was struggling with the same issues

Figure 2. Nonstop International Destinations

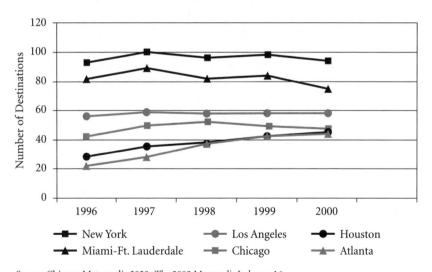

Source: Chicago Metropolis 2020, *The 2002 Metropolis Index,* p. 16.

of high operating costs and the decline in air travel, a fallout from the September 11, 2001, terror attacks on New York and Washington, D.C. These carriers' problems were so severe that the plans to expand O'Hare were put on hold, though they are now active once again.

Continued development of air travel will be needed because of the importance of air connections in the siting of high-level offices and corporate headquarters jobs. Surveys show that both corporate headquarters and regional division offices rank air transport facilities as the number-one reason to locate, ahead of labor, taxes, energy, and regulations. A 1992 report by the Federal Reserve Bank of Chicago noted, "The importance of airport infrastructure to service firms helps to confirm an important economic trend. Increasingly, service-generating industries have become the engine of economic growth in many large metropolitan areas, including Chicago."

On balance, studies indicate significant future losses if Chicago fails to add to the region's air capacity—an important projection to remember as Chicago struggles with economic setbacks. The findings suggest that without additional capacity, employment losses (jobs that would otherwise have been expected to locate in the Chicago region) would rise to 522,000 by 2018 (11 percent of estimated jobs for that year).

International travel to and from Chicago has been the fastest rising component of air travel. From 1993 to the year 2000, domestic flight operations were essentially flat while international flight operations grew by almost three-quarters. In 2002, O'Hare welcomed 8.9 million international visitors—a jump to one international passenger for every six domestic travelers, from under one international passenger for every nine domestic passengers in 1993.

Who are these travelers? Significantly, they are international business travelers. Of Chicago's 1.35 million overseas visitors in the year 2000, 56 percent, or 760,000, arrived with business as their primary purpose. Such visitors have easily been the fastest growing part of Chicago's increasing visitor population, registering a growth of 11.8 percent from 1999 to 2000.

Local overland transportation is equally important to face-to-face communication as it relates to a global city's business health and success. Like other U.S. metropolises, the center city of Chicago has spilled out over its boundaries to configurations of office space in suburban and exurban locales. Unlike some cities that are hemmed in by both water and mountains, and despite the barrier of Lake Michigan to its east, Chicago has ample and functional space for expansion of both jobs and residences. This helps to keep housing costs affordable for workers who have occupations that do not command the stratospheric salaries of many of those in the downtown jobs and in corporate headquarters.

The flip side of this accessibility is that it creates a high volume of traffic. Roadway congestion has begun to make the city a more costly place to assemble office workers and business meetings. Vehicle delays are estimated to have increased on average from thirty-one hours per driver per year in the Chicago area in 1990 to forty-four hours in 1997. Attempts are being made to alleviate some of the congestion through a regionwide dialogue and effort aimed at issues of land use, housing, transportation, and fiscal structure.

The Idea Exchange

Also undergirding Chicago's restructuring into a global service center is its burgeoning travel/hotel/meeting industry. Chicago grew into a world-class center for business meetings and conventions, hosting more conventions, trade shows, and corporate meetings than any other city in the world. Paul O'Connor, executive director of World Business Chicago, reports, "The McCormick Place Complex in Chicago, with 2.2 million square feet of exhibit space, is still and will remain the largest convention center in North America."

This sort of meeting activity complements Chicago's local business-service firms in a couple of ways. First, the added travel activity associated with these conventions and meetings increases the scope of the region's air transportation. For inbound customers of Chicago's business services, and for outbound Chicagoans in these industries, too, convention travel increases the number of commercially viable flight destinations and frequencies.

Second, in today's global business environment, the value of exchange of information is magnified. These numerous local professional convention meetings are one more element that makes Chicago's business-service firms more productive. They help make Chicago a place where "the ideas are in the air," to be plucked and shaped by circulating gabbers, hustlers, and entrepreneurs as they practice the art of networking and the art of the deal. Such a convergence of learning and the exchange of information is critical for another Chicago strength, the attraction of the corporate headquarters operations of large companies.

Just as cities must adapt to changes in globalization and technologies, business organizations must adapt to the same circumstances. For this reason, corporate headquarters have historically chosen to locate in very large cities, where the information they need about the latest business trends is in the air, and highly developed and complex financial and other business services are available. As a metropolitan area, Chicago remains second only to

New York as a U.S. headquarters city for large, publicly traded companies with at least 2,500 employees.

However, along with much of the Northeast and Midwest, Chicago has lost prominent headquarters as manufacturing and other industries have drifted away to regions in the Sun Belt. Once-notable Chicago names such as International Harvester, Inland Steel, Morton, Pullman, Helene Curtis, Amoco, and U.S. Robotics have been lost to reorganization or to mergers. These losses have caused concern that the city is rapidly losing its place in the pecking order of global business affairs. While alarm is not entirely misplaced, it appears to be somewhat overdrawn.

There tends to be "churn" among headquarters in most cities, which sometimes gives a false sense that the bottom is falling out. For Chicago, the prominent brand-name losses obscure an underlying trend, which is that Chicago is *gaining* headquarters rather than losing them. Far from moribund

Table 1. Headquarters in Top Metropolitan Areas, by 2000 Population

Metropolitan Area	2000 Population (thousands)	2000 Headquarters	Net Change in Headquarters from 1990	
			Number	Percentage
New York/northern New Jersey/Long Island, CMSA	21,200	239	16	7.2
Los Angeles/Riverside/Orange County, CMSA	16,374	85	4	4.9
Chicago/Gary/Kenosha, CMSA	9,158	109	13	13.5
Washington/Baltimore, CMSA	7,608	66	22	50.0
San Francisco/Oakland/San Jose, CMSA	7,039	91	39	75.0
Philadelphia/Wilmington/Atlantic City, CMSA	6,188	70	15	27.3
Boston/Worcester/Lawrence, CMSA	5,819	66	11	20.0
Detroit/Ann Arbor/Flint, CMSA	5,456	34	1	3.0
Dallas/Fort Worth, CMSA	5,222	76	18	31.0
Houston/Galveston/Brazoria, CMSA	4,670	70	29	70.7
Atlanta, MSA	4,112	53	25	89.3
Miami/Fort Lauderdale, CMSA	3,876	31	16	106.7
Seattle/Tacoma/Bremerton, CMSA	3,555	19	−1	−5.0
Phoenix/Mesa, MSA	3,252	23	12	109.1
Minneapolis/St. Paul, MSA	2,969	50	12	31.6
Cleveland/Akron, CMSA	2,946	35	−4	−10.3
San Diego, MSA	2,814	18	8	80.0
St. Louis, MSA	2,604	39	12	44.4
Denver/Boulder/Greeley, CMSA	2,582	27	12	80.0
Tampa/St. Petersburg/Clearwater, MSA	2,396	20	9	81.8
Pittsburgh, MSA	2,359	21	0	0.0
Portland/Salem, CMSA	2,265	13	−1	−7.1

Source: Thomas Klier and William Testa, "Location Trends of Large Company Headquarters during the 1990s," *Economic Perspectives* (2nd quarter, 2002), table 2.

as a corporate headquarters locale, Chicago gained thirteen headquarters of large companies (those employing over 2,500 workers) between 1990 and 2000.

The city's morale was given a strong boost in 2000, when Chicago snagged Boeing, a global giant, over rival cities Denver and Dallas after a keen competition. As attested by the vigor with which civic leaders in each city competed for the Boeing facility, headquarters operations of large multinationals are a highly valued asset to local economies.

In commenting on the choice of Chicago, John Warner, the Boeing executive who spearheaded the relocation of its headquarters, noted Chicago's attributes as a place for global business operations. He said, "I listened very carefully to what people were talking about. How they talked to each other. The conversations were about global business. Dallas will say, we do global business, and they are right; there is just a heck of a lot more of it here."

Chicago Transformations

Not all large firms are globally oriented, but Warner is correct in noting that a great deal of globally focused corporate decisionmaking takes place in the Chicago area. The region also boasts headquarters of similarly sized companies having such global scope, namely McDonald's, Motorola, Abbott Laboratories, United Airlines, Sara Lee, Baxter International, and Illinois Tool Works.

Despite the continued prominence of global headquarters operations in Chicago, there are warning signs that Chicago and other U.S. cities that enjoy a headquarters legacy should avoid complacency. According to a recent appraisal of headquarter location trends, the corporate control functions of global companies are becoming more dispersed, suggesting that they are shifting toward midsized U.S. metropolitan areas having a population in the 1–2 million range. This contrasts with the business-services industry, which, as mentioned, continues to concentrate in the very largest cities. It also runs somewhat contrary to earlier thinking that the largest cities should be gaining headquarters because of the expansion of global markets due to broader international trade pacts and lower costs of communication and transportation. The contrary trend echoes the findings of the sociologist and globalization expert Saskia Sassen, who observes (see chapter 1) that many of the largest cities worldwide have been losing headquarters of the world's largest companies for over three decades.

The management consultant Peter Drucker once advised firms to "sell the mailroom"; Sassen claims that they are now selling both the mailroom

Table 2. Foreign Sales of Chicago Headquarters

Rank	1990 Company Name	SIC	1990 Foreign Sales ($ millions)	1990 Percentage of Total Sales	2000 Foreign Sales ($ millions)	2000 Percentage of Total Sales
1	Motorola Inc.	3663	$5,896	54.2	$26,907	87.0
2	Sears Roebuck & Co.	5311	4,221	7.5	NR	NR
3	Sara Lee Corp	2013	3,323	28.6	7,857	39.3
4	UAL Corp	4512	3,010	27.3	5,451	30.2
5	McDonald's Corp	5812	2,769	41.7	8,166	61.6
6	Abbott Laboratories	2834	2,245	36.5	4,887	37.1
7	Baxter International Inc.	2834	1,855	22.9	3,459	54.2
8	Quaker Oats Co.	2000	1,653	32.9	1,091	23.1
9	Illinois Tool Works	3089	1,160	45.6	3,138	33.6
10	Household International Inc.	6141	931	21.6	1,209	12.7
11	FMC Corp	2800	778	20.9	2,330	56.7
12	Wrigley (WM.) JR Co.	2060	449	40.4	1,202	58.3
13	Molex Inc.	3678	422	71.1	1,127	65.8
14	Whitman Corp	2000	408	17.7	187	8.7
15	Brunswick Corp	3510	365	14.7	831	19.4
16	USG Corp	3270	357	18.6	486	13.5
17	Outboard Marine Corp	3510	353	30.8	244	21.9
18	AON Corp	6321	350	13.3	2,939	41.6
19	Navistar International	3711	343	8.9	947	11.0
20	ITEL Corp[a]	5063	290	14.6	863	32.3

Sources: Compustat, company Web sites, author's calculations.
Note: Table ranked by level of foreign sales in 1990; included are only large companies surviving in same metro area. NR indicates that data were not available.
a. ITEL is now ANIXTER Intl.

and the boardroom. Accordingly, the concentration of business-service companies in a city rather than headquarters has become the key feature by which to identify dominant "global cities."

Service Industry

Chicago has been transformed by the service industries of the so-called new economy, or information economy, and this has served as the basis for its continued prominence among world cities. Does Chicago's success look promising enough to place it at the pinnacle among its peer cities? Is it, then, poised for future growth? Or is its business-service transformation something less, something welcome but not so promising?

If not yet dominant on the scene, Chicago has experienced a more profound transformation—from "stacker of wheat" to "service city"—than have other large metropolitan areas in the United States. From 1977 to 1997, a period for which we can accurately assign job growth to specific industry sectors, Chicago added over 328,000 jobs in business services, financial sectors, and legal services.

That this happened while the greater Midwest region was stagnating and the city's manufacturing growth was shifting elsewhere makes the gains all the more dramatic. Concentration in this overall business-service sector climbed from 16 percent above the national average in 1977 to 22 percent above by 1997. Though Chicago continues to trail New York and San Francisco in concentration of such services, it was the only one of the major cities to record an increase in that period.

Banking and Niches

In looking at the business-service subsectors in search of Chicago's niches and specialties, we find striking differences among leading metropolitan areas. Chicago leads other cities by a significant margin in commodities exchanges and derivatives industries, recording a concentration that is over ten times the national average. No other national or regional capital city comes close. Chicago has also gathered itself as the capital city of Real Estate Investment Trusts, with an employment concentration that is almost three times the national average.

With respect to other financial industries, Chicago's concentrations of employment are healthy but unexceptional. Its concentration in insurance industries is strong and notable, but not dominating. Likewise, commercial banking is strong but not dominant, although Chicago does edge out its peer midwestern cities in this regard, through a combination of foreign bank branches—it hosts forty—and, until recently, the national headquarters of Bank One (the fifth-largest commercial U.S. bank as ranked by assets), along with many middle-market and small *de novo* banks that have sprung up to serve the city and its communities. Early in 2004, a merger was announced between Bank One and J. P. Morgan Chase of New York. The headquarters of the newly merged company will be in New York City rather than Chicago. While Chicago will retain many important operations and functions of the company, the loss of headquarters activities is a sharp blow to the city's stature in the financial arena.

Companies engaging in capital market originations—ranging from private company equity offerings to venture capital to the underwriting of public securities—are highly valued in economic development terms. This is because many of these sources of capital are the lifeblood of new companies or young, fast-growing companies. In investment banking and related activities, New York undisputedly remains at the top of the heap, followed by the San Francisco Bay Area, where underwriting and venture capital for high-tech industries remain strong. Chicago runs modestly above the national average in this overall category, though better than Atlanta, Dallas, Houston, Los Angeles, and Miami.

Chicago's venture capital share lies much closer to the average of the high-tech-mecca wannabes in the world. Indeed, Chicago's share of fast-growth companies, at 2.8 percent of the national total in 1999, is close to the national average.

Chicago's activity in the "new economy" is healthy and diverse, although it tends to fall short of the high expectations of many local observers. Measures that are based on absolute numbers without discounting for Chicago's mammoth size tend to lift the region into the top ten in high-tech or innovative capacity rankings. When those measures are weighted or shaped by the size of innovative or high-tech activities in relation to the size of the city, Chicago falls to a respectable middle-of-the-pack position. One notable, comprehensive study places Chicago nineteenth out of fifty large U.S. metropolitan areas as measured by sixteen "new economy" indicators ranging from venture capital to worker education to telecommunications infrastructure to patents issued to high-growth firms.

Meanwhile, as in other aspiring metropolitan areas, the Chicago region's policy makers are striving to make more of Chicago's assets and potential. For example, the Mayor's Council of Technology Advisors has identified four sectors in which it believes the region can excel, if only it can shape the environment. These are biomedicine (including biotechnology, medical diagnostics, and medical devices); wireless software; software development; and emerging technologies, including nanotechnology (manipulation of structures at the atomic level that may affect, among other areas, computing and medicine).

On the more mundane levels of the information age, Chicago is not a dominant media center on the order of New York or Los Angeles. It registers high neither in publishing concentration nor in broadcast and communications industries.

In overall "professional and technical services," Chicago is strong but not dominant. The rapidly growing legal sector in Chicago now records an above-average employment concentration, but it is dwarfed by those of New York City, Miami, and, to a lesser extent, the San Francisco area. By some accounts, the rising importance of global connections for many legal firms is motivating some Chicago law firms to initiate merger or affiliation arrangements with New York firms. This same theme is echoed in advertising. The strength of Chicago's advertising industry, with a concentration 80 percent above national norms, may surprise some observers. Still, Chicago's prowess in advertising is threatened by the trend toward product ad campaigns and messages that are harmonized across the globe. New York City, for one, presents a stiff challenge to Chicago as the domicile of such creative work in advertising.

Computer-system design and related services employment are 40 percent more concentrated in Chicago than the national average, but this ranks Chicago only fourth, behind Atlanta, Dallas, San Francisco, and New York. However, in this and other instances, it is true that size matters. World Business Chicago reports that, in an occupational ranking across all industries, the Chicago metropolitan area leads all others in the sheer numbers of employees engaged in computer programming ("over twice as many as Silicon Valley").

Finally, Chicago excels in one of the particular industries that have been identified as paramount to world business-service prominence. In 1999, over forty-five thousand people were reported employed in Chicago in "management-consulting services," which amounts to the second-highest concentration, behind that of Atlanta. With regional head offices or significant operations of such firms as Accenture, McKinsey and Co., Boston Consulting Group, Peat Marwick, and A. T. Kearney, Inc., and despite the post-Enron loss of Arthur Andersen, Chicago's concentration is two and one-quarter times higher than the national average.

On the strength of such activities, the city stands as a major control center in administering and setting strategic directions for the Midwest's firms and industries. Further, the city hopes that some of these firms can also provide a springboard for "new economy" industries such as wireless software and biomedicine.

Hauling and Manufacturing

Although services and information industries are ascending in Chicago's business scene, the manufacture and distribution of goods are highly significant and likely to remain so. And, though few in Chicago may realize it, to speak of Chicago's economic growth and well-being outside the context of the Midwest and its dominant manufacturing base would be severely misguided. Chicago's transportation, financial, and business-service sectors grew in tandem with manufacturing and as a market maker and shipper of the greater region's natural resources. Today, Chicago's active business-service firms continue to sell their wares to the surrounding Midwest region's manufacturing companies. And although manufacturing itself has waned in the Chicago region as it has in the very largest U.S. cities generally, Chicago remains an important, even prodigious, manufacturer.

Measured in "real" terms—not in dollar prices but in physical units or by comparable qualitative properties—manufacturing output has held roughly steady at around 20 percent of overall U.S. output over the past fifty to sixty years.

However, jobs in manufacturing are another story. While jobs in services have been growing apace with or above the rate of population growth in the United States, jobs in goods production have stagnated or slightly declined. In the United States, jobs in the manufacturing sector have increased by only 5 percent since 1969. More worrisome for Chicago and the Midwest, as of early 2004, manufacturing jobs nationwide had fallen by 2.7 million since the year 2000.

Workers in the American Midwest (and adjoining Ontario) continue to be much more concentrated in manufacturing industries than the national average. Accordingly, they tend to experience displacement as individual industries such as steel, consumer electronics, and autos feel the impact of trade and technological change, and as markets for new products shift.

As the Midwest industrialized in the late 1800s and became the national and world center for manufacturing, its residents enjoyed high and rising incomes. Today, while the Midwest's economy has been restructured toward services production and services paychecks, the region's personal income remains much more highly concentrated in manufacturing—again, not in absolute numbers as compared to yesteryear, but in comparison to the rest of the country today. This is especially true for its capital goods industries— farm machinery, heavy trucks, construction machinery, and others. This, along with consumer goods such as appliances and autos, means that the region remains the center of the continent for durable goods manufacturing, with Wisconsin, Indiana, and Michigan the three most durable-goods-intensive among the fifty states. Despite this concentration, the relative size of the overall midwestern economy as a share of U.S. economy sagged in the 1970s and 1980s precisely because the overall manufacturing sector's nominal share of the national economy fell. Even so, the Midwest began regaining a national share of manufacturing employment and output beginning in the late 1980s. It did so as its companies revamped themselves to become competitive with global standards.

This manufacturing intensity affects Chicago both directly and indirectly. Directly, the Chicago metro region itself remains a manufacturing behemoth; its production and overseas exports are prodigious. Indirectly, much of Chicago's business-service activity derives from or is connected to regional manufacturing and, to a lesser extent, agriculture. For example, advertising firms in Chicago sell to manufacturers of processed foods; Chicago investment banks may underwrite or secure the financial debt of makers of construction or farm machinery; management consultants may be dispatched to advise engine makers on production-line efficiencies or tax matters.

Estimates from economic models suggest that for every dollar of goods output—manufacturing and agriculture—in the surrounding Midwest region, an additional forty cents is stimulated in Chicago's services sectors. In this way, the Midwest's manufacturers and the outlying businesses that serve them underpin the Chicago economy.

Another characteristic of the robust manufacturing trade between Chicago and midwestern states is that the region is highly interdependent. Just as a city survives by the working together of highly specialized parts and functions, so do the region's manufacturers flourish over a broad, multistate landscape.

Overland transportation, then, is critical to the efficient functioning of this interdependent, goods-oriented economy. It is not surprising to find that the land transportation infrastructure and the Midwest's transport-distribution sector are highly developed, having been hallmarks of Chicago's economy from its beginning.

In recent years, Chicago has capitalized on the legacy of its historic position as a railroad transfer point where all major U.S. trunk line railroads converge. In particular, the Chicago area has become North America's center for overland "intermodal" transport. Such transportation, whereby cargo is transferred from, for instance, ship to truck or truck to train, has been growing rapidly as "containerization" has been standardized, refined, and adopted. Containerization is the process by which shipped goods are boxed in standard-size metal containers, thereby facilitating cheaper loading and unloading. This, in turn, has put Chicago in a favored position to take advantage of increased global trade. Chicago is the nexus for a great volume of transcontinental transfer of containers, more than anywhere else in the United States.

In 1999, for example, the Chicago region "handled" over 11 million containerized "lifts," or cargo transferals. An earlier comparison among North American cities found Chicago's capacity more than double that of its nearest competitor, Los Angeles–Long Beach. A ranking of the world's waterborne ports would now show Chicago's land-based facilities ranked third, behind the ports of Singapore and Hong Kong.

Chicago also maintains a collection of maritime facilities along navigable waterways, the so-called Port of Chicago, although the importance of such facilities has diminished severely.

Figure 3. North America's Intermodal Hub

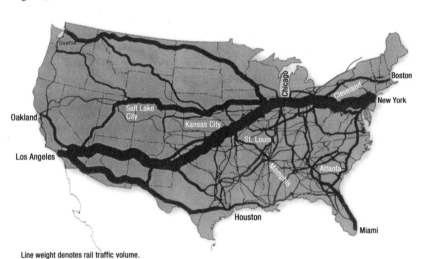

Line weight denotes rail traffic volume.
Source: www.globalchicago.org, PowerPoint by Jon Devries, Arthur Anderson

Like other favored positions in the global economy, Chicago's continued niche in distribution is far from assured. Many of its intermodal freight yards date back more than a century and are located close to the urban core, where truck movement of containers is impeded by dated and low-hanging underpasses and other infrastructure deficiencies. The saying goes that it takes goods two days to get to Chicago and another two days to get through Chicago.

Transfer times within the Chicago area are the source of much complaint among freight haulers. In response, competitive intermodal yards have been developed to bypass Chicago, and others are on the drawing board elsewhere on the midcontinent. The Chicago area has responded with its own local improvements and new developments, including a forthcoming 612-acre intermodal center at the former Joliet military arsenal, located in the southwest quadrant of the region, away from the urban core.

Air cargo facilities have also become more prominent as world commerce shifts toward lighter and higher-value manufactured traded goods, in comparison to the bulky natural resource commodities of yesteryear. Chicago's O'Hare Airport ranked sixteenth in total air cargo worldwide in the year 2002, with 1.28 million metric tons, domestic and international cargo combined, down from 1.47 million tons (and a twelfth-place ranking) just two years before, preceding the manufacturing-led recession of 2001. O'Hare ranked fourth in international air cargo among U.S. airports in 2002.

Table 3. International Freight Rankings for U.S. Airports, 2002

Rank	Airport	City	International Freight (millions of U.S. tons)
1	Miami International (MIA)	Miami	1.38
2	New York Kennedy (JFK)	New York	1.28
3	Los Angeles International (LAX)	Los Angeles	0.96
4	O'Hare International (ORD)	Chicago	0.81
5	San Francisco International (SFO)	San Francisco	0.34
6	Hartsfield Atlanta International (ATL)	Atlanta	0.30
7	Newark International (EWR)	Newark	0.18
8	Memphis International/FedEx (MEM)	Memphis	0.18
9	Dallas–Ft. Worth International (DFW)	Dallas	0.17
10	Washington Dulles International (IAD)	Washington, D.C.	0.14

Sources: Miami International Airport, <http://www.miami-airport.com/html/cargo_rankings_.html>; Airports Council International (ACI) and respective airport traffic reports.

Exporting

While transportation and distribution generate much income and employment for Chicagoans, these industries also favor Chicago as a place to manufacture and sell abroad. Historically, Chicago manufacturing activity has been accompanied by export overseas, and this is still the case. Despite the robust growth of international trade in services (now 30 percent of overall U.S. exports), manufacturing continues to dominate trade flows—and U.S. exports have grown as a share of gross production from 4.5 percent in 1970 to 11.6 percent in 2001.

As the continuing geographic center of U.S. durable goods production, the Great Lakes region is strongly tied to world markets through both imports and exports. On the export side, 7.6 percent of the product of the six-state Great Lakes region in 1999 was comprised of manufacturing exports. This was slightly more than the national percentage. The Chicago (and Illinois) manufacturing export shares are lower than those of both the overall United States and the region, owing to the city's importance as a business-service and transportation center. However, in a broader context, business and transportation services are actually embedded in the value of reported exports, and for this reason the numbers are deceiving: exported midwestern products often contain financial, advertising, and legal-service value produced in Chicago.

Taken one by one, the Chicago and midwestern manufacturing industries tend to be less export-oriented than those industries that are concentrated in other U.S. regions. Nonetheless, what it lacks industry by industry in export orientation, the Midwest makes up for with the sheer size of its overall manufacturing sector as compared to the rest of the nation. The export intensity and sensitivity to the ebb and flow in global markets are

Table 4. Manufacturing Exports/Gross State Product (in percent)

	United States	Midwest	Chicago Area
1993	6.5	7.1	5.1
1999	6.9	7.6	6.7

Sources: United States and state export data are from the MISER database. Chicago export data is from the U.S. Department of Commerce, International Trade Administration. United States and state GSP data are from the U.S. Department of Commerce, Bureau of Economic Analysis.

achieved because the region's manufacturing sector income is 50 percent larger as a share of its surrounding economy than that of the nation as a whole. Important export industries from the Chicago region by category include electric and electronic equipment (including but not limited to telecommunications); industrial machinery; chemicals (including both industrial chemicals and pharmaceuticals); and transportation equipment (including autos and railroad equipment).

The categories of Chicago's manufactured products reveal less about them than do the marquee names of the specific companies associated with the products. "Electronic and Electronic Equipment Sales," leading the pack at $4.8 billion in 2000, is largely accounted for by Motorola, maker of cellular phones, microchips (elsewhere), and many other communication devices and components. Though smaller in size, Tellabs, which produces a broad array of telecommunications products and services, also adds to this mix.

Further down the list, "chemical products" represents Fortune 500 companies Abbott Laboratories and Baxter International, makers of pharmaceuticals and health industry products. These companies are large multinationals headquartered in Chicago, but they also conduct substantial research activity—especially Abbott Labs—and have production facilities in the Chicago area. "Food products" is also well represented as an export industry in the Chicago area, at almost $687 million in 1999.

Chicago's extensive freight railway system still makes the city a natural center to bring in raw products, process them, and send them back out across America as meat products, cereals and packaged foods (e.g., Kraft, Sara Lee), and candy-confectionery (e.g., Tootsie Roll and Leaf). In fact, the Chicago metropolitan area has approximately one hundred candy companies, enough to lead some interested local parties to call it the "premier candy center" of the United States. Chicago, however, may eventually lose this distinction because a combination of federal quotas on the import of sugar and price floors for domestic sugar farmers has resulted in domestic sugar prices that are double that of the world market. This has increased production costs for local candy companies to the point where longtime candy producers such as Archibald and Brach's have closed shop and moved production abroad, where lower sugar (and labor) costs allow them to compete with foreign candy manufacturers.

In its global trade, the Midwest is oriented with Canada to a much higher degree than the rest of the nation. Canada is both the United States' and the Midwest's largest trading partner. Indeed, the trade between the Great Lakes states and Ontario has been aptly described as the "nucleus" of the

Canada-U.S. trade relationship. The volume of exports and imports changing hands around the Great Lakes amounted to almost $100 billion in 1998.

As Mexican industry develops and the Mexican people become more prosperous, they turn to a greater variety and volume of American products, thereby enriching both themselves and midwestern industries and workers. Of course, with open markets comes the intermittent upheaval of industries and their workers, but it must be recognized that in market economies, such upheaval takes place in any event in response to domestic competition and technological change.

Still, the opening of markets can add to displacement and dislocation so that the human and social costs, if not mitigated by careful government policies, are borne by a small subset of workers for the benefit of the greater population. But for Chicagoans, upheaval from increased trade with Mexico has probably been fairly minor, dwarfed by the tumult of the technological changes taking place in industry overall. If anything, net manufacturing activity in the Chicago area may well be greater than it would have been in a non-NAFTA world, with exports to Mexico more than doubling since 1993 (to over $2 billion per year).

While the Chicago metropolitan region by itself represents a hefty manufacturing economy, its employment base in this sector is far from what it once was. The metropolitan area has lost over three hundred thousand manufacturing jobs since 1967, and two out of three such jobs since 1954, when its economy was significantly more concentrated in manufacturing. Though the manufacturing-job share of its economy, at 13 percent, is now only slightly above the national par, the share exceeds that of other large metropolitan areas.

Table 5. Chicago Metropolitan Area's Merchandise Exports to Selected Destinations

	1993 (thousands)	1999 (thousands)	Growth since 1993 (thousands)	Change
World	$14,446,576	$21,144,095	$6,697,519	46.4%
Canada	2,978,126	5,012,949	2,034,823	68.3
Mexico	1,021,119	2,103,563	1,082,444	106.0
Japan	1,608,057	1,882,841	274,784	17.1
Rest of Asia	2,836,879	3,083,087	246,208	8.7
United Kingdom	794,775	1,154,033	359,258	45.2
Germany	766,796	1,106,526	339,730	44.3
Rest of Europe	2,377,357	3,543,227	1,165,870	49.0
Africa	242,474	231,388	−11,086	−4.6

Sources: U.S. Department of Commerce, International Trade Administration. All figures show sales by exporters of record located in the indicated area. The sales location may or may not coincide with the location of production.

The upshot is that the absolute size of Chicago's manufacturing sector makes it supreme among metropolitan areas—if one excludes the consolidated New York–New Jersey–Connecticut metropolitan area, which, in fairness, is more "eastern seaboard" than a single urban area.

As a direct exporter of manufactured goods, Chicago was credited with an international merchandise export volume of $21 billion in 1999, placing it sixth among metropolitan areas, behind Seattle, San Jose, Detroit, New York, and Los Angeles in value of exports shipped. These manufactured exports as a share of its local economy, at 6.7 percent in 1999, are just about on par with the overall United States economy.

Importing

The Midwest's high concentration of durable-goods manufacturing ensures that a large share of U.S. imports of durable goods finds its way to the region, since interindustry trade is highly developed. Estimates by the Federal Reserve Bank of Chicago suggest the Great Lakes region receives about 30 percent of the nation's imports of durable goods, about twice that of the next-highest region. This is not surprising if we consider that the vast majority of trade occurs between and among industrial sectors. Most trade, contrary to popular belief, takes place not between developed and less-developed countries, but between highly developed economies and their multinational companies. In manufacturing especially, sophisticated trade in small, specialized submarkets is the norm. Such imports and exports among manufacturers

Table 6. Top Ten Metropolitan Areas Ranked by Value of 1999 Exports

Metropolitan Area	Value of Exports (thousands)	Change since 1993
Seattle/Bellevue/Everett, Wash.	$32,356,050	35.9%
San Jose, Calif.	28,255,739	74.7
Detroit, Mich.	28,008,260	66.9
New York, N.Y.	24,484,725	−13.2
Los Angeles/Long Beach, Calif.	23,904,708	19.4
Chicago, Ill.	21,144,095	46.4
Houston, Tex.	18,967,586	54.4
Minneapolis/St. Paul, Minn./Wis.	12,401,331	37.7
Miami, Fla.	11,942,051	44.5
Boston, Mass./N.H.	10,426,980	61.1

Sources: U.S. Department of Commerce, International Trade Administration. All figures show sales by exporters of record located in the indicated area. The sales location may or may not coincide with the location of production.

often indicate healthy specialization and wealth creation for participating countries, and trade activity often precedes or accompanies transfers of new technology and investment around the world.

Foreign Investing

It is not only trade that has expanded globally, but also ownership and control of the means of production. Much global trade and shipment takes place between and within subsidiary operations or facilities of multinational companies. Such companies usually originate in a single country before branching into foreign investment or assets abroad. The degree to which foreign companies and individuals take ownership positions in U.S. productive assets, either by purchasing or building businesses here, is generally—though not universally—viewed as a favorable sign.

Investment from abroad usually means healthy infusions into the local economy. In addition to job creation and increased income, new technologies and management ideas often accompany the flow of direct investment, some of which may revive moribund domestic industry. Such has been the case with the siting of Japanese auto-assembly operations in the United States. While the incursion of Japanese auto makers into the Midwest in the 1980s was viewed with antipathy in some local quarters, the overarching perspective tells us that the region was fortunate to have been a location of choice for such investment.

To a large extent, the just-in-time (JIT) production technologies and inventory management of Toyota (also called "lean manufacturing") have become an important innovation for midwestern manufacturers and distribution companies. In turn, U.S. companies have proven successful in adopting JIT to corporate and labor cultures and community and regional conditions in the Midwest.

Although there is some information available about the largest foreign-owned Chicago companies, we know much less about the total amounts of foreign-owned or foreign-controlled assets in the Chicago area. The federal government tracks these transactions, but it compiles and reveals the aggregate data for states, not for cities or counties.

Still, since the Chicago area comprises three-quarters of the Illinois economy, the state-level statistics are broadly indicative of trends, sources, and origins of foreign direct investment flowing into Chicago. These data suggest that Illinois and the Chicago area have attracted foreign investment about on par with the overall United States. For 1999, Illinois employment at foreign affiliates totaled 283,500 by the reckoning of the U.S. Bureau of Economic Analysis, representing 3.9 percent of Illinois total employment.

This tops other midwestern states, although it must be remembered that Illinois's overall economy is proportionately larger as well. Employment at foreign-owned establishments has increased by four- or fivefold in the Midwest since 1977. This healthy growth spurted in the late 1980s, as automotive and other manufacturing companies, many of them Japanese, moved or made acquisitions in the region.

Chicago has shared in the resiliency of the automotive industry. Its Torrence Avenue Ford plant remained robust in the 1990s, for example, building the company's number-one car, the Taurus/Sable. While production of that model is currently being phased out, the plant's future looks assured, as it has adopted lean production technologies and has partnered with the city of Chicago and state of Illinois in establishing an adjacent "supplier park" and training facility.

The declining steel sector has been much more problematic for Chicago's South Side, and for adjacent northwest Indiana, too. The U.S. Steel plant along Chicago's south shore, along with Wisconsin Steel, was shuttered in the early 1980s, while more recently, the Indiana Harbor LTV plant in northwest Indiana closed its doors prior to declaring bankruptcy.

Integrated steel firms have continued to erode. Consequently, merger-acquisitions have taken place, such as that between Inland Steel and Ispat International N.V., a holding company based in Rotterdam. There have been outright failures and downsizing reorganizations, such as those of National Steel and LTV Steel Company. The large integrated mills in the Chicago region have withered under competition from U.S. domestic "mini-mills" that produce steel by recycling scrap, as well as from imports from around the world where steel-making capacity has been overbuilt, subsidized, and treated more tolerantly with regard to fouling the air and water.

Nowadays, foreign direct investments in the Chicago area are increasingly being made in cleaner manufacturing industries or in business services, finance, sales, clerical work, or administration. Foreign direct investment by a company usually begins with an overseas branch, often a production plant or service operation that is directed from abroad. But as a foreign-domiciled company becomes more comfortable and/or widens its operations in the United States, it commonly establishes an overseas headquarters or "regional headquarters" in Chicago. The rich array of available business services, premier air travel connections, and a cosmopolitan living environment make the Chicago area a preferred administrative locale.

The contribution of foreign-based investment to Chicago's ongoing growth and well being is keenly recognized, so much so that an active organization has recently been launched to attract investment, both domestic and from around the world. According to World Business Chicago, "Chicago has more foreign-owned firms than any other U.S. city but New York. There are over 1,200 foreign-owned firms at more than 3,000 locations around the Chicago PMSA, employing approximately 200,000 people. These companies involve virtually every type of economic activity. Two large employers in the finance sector are a Dutch firm, ABN AMRO (parent of LaSalle Bank), with 10,000 employees, and from Canada, the Bank of Montreal (parent of Harris Bank), with 6,100 workers. Some large foreign firms are familiar names with long ties to Chicago—BP Amoco, for one. Or Hinckley Springs, owned by Suntory International of Japan, or American Can, owned by Rexam of the U.K. The ten largest foreign-owned employers alone account for some 40,000 jobs in the Chicago area, representing a range of activities including finance, energy, consumer goods, electronics, and food processing."

Chicago as a Direct Investor Overseas

Just as Chicago is a center for large company headquarters, Chicago-based companies also control, own, or source extensive direct investments overseas. Reporting on foreign assets is spotty, and the figures for metropolitan areas often swing dramatically by year, according to the inclusion or exclusion of a single company in any given metropolitan area.

Among the names of Chicago's global companies, it is startling to find the companies that have created the very tools and products that have allowed and incited world commerce to globalize. These would include Motorola's global communications systems, such as radio, satellite, and cellular communication, and now Boeing's commercial jetliners. Our corporate landscape includes the pioneering company to export a cuisine within a single corporate identity—McDonald's Corporation of suburban Oak Brook, Illinois. While these investment initiatives have been daring and innovative, the public reaction to overseas investment is not always hospitable. When U.S. companies invest overseas, popular opinion sometimes takes the view that, after enjoying the comforts and labors of the home country and its workers, these companies are "exporting" their jobs.

Although there is no denying that the ebb and flow of investment—whether across international borders or across county lines—can be disruptive and

Table 7. Foreign Assets by Metropolitan Area, 1990

| | | | Foreign Assets | |
Rank	Metropolitan Area	Total Assets ($ millions)	Amount ($ millions)	Percentage	Percentage Excluding Largest Company
1	New York/northern New Jersey/Long Island, CMSA	$6,616,822	$715,893	10.8	12.1
2	Detroit/Ann Arbor/Flint, CMSA	1,031,080	44,692	4.3	5.9
3	Chicago/Gary/Kenosha, CMSA	962,420	46,123	4.8	6.5
4	Charlotte/Gastonia/Rock Hill, MSA	941,811	0	0.0	0.0
5	San Francisco/Oakland/San Jose, CMSA	754,261	8,003	1.1	1.5
6	Washington/Baltimore, CMSA	739,361	59,294	8.0	16.8
7	Philadelphia/Wilmington/Atlantic City, CMSA	658,734	19,667	3.0	4.9
8	Dallas/Fort Worth, CMSA	579,111	66,939	11.6	15.4
9	Boston/Worcester/Lawrence, CMSA	495,830	13,721	2.8	4.5
10	Houston/Galveston/Brazoria, CMSA	443,491	6,212	1.4	1.9
11	Atlanta, MSA	423,389	15,189	3.6	4.6
12	Hartford, MSA	376,057	0	0.0	0.0
13	Seattle/Tacoma/Bremerton, CMSA	345,462	1,909	0.6	1.6
14	Cleveland/Akron, CMSA	310,340	1,495	0.5	0.7
15	Los Angeles/Riverside/Orange County, CMSA	307,081	22,949	7.5	8.1
		$14,985,250	$1,022,086	6.8	
	Chicago including Boeing	$ 998,567	$ 46,123	4.6	

Sources: Compustat; author's calculations.

sometimes harmful to the lives of workers and communities, the aggregate net effect tends to be beneficial rather than detrimental. For example, formal studies show that when a domestic company has affiliates overseas, the home country tends to be a very active exporter to the affiliate or its overseas region. Such exports are generally associated with highly paid production jobs, as jobs and investment at home are channeled into the higher-paying and more competitive export sectors. In addition, the home company often administers, directs, or services its affiliates located abroad, thereby adding highly paid corporate headquarters jobs to the mix in the United States.

On the other hand, there are often underlying, countervailing trends that dislocate or impoverish specific groups of domestic workers and households. In particular, if U.S. companies tend to open plants abroad for their most labor-intensive (and often low-wage) operations, demands for workers with low skills at home may fall, along with the wages and incomes of this segment of the workforce.

While U.S. companies are no longer compelled to report on assets abroad, many of them do so voluntarily. Among those at the top of the list of foreign assets and reporting in the year 2000 was Motorola, Inc. In its annual report for 2000, Motorola reported over $15.4 billion in foreign assets, comprising over 40 percent of the firm's capital stock. Motorola has eighty-five manufacturing, R&D (research and development), software development, and design centers worldwide, not including sales and service locations.

McDonald's is another homegrown global giant, which opened its first Chicago restaurant in 1955. The company, with over $12 billion in assets abroad, has been among the most aggressive and certainly among the most successful pioneering U.S. multinational companies. By 1994, its foreign sales had reached one-half of its total sales.

Aerospace is perhaps the quintessential global industry, and in 2001, after careful consideration and evaluation, Boeing chose to relocate its headquarters in Chicago. The development of new jetliners involves collaboration with customers—Boeing claims 145 countries worldwide—as well as suppliers spread throughout the world. Suppliers produce not only incidental parts for aircraft, but engines, subsystems, and design elements. On the technical side, Boeing's Office of Technology has formal affiliations with universities and technical institutes around the world.

Boeing has long maintained design and production centers across the globe, and it recently began an accelerated R&D initiative to establish overseas research centers such as the one it opened in Madrid, Spain. Boeing is arguably the grandaddy of global companies in terms of sales and sourcing.

Along with Airbus of Europe, it virtually dominates the world market in sales of civil aircraft. It is the largest exporting company in the United States and, most symbolically, essentially invented and developed the commercial jetliners that have carried globalization's personal travel activity.

Health-services and pharmaceutical companies are fast becoming the most global of enterprises. Mergers, acquisitions, and partnerships have characterized the drug and pharmaceutical industry in recent years as the costs of development and market introduction for new drugs have increased dramatically. This has meant that, to be profitable, firms have become compelled to sell to as broad a market as possible.

Like its competitors, Abbott Laboratories, located in the northern suburbs of Chicago, has been expanding its sales and markets around the world. As one of the largest U.S. companies (with $16 billion in sales for 2001), Abbott Labs reported that 38 percent of its sales were international (to 130 countries). So, too, it has been expanding its assets abroad; for example, one of its latest and most prominent acquisitions was Hokuriku Seiyaku of Japan, a fully integrated pharmaceutical company.

The pharmaceutical industry is also noteworthy because it illustrates the many and expanding global issues and public policy environments in which multinational companies must operate. It is one more sign of the global nature of international commerce that Abbott, along with other big pharmaceutical companies, has been asked to do more in lowering the price of diagnostics and treatments for HIV/AIDS in impoverished regions, especially sub-Saharan Africa. For the sake of goodwill, the company already sells its treatments at "below cost" (cost of production and shipment) in Africa, versus treatment costs that are ten times higher in the United States. Issues like these involving local multinational companies bring the world's public policy problems and issues to Chicagoans' front door. Chicago-domiciled large companies are in the vanguard of the rapid changes in health, technology, communications, travel, and culture.

At the same time that they bring global changes, peoples, cultures, and issues closer to our attention, foreign investment and operations abroad bring jobs—often highly paid jobs—to Chicago. In an effort to keep their operations competitive, Chicago's companies are developing strategies to draw on the talents of the best workforce in the world. This often involves initiatives like Boeing's establishing a research center in Spain to affiliate with the best research talent around the world, but Chicago companies must often induce global talent to relocate to Chicago.

Immigration and the Workforce

Chicago has long been a magnet for immigrants, dating back to the 1840s. Strong immigration continued through the later nineteenth century and into the early twentieth century, with a kaleidoscope of nations and cultures represented. The later waves of immigrants were largely from eastern and southern Europe. As reported in the 2000 census, over one-half of Chicago-area residents considered themselves to be of Irish, German, Polish, or Italian ancestry (approximately evenly split among the four).

In recent decades, Chicago immigration—both legal and illegal—has been dominated by Mexico and Central America, and there has been a steady climb in the number of immigrants from Asian countries. Chicago remains the most popular midwestern destination for immigrants to the United States. As of 1990, the foreign-born population of the Chicago region approached 17 percent—in comparison to that of its closest urban competitor in the Midwest, Minneapolis–St. Paul, at slightly over 6 percent.

The Chicago region, with about 3.5 percent of the overall U.S. population, has drawn especially from Poland (36.8 percent of the total of Polish immigrants to the United States), India (8.2 percent of Indian immigrants), and the Americas—especially Mexico (6.5 percent of the very large Mexican

Figure 4. Foreign Born as a Share of Total Population in Metro Areas

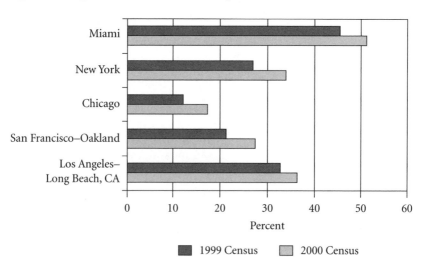

Source: U.S. Census Bureau, data are for PMSA's.

immigration). By the late 1990s, Chicago was drawing 38 percent of its work-ing-age legal immigrants from Latino countries and 31 percent from Asia, as compared to 22 percent from Latino countries and 7 percent from Asia pri-or to 1965. At 29 percent, Mexican immigrants dominate both in absolute numbers and in share.

The recent surge in numbers of immigrants to the Chicago region has been the largely untold secret behind its revitalized growth in the 1990s. The population of the Chicago metropolitan area grew by 869,000 (11.6 percent) between 1990 and 2000. This has been the strongest decade of growth in thirty years. Metropolitan area growth by immigration has been partly offset by emigration of native-born households. In this, Chicago joins some other large metropolitan areas—New York City, Los Angeles, and San Francisco—that are experiencing offsetting out-migration of domestic households to other regions of the United States while receiving a sizable influx due to immigra-tion from abroad.

Following the experiences of prior eras, the central city has been the beneficiary of such immigration. Owing to recent immigrants and their U.S.-born offspring, the city of Chicago's population gain of 112,000 during the 1990s was the first in more than fifty years. This renaissance can be plainly seen in the revival of many older urban neighborhoods. However, the cen-tral city's recent population growth is not quite as robust as it might be be-cause many immigrants have immigrated directly to the suburbs or have moved there from the city.

A growth in the Latino population exceeded gains of white and black populations in both the city and the Cook County suburbs, while also con-tributing over 200,000 in population gains to the remainder of the Chicago region. In the city itself, population gains can be wholly attributed to the Latino population, as both the white and black central-city populations de-clined over the decade. According to Ken Johnson, a demographer at Loyola University, "Much of this growth was fueled by immigration and natural increase, with Hispanics contributing disproportionately to both." More than two-thirds of the growth in Hispanic population was due to natural increase, rather than to immigration.

The strength of recent immigration directly to the suburbs and the at-tendant natural increase have been surprising given the historic tendency of immigrants to disembark in the central city before ultimately climbing the socioeconomic ladder upward and moving outward toward suburbia in sub-sequent generations. New, highly skilled immigrants to the Chicago area have increasingly bypassed the city for the suburbs. Computer programmers and engineers, for example, have gone to work for fast-growing high-tech and telecommunications companies located in the western and northern suburbs, such as Naperville and Western Springs.

The federal government significantly expanded immigration ceilings and positions for those having occupational skills sought by employers in the 1990s, and Chicago companies such as Lucent, Tellabs, and others have been the workforce beneficiaries. In addition, both lower-skilled service-sector jobs and more traditional manufacturing jobs in the suburbs have been eagerly filled by recently arrived workers.

Despite some easing of entry restrictions intended to bring high-tech workers into the United States during the 1990s, the bulk of recent immigrants has been exceptionally low skilled. The most recent immigrant wave has been characterized by a deep deficit in years of schooling completed, as compared with that of the existing U.S. workforce and population. For example, native-born males aged twenty-five to sixty-four in 1998 had completed 13.4 years of school; their counterparts from Mexico reported an average of only 8.6 years. (The gap for females was marginally higher than that of males.)

Schools and school systems throughout Chicago are struggling to adapt to the requirements of the many different languages and family backgrounds of immigrant and first-generation students. Approximately sixty thousand children in the Chicago Public Schools District—one in seven—are enrolled in Limited English Proficiency courses. Even second-generation students, and there are plenty of them, are reported to be lagging in achievement. While Chicago schools have much experience with foreign-born students, a lack of political participation by recently arrived Hispanic families may be a weakness in directing public resources and programs toward Hispanic immigrant communities.

Most reputable studies show that immigrants are not, overall, a fiscal burden; they tend on average to pay more in taxes over their lifetime than the cost of government services received. However, public school systems in Illinois (and in some other states) rely heavily on local rather than state funding, meaning that suburban schools that receive a large number of high-cost and property-poor immigrant families with children will be fiscally strained as they attempt to meet the needs of such children.

A failure to bring immigrant children up to speed quickly, despite the challenges, will mean that the Chicago-area labor pool may one day be burdened by a subset of people with lower skills than are needed. Household income disparities will remain large, and the most recently arrived Chicagoans will make slower progress than those who preceded them.

Like newcomers before them, Chicago's new immigrant workers struggle to upgrade their skills and jobs at the workplace. One common method is by moving from low-skilled service jobs to manufacturing. By one report, many Chicago-area manufacturing jobs are now held by Hispanic workers, who are often viewed as cheaper labor. Training to qualify workers for manufacturing jobs is taking place both in local community colleges and in factories, with many initiatives led by community organizations.

Beyond the training requirements, the lower-on-average skills of the immigrant workforce are a concern of those who feel that the recent surge of immigrants is depressing wages for indigenous households of limited means. Many foreign-born workers are undocumented, or "illegal aliens," which may make them vulnerable to abuses of U.S. standards for health, safety, and compensation. A survey conducted across twelve immigrant and low-income communities during 1999 in the Chicago area uncovered abuses of overtime pay, minimum wage, and hazardous working conditions.

Analysts of the wage-depressing effect of immigrant workers in Chicago and around the United States remain divided as to its existence and extent. At first blush, it seems logical that a larger supply of lower-skilled workers will tend to depress wages. But in considering the impacts of immigration on indigenous low-income households, some of these analysts offer a countervailing argument that immigrants spend significant amounts of their wages, which in turn creates jobs and lifts general wage levels.

It is also true that income generated by immigrant workers flows back to their home countries in significant amounts. While there are no estimates of the total sent from Chicago, Mexico is the destination for the bulk of U.S. remittances abroad, with $6.3 billion going from the United States to Mexico in 2000.

Such monies can be important, of course, not only to support the basic needs of those remaining behind, but also to encourage growth and development abroad. Reports on the remittances made by Chicago immigrants show that villages in Mexico and Nigeria are using these funds to support basic infrastructure and education, and to develop businesses in the home country. From a self-interested perspective, growth and development abroad not only improve relations with the United States, but also result in increased spending on goods and services from Chicago and the remainder of the country.

Immigrants also add to the very fiber of entrepreneurship that sparks economic growth in Chicago. Many immigrants or first-generation Chicagoans historically enjoyed a meteoric rise to the top of new industries. Julius Rosenwald purchased and built Sears, Roebuck and Company, founding the industry of mail-order retail sales. The company remains a Fortune 500 company today. An entire global industry rose around Sears, with Chicago's Montgomery Ward and Spiegel also taking up catalog sales. On a less heroic scale, Antonio Pasin, a nineteen-year-old Italian immigrant, began building wooden wagons, an activity that soon spawned the Radio Flyer line of toy wagons, which were built here for eighty-seven years.

Not all Chicago entrepreneurs remained in place, but rather went on to improve the lot of humankind in another place. For example, Max Palevsky, the son of Polish immigrants from the Northwest Side of Chicago, moved to California and founded Scientific Data Systems and eventually Intel Corporation, a leading maker of semiconductors and computer hardware. But the rhythmic beat of entrepreneurship carries on today in Chicago. Ilya Talman, a Soviet émigré, left Ukraine for Chicago in the 1970s. Following a series of ventures in employee placement and administration, Talman founded a successful local tech-recruiting business, which reached a yearly revenue of $3.5 million prior to the recent tech downturn.

Meanwhile, some first-generation entrepreneurs have displayed the talent that the city fosters in creating business organizations to improve on the mundane services of living. Arthur Velasquez, the son of Mexican migrant workers, founded Azteca Foods in the 1970s, which has its manufacturing plant on Chicago's Southwest Side. The company's revenues now exceed $30 million, with supermarket sales in thirty-five states.

Chicago has a deep culture of dealmaking and business-building that has been greatly enriched by immigrants. Chicago's efforts to assimilate its newest arrivals can be seen as something of a bellwether as to its ultimate success in its reinvention as a global city. The overarching question is whether Chicago's location, culture, people, and business climate are sufficient to generate the rapid growth that is needed to keep pace with an America that has entered a "new economy." Though the outcome is far from certain, the continuing inflow of immigrants into Chicago must be seen as a positive sign in this regard. More than elsewhere, the United States is a nation of people who vote with their feet and then go on to build business empires.

Conclusion

Globalization is adding to Chicago's challenges, just as it is presenting new opportunities for reinvention. As always, the question comes down to what the urban region can make of its legacy and its opportunities. Taken one by one, Chicago's challenges seem as daunting as its prospects are promising, but confronted strategically, systematically, intentionally, and together, they are surely manageable.

In recent decades, Chicago, in contrast to many "sunrise" cities in newly developing regions of the United States, has had the painful task of working off its historical concentration in manufacturing. However, almost since its inception, Chicago's economy has been diversifying toward high-level functions in finance, business services, and information and transportation infrastructure, and these are the underpinnings of reinvention.

Chicago has done well to hold its own as one of the nation's premier centers of commerce, and as an important place in the global hierarchy of cities. It remains host to many significant corporate headquarters and to a highly developed set of business-service activities, such as meeting and travel, legal, finance, and management consulting operations. Its prodigious air travel infrastructure has been crucial—and it will be necessary to continue building on this asset as its physical capacity becomes strained in the near future. The growth of business-service firms has been outstanding, and global travel connections are a key part of the information trade on which such industries thrive. In addition, these firms will rely on their ability to keep recruiting the best and brightest from throughout the world, an effort for which the quality of life in the metropolitan area matters greatly.

Looking farther afield, the need for a stronger Chicago voice has become apparent as the market for Chicago's products and services has broadened. Chicago must remember the importance of clarity of voice and of purpose, as it moves even more aggressively onto the global economic stage.

3   The Political City

RICHARD C. LONGWORTH

PICTURE THE AMAZEMENT of Rip van Winkle, waking in Chicago's city hall after a twenty-five-year snooze. The mayor's name is still Richard Daley and he's a tough Irish politician, given to bluster and malapropisms and a fierce devotion to family. The city council is still largely a civic joke, rife with corruption, a willing rubber stamp for the mayoral whim. The Democratic Party still rules the city's politics, and the Republican Party barely exists. Poor Rip could be forgiven for asking: Has anything changed here?

The answer is an unambiguous yes. In the quarter century since the death of Mayor Richard J. Daley, even since his son, Richard M. Daley, became mayor in 1989, everything has changed. Chicago, once the capital of the Midwest, has become a global city, competing more with Frankfurt and Shanghai than with Detroit or St. Louis. Workers labor at computer terminals, not blast furnaces, and only traditionally green cities like Seattle have cleaner air. Bistros and three-star restaurants have replaced diners and pizzerias at the center of Chicago cuisine, and a city once famed for its grit and gangsters has blossomed with miles of flowering planters.

Neighborhoods long abandoned to street gangs and drug runners are drawing in new housing and new residents. The children and grandchildren of the Chicagoans who fled the city for the suburbs are returning now, and the icon of residential architecture is no longer the bungalow but the loft—or the rehabbed bungalow. Around the world the most famous Chicagoan these days is no longer Al Capone but Oprah Winfrey.

In the years immediately following the death of Daley I, most press coverage of Chicago carried headlines like "Beirut-by-the-Lake" and "City on the Brink." In the era of Daley II, the world press is more likely to rave about the city's vitality, its cultural scene, and its restaurants. Chicago virtually symbolized the industrial era, and its fortunes rose and fell as that era came and went. When Rip van Winkle nodded off, Chicago was sliding downhill economically, along with the rest of the Rust Belt.

New Wine, Old Bottle

Just as Rip van Winkle awoke to find he was in a new era in which the most important George was no longer George III, but George Washington, Chicago has awakened to a new era—the global era—in which the city most definitely has survived and is now competing to thrive. And yet Rip would be right to be astonished. The shape of politics in Chicago—the dominance of a Daley and the Democratic Party—lives on, virtually unchanged, even as the city itself changed utterly. If ever there was a case of new wine in an old bottle, this is it. The structure of Chicago's city governance under Daley II looks just like that under Daley I, but the son uses it to respond to entirely new issues and needs, and this makes all the difference. "The things that government does are different," says Don Rose, a veteran political analyst, "but the people that do it are not necessarily different."

Put simply, city government under Daley I delivered jobs; under Daley II, it delivers amenities. Once, people came to Chicago for jobs that were already here. Now they come because it's a good place to live; they look for a job, or start a business, once they get here.

Forty years ago, the "machine" itself delivered some of those jobs, in city government and its agencies. As Terry Nichols Clark, Richard Lloyd, Kenneth Wong, and Pushpam Jain have written in their article "Amenities Drive Urban Growth," in the *Journal of Urban Affairs:* "City agencies in Chicago were regarded as job banks for machine loyalists. Even the agencies the mayor did not directly control, such as schools, were not exempt from patronage politics. Chicago's machine organization rewarded people who re-elected the mayor by handing out city jobs, which expanded the local government."

Thousands of other jobs existed in the giant steel mills, stockyards, metal fabricating plants, and other industrial behemoths. These industries, being both big and concentrated, were easy to organize politically: both their management and their unions kept close ties to city hall. Immigrants flooded into Chicago, following the earlier waves of immigrants, and tended to settle in the same neighborhoods. Again, these communities of immigrants, large and geographically concentrated, were easy to organize politically. Often, the first Chicagoans the new arrivals met were precinct captains who greeted them at the train station or bus depot. African Americans from the South flowed north into ghettoes and then into housing projects under the eyes of black aldermen tied into the machine.

Services—jobs, schools, help with the bureaucracy, political pressure—were channeled to constituents by the machine, through aldermen and ward committeemen. Constituents repaid the favors by voting for the machine, which kept it in power. It wasn't textbook democracy, but it amounted to a social contract—votes for services—between government and governed. In the heyday of Daley I, it worked. When Chicago boosters talked about their town as "The City That Works," this tightly run, smoothly functioning political production line was part of what they meant.

An Era of Decline

Daley I's Chicago stopped working long before his death in 1976. Heavy industry declined or decamped to the Sun Belt. The city bled jobs, about 150,000 of them in the first half of the seventies. White flight accelerated: in those years, the city lost about 200,000 persons, many of them middle class, well educated, the kind of people who could afford to move, the kind of people the city needed. Tax revenues shrunk, and so did city services. Public schools, largely abandoned by city hall, grew worse and worse, encouraging the flight of both companies and their employees to the suburbs.

"How many trees do they plant?" the old mayor scoffed at his critics, but the fact was that his city was planting fewer trees, filling fewer potholes, repairing fewer bridges, running only as many libraries as it did before. The Loop remained vibrant and provided a façade of vigorous prosperity, but behind this façade the city crumbled and emptied. Much of this was inevitable.

Chicago, as the capital of the Rust Belt, could not avoid the economic crisis that swept the region in the 1970s. But relentless boosterism from city hall and downtown businesses kept the critics quiet, letting Daley pretend that all was well while problems went unmentioned and, hence, untreated.

Rust corroded Chicago politics, too. It's true that the machine's grip weakened after a 1969 lawsuit against patronage employment brought about the Shakman decree of 1972, a federal ban on political firing. The machine was dealt a further blow in 1983 when Mayor Harold Washington signed a companion ban limiting patronage hiring by the city. But the economic decline probably was more important to the political revolution taking place. As businesses moved or closed, political organizing became harder. With tax revenues down, city hall had fewer city services to offer as a quid pro quo for votes. Second-generation immigrants moved to the suburbs and took their votes with them.

When the first Mayor Daley died, his successors inherited an ineffective government and a rusted machine. The decline in services hit all neighborhoods but struck hardest at African Americans, and they rebelled against the machine. First, their votes helped oust Daley's heir, Michael Bilandic, after a campaign in which Jane Byrne trumpeted the hollowness of city government. Blizzards proved her right by bringing Chicago to its knees, and Byrne became mayor. Four years later, Byrne herself was driven out by a massive swing of black votes to the first African American mayor, Harold Washington. The machine, once a political rainbow of races and ethnic groups all feeding from the same trough, split into black and white factions, and "Council Wars" began. Washington eventually triumphed, and then died at his desk. By 1989, when Daley's son became mayor, he commanded a city in crisis.

Another Daley and a Revival

Chicago still has its problems—segregation, schools, crime, drugs, neighborhoods that never recovered from the earlier collapse, growing inequality between the newly rich and the embedded poor. But it would be absurd today to call Chicago a city in crisis.

Overall crime is down, schools are better, the economy booms, many neighborhoods have hit bottom and are recovering. But mostly there is an air about town, a mood of optimism, an appreciation of the city that amazes longtime residents used to balancing boosterism with a sort of "second-city" defensiveness. Young singles flock to the city for its jobs, beaches, and culture. Young families, no longer deterred by schools, buy into once-stagnant neighborhoods. Old timers who fought the father and dreaded the son agree now that Daley II is doing a good job. Chicago, they say, is simply a great place to live.

If Chicago is not yet a polished global city with the confidence of a London, New York, or Paris, it is a place where global things happen. It possesses formidable global assets—powerful multinational corporations, vibrant ethnic communities, great universities, forums devoted to foreign affairs, wealthy markets, law firms and hospitals and consulting firms that deal daily with the world.

Too often these global assets operate in isolation, seldom interacting, never leveraging their individual strengths to create a stronger whole. But the city is attracting assets, not losing them as it was twenty-five years ago. Its global contacts expand each day. Chicago, locked midcontinent a thousand miles from saltwater, struggles to cast off its midwestern mentality and see itself as a player in the world. It's more global than it was, but nowhere near as global as it's going to be.

Some of this revival under Daley II, like the decline under Daley I, may have been inevitable. As the global economy grows, a city with global connections must grow with it. But part of the credit goes to a shrewd city government, which responded to the new challenges of the global era without really changing the structure it acquired in the industrial era.

This Mayor Daley has never articulated a global strategy for his city. But his actions have changed the thrust of governance in Chicago, recast the whole purpose of city government, and repositioned the city to compete in a global economy. *The Almanac of American Politics,* in a piece about Chicago and its mayor, said that Daley "came to office with a reputation as an inarticulate heir. [He] has proved to be an innovative, thoughtful and effective mayor, one of the most successful Democratic officials in the country." Chicago itself, said the almanac, "has marvelous vitality."

Comforts, Not Jobs

The key to this change is the shift from city government as a provider of jobs to city government as a provider of amenities. This change is not widely understood in the city, but several academics have written about it, none more extensively than Terry Nichols Clark of the University of Chicago, whose book has the whimsical title *Trees and Real Violins: Building Post-Industrial Chicago.* Clark notes that Daley II claims to have planted more trees than any other mayor in the world, and that Chicago's global image has shifted from that of Capone-era gangsters packing machine guns in violin cases to that of the Chicago Symphony on tour, packing real violins in violin cases.

But the book's true focus is the way Chicago's government works. "Building the city and finding Chicagoans jobs were the elder Daley's central aims," Clark says. "He pursued both via massive public works projects." By contrast, "the younger Daley has increasingly stressed making the city a good place to live, as well as work." The difference between the two is symbolized by Meigs Airport. Daley I tried, unsuccessfully, to expand the small airstrip on the lakefront into a true airport on the lake. Now his son has shut it down and wants to turn it into a park.

Why this difference?

Industrial Chicago was a labor pool before it became a city. Giant industries grew up here, and people came from around the world to work in them, and so the city grew and became a civilization. But the key always was jobs. That was why Chicagoans came to Chicago in the first place: they came to work. Global Chicago responds to a different era. "People no longer just move to jobs," Clark says. "Many first choose a city to live in, and then look for a job there, or make the two decisions jointly." In other words, they come to live.

So the availability of an existing job is no longer the key. Earlier generations, especially immigrants, didn't know the word "lifestyle" and couldn't have afforded it if they had. Today, people come to Chicago because of the amenities of life and assume the urban economy will support them. If it doesn't, they will start a business of their own. In this way, the city's economy grows as its population grows.

Other cities, of course, are fighting the same competitive battle, but without the albatross of Chicago's weather. So Chicago must be more beautiful, more vibrant, more fun. This is the campaign that the dour, defensive mayor in city hall is waging—and, so far, winning. In industrial Chicago, the big industries were here because of geography. Chicago was the heartland city at the tip of Lake Michigan, the focus of railways, the midpoint between great lodes of iron, steel, livestock and crops, all of which came by boat or train to be processed here and then shipped out again by boat or train to a world that needed what it supplied.

Today, employers come here because the city offers sweeter but less tangible attractions. An entrepreneur wanting to start a high-tech or global service firm looks for a place with smart, educated workers and the kind of amenities—housing, restaurants, culture—that will attract and keep them. A French company looking to set up a U.S. subsidiary has a limitless choice of American cities to choose from and will pick a place where his employees feel comfortable, a place with good food and good museums and French-language elementary schools and direct flights back to Paris.

A City Freed of Its Geography

Once, geography was destiny. Chicago was irremediably midcontinental, the capital of an inland empire. If you wanted to reach the Middle West, you came to Chicago. If you wanted to reach the great world out there, you went to New York or San Francisco. That's where the ports were and, in an ocean-linked world, everything—goods, people, ideas—flowed through these ports. Chicago was not only the Second City but a second-hand city, getting the world's largesse after the two coasts were done with it.

This is no longer true. In a space-linked world, every place with a satellite dish or a decent airport is a port. Chicago still sees itself as isolated, remote from the world, but in fact it gets the goods, people, and ideas as fast and as fresh as any city. Any investor who wants to go global can do it as quickly from Chicago as he can from dozens of coastal cities. Geography no longer is destiny, nor decisive.

This is why the Art Institute and the Chicago Symphony, the restaurants on West Randolph Street and in River North, the lofts and townhouses in the South Loop and Near West Side are crucial to economic development. It is also why the kind of amenities that city hall provides—low crime rates, better schools, flowering streets, even gondolas and wrought iron—are as important to Chicago today as good railways and compliant unions were in an earlier era.

Chicago during Daley I "was a blue-collar town," Clark has written. "It's political life was . . . dominated by clientelism, patronage, jobs and contracts. Fights over these were like slicing a fixed pie. Now politics turns on multiculturalism and efficient services: relatively universal public goods such as lakefront aesthetics receive more emphasis than the older private goods." As the city changes, so its political priorities change. Today, Chicago's biggest industry is neither steel nor stockyards but entertainment, which encompasses tourism, conventions, and the giant hospitality mill of the city's hotels, restaurants, blues bars, and sports arenas. Clark notes that the most visited park in the United States is not Yellowstone or the Grand Canyon, but Chicago's lakefront.

If terrorist attacks produce a long-term downturn in tourist and business travel, Chicago could suffer disproportionately. The vast hospitality industry around O'Hare Airport—the hotels, restaurants, conference centers, meeting organizers, and convention hosts—depends on business travel. The Loop and the lakefront thrive on tourist travel. Any prolonged impact on this travel means hardship for Chicago and, especially, for the mostly low-wage Chicagoans, many of them immigrants, who serve this industry. A silver lining may be the fact that, despite its efforts, Chicago still does not draw international travelers in the numbers that flow to, say, New York, San Francisco,

Washington, or Orlando. Most of Chicago's tourists come from the Midwest, and presumably they will keep coming.

Huge public projects still dominate Chicago's political life and political scheming, and proximity to the mayor's ear and affections is still the key to prosperity in the city's construction industry. But while his father built highways and promoted the commercial palaces of the Loop, the son builds lakefront paths, bike stations, and a band shell. Highway contracts went to the pals of Daley I and the projects seldom came in on time or on budget. Contracts for Millennium Park went to the pals of Daley II. And it ran late and was over budget.

But if the methods don't change, their purpose—to define the mayor's vision of his city—has changed radically. Daley I built places to work. Daley II, in his encouragement of new lofts and townhouses near the Loop, is building places to live. He even moved into one of them himself.

If this is new wine in old bottles, it comes from a global vineyard. Many analysts agree that the current mayor and his government are responding to global pressures that have put Chicago into competition with cities around the world. Its LaSalle Street markets virtually invented the global economy, and the current threat to them comes from Asia and Europe, not the Sun Belt. Immigrants, especially from Latin America and Asia, are reviving whole neighborhoods. Other immigrants flock to the city's global industries, finance, law, consulting—there are so many Indonesians moving in and out of the Loop that an apartment in Presidential Towers in the West Loop has been turned into an Indonesian church.

Power Politics

The key to politics anywhere, but especially in Chicago, is power. Shortly after the first Mayor Daley died, a reporter from the *Economist* magazine of London wrote that in its politics, Chicago was much like Thailand: the Democratic Party might rule here, just as a royal or military government might rule in Thailand, but it was useless to draw any ideological conclusions from this. Politics in Chicago was not about ideas but about power—who had it and how effectively they used it.

Power still flows from the mayor's office on the fifth floor of city hall. But those who share in it have changed utterly. In a machine-dominated city, power flowed through aldermen to ward committeemen to campaign workers. This was a low-tech politics that relied on armies of precinct workers knocking on doors and distributing literature and favors. The payoff, as all these precinct workers knew, was a soft, safe job with the city or with one of its branches, like the Chicago Park District. The process needed lots of people but a surprisingly modest amount of money.

The Shakman decree of 1972 outlawed most city patronage. The younger Daley does not even hold an official post in the local Democratic Party. Hispanic neighborhoods still retain traces of the old Chicago politics, with strong ward organizations, personal campaigning, and politicking through churches (although in these neighborhoods, as in other low-income areas of the city, voter turnout remains relatively low). But elsewhere, the key to success has become not people but money, lots of it.

Dick Simpson, the former reform alderman, wrote a book about Chicago politics called *Rogues, Rebels, and Rubber Stamps,* in which he charted, among other things, the growth of money politics in Chicago and the radically changing nature of political donors between the two Daleys. "Most of the older downtown commercial, real estate, and financial businesses that had supported his father are no longer central to the new regime," he wrote. "Of the 21 companies that had composed the powerful Chicago Central Area Committee in the 1950s and 1960s, only a couple contributed a total of a few thousand dollars to Richard M. Daley's multimillion-dollar 1999 campaign. Daley's support, at least in terms of financial contributions, now comes more from wealthy lawyers, lobbyists, bankers, stock traders, and the construction firms and unions that depend on contracts from city hall. In 1999, bankers, lawyers, and stock and options traders gave Richard M. Daley more than $463,000 to run a modern Clintonesque campaign."

Simpson's list of the twenty-one mighty firms that helped bankroll Daley I in the 1950s and 1960s makes mournful reading today. It is a roll call of vanished or weakened Chicago business powers. The list included Sears, Roebuck; First Federal Savings and Loan; Carson Pirie Scott; Commonwealth Edison; Peoples Gas; First National Bank; Hart Schaffner & Marx; Standard Oil; Skidmore, Owings & Merrill; Hilton Hotels; Illinois Central Industries; Chicago Title and Trust; Harris Bank; CNA Financial; Continental Bank; Inland Steel; Scribner; Marshall Field's; Northern Trust; and Real Estate Research Corporation. A few of these firms survive but no longer wield political clout. Most have gone to the suburbs, been bought up by non-Chicagoans, or simply vanished.

John Kass, a *Chicago Tribune* columnist, has quoted the younger Daley as saying, "People aren't what they used to be. People don't vote for parties.

They vote for the person. It's all television money and polling now. It's not parades. It's not torchlights and songs."

Or as Don Rose, a political operative and longtime observer, puts it: "Under the old Daley, politics was labor-intensive—people ringing doorbells. Now, under the new Daley, politics is cash-intensive. Under the old Daley, black aldermen like Bill Dawson who approved housing projects in their wards did it to have a concentration of bodies dependent on government. Dawson didn't want any $15,000-a-year lawyer's jobs, he wanted a lot of $3,000-a-year postal jobs." In this new world, the mayor can't deliver many jobs at all. But he desperately wants as many lawyers and other high-wage residents in the city as possible. Thus, Rose says, the old concentration of bodies just isn't as important as it used to be. If the housing projects were built because they were politically useful, they're being torn down now because they have outlived that usefulness.

Daley spent $3.41 million in his campaign for the 1999 primary—still the only election that counts. Of this, 68 percent went for consultants and promotional material. "These modern, high-tech, media-based mayoral campaigns require huge sums of money for consultants, media, and professional staff," Dick Simpson says. "The days of precinct captains delivering simple brochures and campaign promises door-to-door are gone."

Kevin Michael DeBell, a political scientist, wrote that, if the first Mayor Daley provided jobs and contracts to supporters, his son "seems intent on service delivery as a way to keep political allies and win votes. His regime comprises regional business interests, special interest groups fighting tax increases, large-scale investors and city agencies which must optimize services under tightly controlled budgets." As Simpson and others have noted, the old jobs-based patronage of the pre-Shakman era has become "pinstripe patronage," with large city contracts going to big donors. Simpson says, "Although the new regime that surrounds Daley includes some party hacks and wheeler-dealers from the past, more prominent are wealthy lawyers, bankers, and investors who make up the new business elite of the city."

The big losers in this process have been ward committeemen and other neighborhood satraps, who have been left with little to do and little to give. Aldermen also are more marginal to city government, although they still control much of what goes on in their wards, giving them some leverage over contracts and favors. Some aldermen and other local politicians—Aldermen Edward Burke and Richard Mell and County Board President John Stroger are examples—can still turn out the vote; in their wards, committeemen still have clout. But not even these politicians enjoy reputations for independence from the mayor. In the governance of the city as a whole, Daley reigns supreme. Judson Miner, a former corporation counsel, comments that, "with few exceptions, the current aldermen are a bunch of puppets, doing what they are told. According to reports, the mayor is vindictive to anyone who opposes him. There is no thoughtful debate or discussion." Nor are these aldermen models of civic probity; between 1973 and 2000, no less than twenty-six of Chicago's aldermen were convicted of corruption.

A Brighter Side of Chicago

Other arms of city government are delivering impressively on the civic campaign to give Chicago the amenities and services it needs to compete in the global arena. The park district, once a patronage pit, has become a professional service that has literally greened the city. The city's schools are improving, as they must if it is to attract the middle-class families it so badly needs. In these and other areas, Daley has put the delivery of services and good government above payoffs and patronage.

He did this by reversing years of patronage-based abuse of the two systems. As Clark, Lloyd, Wong, and Jain report in "Amenities Drive Urban Growth," Daley persuaded the state legislature to give him control over the park district in 1993 and the school system in 1995. He created a corporate style of management in each, with a board and chief executive, and appointed two of his best managers, Forest Claypool at the park district and Paul Vallas at the school system. Neither had experience in their new areas, but both were former city hall officials with good track records and, more important, good relations with the mayor.

If the *Economist* compared Chicago to Thailand, the Daley II city, say Clark and his associates, "is more like a Japanese corporation, with its powerful local culture and deep personal loyalties and commitments." Both agencies underwent a thorough turnover in top management, with Claypool and Vallas hiring top staff with strong personal loyalties to the two executives. They quickly erased the two systems' budget deficits, partially through downsizing, efficient management, and contracting out. Between 1993 and 1997, Claypool cut the park district's total staff by 27 percent, from 4,938 persons to 3,577, and Vallas trimmed the public schools' notoriously bloated central office staff by 21 percent between 1995 and 1997, from 3,456 to 2,740. The park district increased its spending on two core functions, recreation and landscaping, from 14 to 29 percent of its budget, and Vallas, in his first year, was able to increase the share of the schools' budget devoted to teaching from 53 to 58 percent.

In these and other areas, Daley II seems to be undoing the damage of his father's regime. Daley I abandoned the schools to decades of decline; Daley II has made their resuscitation the keystone of his mayoralty. The reign of Daley I saw the destruction of the city's industry; the reign of Daley II has coincided with the arrival of the global economy. Where Daley I gave Chicago a global black eye by setting his police on demonstrators at the 1968 Democratic Convention, Daley II brought the 1996 Democratic Convention to Chicago and made sure it came off peacefully.

Daley I focused on the Loop while many neighborhoods, especially those that were predominantly African American, corroded and crumbled. Under Daley II, tracts of derelict land long since seized by the city for tax delinquency are being given to contractors who are building the first market-rate housing these same neighborhoods have seen in forty years. Daley I oversaw the construction of Chicago's noisome housing projects and their conversion into all-black warehouses for the poor. Under Daley II, these projects—some of them in the path of the gentrification spreading out from the Loop—are coming down or are being surrounded by $500,000 townhouses that put the city's poorest citizens and some of its richest ones across the street from each other.

The Daleys and Dissent

There is another major difference between the regimes of the two Daleys— the nature of dissent in Chicago and how city hall deals with it. The twenty-one years of Daley I were cacophonous. Political foes, angry professors, African Americans, neighborhood groups, Saul Alinsky, Martin Luther King, the Italian Americans uprooted by the University of Illinois Chicago campus, the war protesters clubbed by Daley's cops at the 1968 Democratic presidential nominating convention, liberals, small business owners, Black Panthers—Daley I either subdued or ignored them. He lavished federal funds on neighborhoods, but on his own terms, funneling them from the top down, through aldermen and committeemen, seldom to the benefit and often to the detriment of the people he claimed to be helping.

By contrast, the era of Daley II has been almost eerily peaceful. Demonstrators still march on city hall waving their placards and bullhorns, but these rallies are forlorn affairs, because most of the demonstrators' natural allies—

the neighborhood groups, the churches, and the like—aren't there. Instead, they're back in the neighborhood, spending their latest grant from city hall. If Daley I ignored protest, Daley II coopts it. The father raised the drawbridge against the besieging hordes; the son invites them in and gives them a good meal.

Under Daley II, the machine is less important and the number of foot soldiers and patronage jobs has shrunk. Probably fewer Chicagoans are directly involved in politics than under the old Daley machine. But many more are being brought in for specific projects and programs. Neighborhood groups, nonprofit and nongovernmental organizations, and special-interest bodies are being asked for their opinion or recruited to help carry out programs. Often, they are nominated by city hall to spend the money and make sure projects come to fruition. Given a piece of the action, they become part of the process.

"These neighborhood groups don't rally downtown any more," Dick Simpson, the former alderman, comments. "They're captive. They get the money. City hall is their patron and it hands out money to these groups for housing programs, CAPS [Community Alternative Policing Strategy] programs, and the like. In this way, Daley is buying off these neighborhood groups. But this has its positive side. The money does go directly to these groups. It doesn't go through committeemen any more, and it's not patronage." For that reason, "there are not that many voices for change in the city."

It's important to stress that this cooperation with citizens' groups doesn't mean that Daley has ceded control to them. Instead, they are brought in to support one of the mayor's projects. Their advice is sought and sometimes even heeded. Great effort is spent getting their support. Their agendas receive attention. And then they are charged with the job of making sure the project works. It's seductive, and successful.

A current example is the attempt to repair the ravaged neighborhoods of Woodlawn and North Kenwood. Both suffered white flight and almost total racial change after World War II and declined into regions of decaying housing, poverty, and crime. Hyde Park, located smack between the two, turned itself into a tense, heavily guarded academic island in the midst of this urban squalor. But in the 1990s, the city and the University of Chicago, working quietly together, hatched a plan to reverse this pattern, to move development out from Hyde Park into the surrounding neighborhoods. The first task was to get neighborhood organizations on board—churches, citizens' groups, block clubs. Some groups, like KOCO (Kenwood-Oakland Community Organization) and the Woodlawn Organization (TWO), had long ruled their neighborhoods, with dissent and angry rallies as key weapons. They were not inclined to surrender their special status and merge their efforts with other groups, including the city government and the loathed university. But both were given key roles in the revitalization program, and money to work with, and eventually they signed on. The result is a broad-based community program in which almost everybody gets something. The city gets derelict property back on the tax rolls. The university gets friendlier neighbors and, for the first time in four decades, lower tension in the streets around it. The neighborhoods get new housing and an influx of middle-class and working-class residents. Longtime residents get better policing and better schools and the promise of good stores.

Not everyone is happy, of course. In North Kenwood, some residents fear the gentrification will raise their taxes and drive out poorer residents. In Woodlawn, dissenters protested the demolition of the old, unused El line down Sixty-third Street. But these few holdouts have been made so marginal by the new, inclusive style of Chicago governance that their protests barely registered.

The result is a city in which many groups—nonprofits, the business-dominated Civic Committee, neighborhood groups, social movements, and the like—have a political voice and a share of political power that they lacked in the first Daley era. But politics in Chicago does not seem to be a finite pie with only so many slices. Rather, as the influence of these groups has grown, so has the power of the second Mayor Daley and city hall. Through some sort of political alchemy, Daley shares power while increasing his own power. There are more passengers to rock the ship of state, but the ship sails steadily on. "The non-governmental organizations like KOCO and TWO are really an adjunct of government," said one former mayoral aide. "Daley truly does listen to them, and then suddenly they get money for his project. Is he buying them off? Or is he improving their neighborhoods? One thing is sure. If you're seen as an organization that can't get along with the mayor, you're not going to get much done."

Perhaps nothing symbolizes this new inclusive style more than Daley's attempts to reach out to Chicago's gay community. Daley, like his father, is old-school Irish, family-centered, strongly Catholic, as far from a 1960s prototype as one can get. Yet he has marched in gay rights parades, openly courts the gay vote, and permitted—possibly even encouraged—his government to install special gay-pride decorations along North Halsted Street, in the heart of Boys' Town. It is impossible to imagine his father doing any of this.

Immigration

New waves of immigrants are revitalizing the city and changing its face and culture. They are also changing its politics—but only by holding themselves aloof from it. If earlier waves of immigrants shaped Chicago politics, the new immigrants remain outside the political arena, neither asking much from it nor contributing much to it. This is a fact of life. What it will mean in the long run to the city's governance is still unknown.

Part of it is the nature of the immigrant communities, and part of it reflects their size, or lack of it. In a way, Chicago always has been a global city. Since its birth, it has taken in workers from around the world and exported their products back to the world. In the early days of the machine, great numbers of Poles, Irish, Italians, Czechs, Slovaks, and other nationalities came to Chicago to work in its industries. Often they settled in geographically cohesive groups that proved easy to organize.

These huge national contingents, once settled in Chicago, had several things in common. They lived in the same neighborhoods in numbers large enough to dominate a ward. By voting as a bloc, they could elect one of their own to the city council. They needed services and, coming from Europe or from the plantation system of the South, were used to looking to government or some other central authority to provide it. They needed help in settling into their new country, and there were plenty of political hangers-on, working almost like block captains, providing a link to the ward office and city hall from which flowed jobs and advice and help with bureaucracy, all in return for votes. These immigrants, by and large, looked to politics for a foothold, and the machine provided that foothold, for a price to be paid on election day.

And so was born ethnic politics in Chicago. Churches, taverns, union halls, precinct workers, and voters all played their parts. For the new immigrants and their children, politics was part of the great process of acculturation to the new world. In turn, they gave Chicago politics the organized, nationalistic flavor of European politics. Young men not only followed their fathers into the mill but voted the way their fathers did. It wasn't really democracy but more a mosaic of Old World villages transported to the New World, organized and generational and responding to authority. Powered by the Chicago economy and the energy they brought to it, the immigrants thrived, and so did their government. Ethnic groups that hated each other back home still didn't like each other very much here, but in Chicago, there was enough to go around and no reason to fight. And so they settled into a wary mutual harmony within the framework of Chicago politics.

It was a flexible structure, but not flexible enough to absorb the greatest immigrant wave of all, African Americans from the South. During and after World War II, hundreds of thousands of African Americans came north to Chicago to work in the industries. They settled in great numbers, sweeping into established ethnic neighborhoods in a process that ignited spasms of racism and violence, even riots. The machine of Daley I was able to bring these new black wards into the system even while many of its white voters fled to the suburbs. Postwar prosperity provided jobs and money enough to keep the wheels moving.

But when Chicago's economy declined in the 1960s and 1970s, this prosperity ended. Unemployment rose, city services became more scarce, and the African American wards rebelled, first by helping to elect Jane Byrne and then by electing Harold Washington, the city's first African American mayor. Ethnic politics hasn't been the same since.

The New Immigrants

Of the new immigrant groups, only the Mexicans fit the old pattern. Mexican-dominated areas of the city have been able to elect Mexican American aldermen, alderwomen, and members of Congress. For voters in these wards, politics is part of the acculturation process of becoming an American. But these Mexican Americans share some of the characteristics of other large recent immigrant groups, especially from Asia, that make them different, politically and culturally, from Europeans who came before. Each of these new immigrant communities maintains close ties with its homeland, and its members often are in closer contact with the country they left behind than with the greater Chicago beyond their own neighborhoods.

Earlier generations of immigrants came to stay. Many were fleeing wars, famine, or pogroms and saw America as a refuge. The later generations more often come mainly for economic betterment, not to reject their homelands or to transfer all their loyalties to the United States. Earlier immigrants may or may not have written home occasionally; the later immigrants have access to the Internet and telephone cards and are in daily or weekly contact with the folks back home. Air travel enables them to go back for vacations or to bring relatives over for visits.

Most of these immigrants live in "transnational space," to use Saskia

Sassen's phrase, rooted neither here nor there, local in two places. Some immigrants can vote in national elections back home. Mexicans cannot do so yet, but Mexican law is changing to permit this, and candidates from Mexico and other countries come to Chicago to campaign.

National governments recognize their citizens in America as a weapon in foreign policy and use them to lobby Washington. The U.S. State Department is aware of this and returns the compliment by working with the Czech, Chinese, Pakistani, and other communities to convey American policy and wishes to elites in those countries. In this sense, these communities exercise real influence over the activities of many governments, including the American one. But apart from the Mexicans, the new immigrant communities play a relatively small role in the politics of Chicago and its suburbs. There is no alderman or other leading politician of Indian heritage, or Vietnamese, or Chinese, or Korean, or Nigerian.

There are several reasons for this. The first is demographic and geographic. For an ethnic group to have clout within a ward, it must make up a significant percentage of that ward's population, and the new immigrants are too thin on the ground to achieve this. Asians make up barely 8 percent of the city's population, and in no ward does any Asian ethnic group approach 20 percent—probably the minimum required for political leverage. While most of the earlier groups settled in the city, the new immigrants—including the Mexicans—are spread across the city into the suburbs. Nearly half the Latino community lives in the suburbs, and so do the Koreans. Most of Chicagoland's Indian population also lives outside the city. Some ethnic groups have high visibility but relatively low numbers: there are probably more than two hundred Thai restaurants in the Chicago region, many more than their low numbers—barely four thousand people—would suggest.

"Major immigrant groups that produced office-holders, like the Poles, Italians and Jews, did so within their own neighborhoods," Don Rose explains. "There is no place even among Koreans or Vietnamese here, where the concentration is sufficient to become an ethnic bloc." And Terry Nichols Clark in *Trees and Real Violins* adds that many of the new immigrants get their foothold in the new society from means other than politics. Many of the Asian groups, like the Koreans, have well-developed self-help mechanisms, including pools of money from which new arrivals may finance a business or a home. Many own their own businesses—no American group, including native-born whites, has so high a percentage of business ownership as the Koreans—and so rely less on others to find them jobs in the huge industrial mills of old, or look less to government jobs to support themselves. Even relatively small communities have strong internal institutions—places of worship, chambers of commerce, clubs—that guide new immigrants into the society and help them find their place. For these groups, politics simply is less necessary than it was for most of the older European immigrants.

Many of the new immigrants, especially from Asia, are educated. Some are professionals. Those from countries like India and the Philippines already speak English, as do many Africans, Pakistanis, and other newcomers. Like earlier immigrants, they can move directly into the succoring surroundings of an existing community here, but not all need even this landing strip.

While first-generation Mexicans and Koreans are likely to live in Chicago's Mexican and Korean neighborhoods, other nationalities such as Indians and Filipinos are scattered across the region. Again, language may be the key factor here. Earlier immigrants came to work in Chicago's giant industries. The new immigrants land in small businesses, like restaurants or Dunkin' Donuts, or big high-tech ones, like Motorola. None lend themselves to the kind of political organizing that built the original machine.

Politicians who represent areas with Asian immigrant populations say that these immigrants do not feel the need for government in their daily lives and are proud of this independence. This, among many other things, makes it harder for government and government representatives to reach them.

This doesn't mean that the new immigrants ignore politics altogether. Like other Chicagoans, they need city services and occasionally they need special help—a bit of clout—from their alderman. Don Rose says that Asian groups have become political donors "disproportionate to their numbers." In the new Chicago politics, this money paves the way to political access. In this as in so many areas, Rose says, Korean immigrants today resemble Jewish immigrants of the last century.

Chicago and Its Neighbors

The relationship of Chicago to its region is a fraught issue that is no closer to solution now than it was under the administration of Daley I. *Chicago Metropolis 2020*, a comprehensive report sponsored by the Commercial Club, noted that the region includes nearly 1,300 units of local government, including 6 counties, 113 townships, 267 municipalities, 303 school districts, and 587 special districts, or single-purpose governments. It calculated that this works out to one unit of government for every 6,000 persons in the region, which is seven times the ratio in New York City. Occasionally, these units of government can cooperate in a productive way: the Regional Transportation Authority is a good example. But mostly, this splintering of government has been the despair of reformers. Who, they ask, is going to oversee the solutions to the intertwined problems of traffic congestion, say, or pollution, or energy? The battle over the expansion of O'Hare Airport has pitted the city against the suburbs—or, rather, against some suburbs. Northern suburbs away from O'Hare's roar are content to let expansion proceed.

Some problems are solvable only at a regional level, but no regional authorities exist to deal with them. "People are confused about who's responsible for delivering which services," one analyst said. Since the administration of Jane Byrne, Chicago and suburban mayors have met periodically to seek common solutions to common problems. The latest incarnation is the Metropolitan Mayors Caucus, a six-county group of regional councils, formed in 1997 by Mayor Daley and suburban mayors. At this point, what can be said about these forums is that they allow useful exchanges of information and may provide a framework to create common solutions, if ever the political atmosphere seems right.

History plays a large role in this. For more than a century, Chicago's suburbs have been seen by many of their residents as a refuge from the big, dirty, corrupt, crime-ridden, and, above all, expensive city at the region's heart. Especially after World War II, these residents fled the city with relief and vowed to have as little as possible to do with it in the future.

The city they left behind them turned increasingly black and poor. Employment fell, crime rose, schools crumbled. Meanwhile, life in the suburbs was grand—spacious and clean, with lots of good jobs in companies that had also fled the city, relatively low crime rates, often first-rate schools. Who needed the city? Not the suburbanites, many of whom built their entire lives— jobs, homes, entertainment, church—in the suburbs and seldom ventured into Chicago, which loomed in their mind as a no-man's-land, a no-go zone of slums and high taxes.

Those who still worked in the city often worked in the Loop and sped daily from their prosperous suburb to the prosperous Loop, barely glancing at the wasteland in between. Chicago, in their minds, looked like a dumbbell, with two lumps of commerce at either end and nothing but a long, thin expressway hooking them together.

Reformers held up cities like Minneapolis as examples of unitary taxation or other systems of tax revenue sharing between central city and suburbs. This idea never gained much traction in the Chicago suburbs, to say the least. Most suburbanites saw no reason to share their tax dollars with a city they viewed as either evil or beyond help. This view often disguised, more or less, a core of racism. Many suburbanites felt that the spread of black neighborhoods, often accompanied by block-busting, had pushed them out of Chicago, and they were little inclined to be generous. Politics also played a big role: the Chicago machine was Democratic and most of the suburbs were Republican.

Some suburbs, of course, are venerable, with deep roots and histories that go back nearly as far as Chicago's itself, like Oak Park and the North Shore suburbs such as Evanston. But many of the other suburbs were virtually created after World War II. Park Forest was the very model for the new, raw, striving suburb in William H. Whyte's *The Organization Man.* In their newness, they could not have been more different from the old, tired, crowded, dirty city.

If there's a solution to the regional balkanization of Chicagoland governance, it may lie in the fact that history is having its little joke on the suburbs. Chicago suddenly is beginning to boom again, but many of the suburbs are struggling. Traffic gridlock in many suburban areas is worse than anything in the city, partially because the suburbs never planned for it. Chicago has cleaner air than many of its suburbs. The descendants of the first suburbanites are moving back to the city, reinvigorating its housing and rejuvenating its schools. In the process, they are shoving up housing costs and property taxes, a gentrification that is doing what the foes of gentrification claim it always does, which is to force out older, poorer, longtime residents. Many of these residents are African Americans. And they are moving increasingly to the suburbs, mostly older, close-in suburbs which are taking in not only the emigrants from Chicago's black neighborhoods but many of those neighborhoods' problems as well.

This process seems certain to continue, with two foreseeable results. Middle-class families who can afford to choose will either flock back into the city, reinforcing its vitality, or flee farther out to distant suburbs, taking their jobs and businesses with them and contributing to the suburban sprawl.

Chicago, in short, is beginning to look like a traditional European city. Many of these cities—Paris, especially, but most European cities fit the pattern—have vibrant and wealthy city centers, inhabited by the best-paid and best-educated, while the suburbs beyond the Peripherique are the warehouses for the poor, many of them living in high-rise housing projects not unlike those that are beginning to disappear in Chicago. Many of these suburban poor are part of a new service caste that waits upon the city dwellers—the cab drivers, waiters, shop attendants, parking valets, maids—who work in the city but cannot afford to live there. This turns the old city-suburban split on its head.

Not so long ago, Chicagoland resembled a bagel, with a lot of dough on the outside and a hole in the middle. Now it's turning into a sandwich, with a layer of poverty in the middle surrounded by the bread of the city and the far suburbs. The present political entities have so far shown absolutely no interest in examining, let alone addressing, this situation. Even today, there is little political interest in *Chicago Metropolis 2020* and its recommendation for a Regional Coordinating Council to "deal effectively with the interrelationships among policies and practices concerning transportation, land use, housing and the environment." In a respectful review of the report, Lois Wille, formerly the *Tribune*'s chief editorial writer, called it "thoughtful and earnest" but admitted it had been greeted by no more than "polite applause" by civic leaders and newspaper editorialists. So far, she said, "there have been no signs of massive blood stirring among the populace" (a reference to Daniel Burnham's original Chicago Plan). Clearly, this is a process that has only just begun.

The report argues, correctly, that the Chicago region is a single unit and that no part of this region is immune from the problems besetting any other part: common solutions, then, are the only solutions. It's hard to dispute this logic. The report's calls for regional planning, regional tax-sharing, and regionally dispersed low-cost housing are certainly radical and controversial and, perhaps for that reason, figure on no politician's platform. Mayor Daley is said to have taken the report's warnings seriously, but to be cool to its agenda. The twin pressures of globalization and demographic shift may revive the mayoral interest, but action now—or even by 2020—is uncertain.

The *Chicago Metropolis 2020* report spawned the creation of a new civic organization, Chicago Metropolis 2020, dedicated to promoting regional cooperation in areas such as transportation policy, land-use planning, affordable workforce housing, and tax policy. The group's tagline, "One Region, One Future," sums up the challenge. At a time when skilled workers are choosing to locate based on quality of life, the region cannot afford internecine squabbling. Many quality-of-life issues such as easing traffic congestion or protecting open space require cooperation among the region's hundreds of municipalities. This will not be an easy political task in the Chicago region or anywhere else.

The Global Future, Chicago-Style

In the absence of a transformation of regional government, what should Chicago be doing to prepare itself for a globalizing world and to position itself as a global city? The job is almost halfway done.

Chicago has achieved the transition from industrial powerhouse to a city dominated by the service and financial economies. Cities, like people, have life cycles, crises, periods of growth and decline, and challenges to be met. The great cities of the world were, like Chicago, mostly founded for economic reasons—as a seaport, or a mining town, or a ford on a river where travelers could be provisioned and taxed. Over time, the seaports silt up or the mines play out, and cities must find new economic raisons d'etre. Those that fail become picturesque backwaters, like Venice or Dubrovnik. Truly great cities reinvent themselves and thrive anew.

Chicago, founded to serve the great mills and rail yards, has just gone through its first reinvention. And it has done this with a political structure that looks antiquated, even ludicrously out of date, but one that has adapted in order to do many of the things that a city must do to compete in this new global world.

Virtually all analysts agree that O'Hare Airport and its expansion, on hold now because of an economic slump, are key to Chicago's future. The terrorist attacks of late 2001 have given airlines and airports a clear challenge that must be overcome if the global travel that has been so vital to the formation of the global economy is to continue. But there is no reason to think this challenge cannot be met, so that O'Hare will continue to be the visible symbol of Chicago's role as a global hub.

As such, it needs to grow, and the apparent breaking of the political stalemate over the airport's future has removed a barrier to that growth. As it grows, it needs to be linked to the city by a dedicated high-speed rail link, similar to those that link major airports to most European cities. The El line between the Loop and O'Hare is useful, but it is not a solution for a global future.

A Chicago Foreign Policy?

Many have suggested the creation of an office within city hall dealing with the city's international ties. Without one, there is no one with regular access to the mayor who can argue for this global dimension when civic decisions are made. Foreign entrepreneurs anxious to invest money in an American city have trouble getting a hearing in city hall. Foreign consuls here often have to wait months to meet the mayor, unless they represent a country, like Poland or Ireland, with links to big blocs of Chicago voters. Many of these consuls say they have trouble locating an appropriate contact at city hall to propose a project that, quite conceivably, could benefit the city globally.

No office coordinates the work of the city's planning and development departments and the World Trade Center Chicago and World Business Chicago. Such an office could be the generator of a foreign policy for this city and its region. Almost everything that happens in the world affects Chicago, but the city has no focused way to affect those events. The United States has a foreign policy, of course, but that policy does not always benefit Chicago. As the nation girds for the fight against terrorism, for instance, it is easy to imagine an anti-immigration backlash that could restrict immigration far beyond any security needs. But immigration has been good for Chicago, which needs this transfusion of skills and energy from abroad. A Chicago foreign policy would fight to keep borders as open as possible.

As globalization progresses, so will the need for Chicago and its institutions to make their voices heard in global forums. These forums—on trade, investment, communications, standards, labor, environment, and many other issues—will make decisions that will affect the life of the city and its people. Global rules on trade and investment, for instance, may affect the ability of the city to frame social policy in such areas as public procurement. The city's custom of mandating a certain percentage of city contracts for firms headed by women or minorities is already vulnerable to NAFTA rules that see such set-asides as a violation of the right of Canadian and Mexican firms to do business here. Similar restrictions have been considered by the World Trade Organization, and Chicago should be making its wishes known. The city's global forums, especially the Chicago Council on Foreign Relations, are the logical places to debate these issues, and city government is the logical place to take the results of these debates and shape them into a global policy for Chicago.

When this policy takes shape, it should be promoted in Washington by the Chicago region's congressional delegation. But the present delegation is ill-placed to do the job. With the single important exception of Henry Hyde, the veteran Republican from the Sixth District who is chairman of the House International Relations Committee, Chicago and its suburbs are all but unrepresented on Congressional committees dealing with foreign policy. Aside from Hyde, the eleven Chicago-area members of Congress focus primarily on domestic issues.

For much of the world's media, Chicago is virtually invisible. Most foreign correspondents in the United States are based in Washington and New York and seldom venture out. When they do, it's most often to the West Coast. Chicago worked hard to reach these correspondents during the 1996 Democratic Convention here, with good results. From time to time, the city has sponsored trips to Chicago by groups of foreign correspondents, and, again, the resulting stories and broadcasts around the world have been gratifying. It is not an accident that the *Economist* has run frequent articles making Chicago and its mayor look good: the *Economist* is one of the few foreign publications with a resident correspondent in Chicago.

The state of Illinois has trade offices around the world to beat the drum for trade with industries and investment in the state. These offices benefit Chicago as part of Illinois but do not focus on it. It may be necessary to post Chicago trade and investment representatives abroad, either in the Illinois offices or with their own missions, to sell the city in a single-minded way that the Illinois offices never can.

This implies a separation from the state of Illinois, in this area at least. Many people have written that in a globalized world, nations will become less important, ceding some of their power upward, to transnational institutions like the World Trade Organization, and some of it down, to cities and regions. Old political boundaries will be redrawn to meet the demands of globalization. In such a world, it is easy to imagine a Chicago linked by its true interests to its immediate region and possibly to Milwaukee and northwest Indiana, in a single lakeside economic unit, while its ties to the rest of Illinois fray and weaken.

Mayor Daley already is traveling abroad on a schedule that his father never contemplated, and most observers think this strengthens the city's image around the world. Some Chicago sophisticates fret that their often tongue-tied mayor lacks the social graces to deal with, say, the mayor of London. Perhaps these sophisticates have never met the mayor of London, who is a tough, plainspoken, and results-focused old Labour Party pol named Ken Livingstone. The two mayors definitely talk the same language, such as it is.

Why shouldn't Chicago get in the habit of hosting international meetings with high visibility? It already is the convention capital of the nation, but it seldom holds conferences that draw the attention of the world at large. A suggestion has been made for a conference of world mayors on the theme of globalization. On the assumption that major cities around the world are all struggling to some degree with the challenges and problems of globalization, an international meeting of mayors would be an ideal forum for these issues.

Chicago is adapting almost instinctively to the new global era, even though most of its citizens are just beginning to appreciate it. The young Mayor Daley inherited a political framework he is using to build a twenty-first-century Chicago that is, once again, a "City That Works," in a way that hasn't been true since many years before his father died.

4   Global City, Global People

RON GROSSMAN

IN ALBANY PARK on Chicago's Northwest Side in the 1950s, I passed through adolescence. It is a stage of life when three meals a day don't suffice, at least for males. By midevening, a teenaged boy needs to eat again, partially because it is an age of tremendous energy expenditure, much of it spent on thoughts of teenage girls. Also, by that time of day, he needs to find refuge from adults and family in the company of his own kind.

Accordingly, around 9 P.M., I'd pick up my best buddy, who lived on Kedzie Avenue near Montrose Avenue. We would walk north to Lawrence Avenue, then turn west to Marie's Liquor and Pizza, one of the first places to serve what was then an exotic Italian import. Our route took us through a largely Jewish neighborhood. We would pass Mt. Sinai Congregation, a storefront synagogue where I was bar mitzvahed, and Ada's Delicatessen, where local families picked up their Sunday morning smoked fish and lox. Or we could cut the journey short by holding our nightly review of life's vagaries at The Bagel restaurant, just north of Kedzie and Lawrence.

Except for Marie's, all those landmarks are gone. The synagogue has been transformed into Jesus House Chicago, a church with a largely West African congregation. The Bagel followed its customers north to Devon Avenue, then to the North Shore. Its older quarters house Holy Land Grocery, a store with a Middle Eastern clientele. Ada's was replaced by a Spanish food market. The *Korean Times* newspaper publishes a few doors down. On the same block, two lawyers, one Greek and the other Arab, advertise their firm's services, each with a sign in the language of his ancestors.

Retracing that route is a mixed experience. Clearly, it is not the neighborhood of my youth. Yet it is not quite something else, either. The letters in which shop-window signs are written may be unintelligible, but the experience they represent is perfectly understandable. Albany Park remains what it was: a place where immigrants and their offspring occupy a mental space about midway between their older and newer homelands. And as such, it is part of the answer to the fundamental question of this book: Is Chicago a global city?

From the vantage point of the railroad apartments piggybacked over the storefronts of Kedzie and Lawrence, and in the two- and three-flats of Albany Park's side streets, the answer is unmistakably clear. Of course Chicago is a global city. It always was.

Connected to the World

Chicago didn't wait for the current fascination with globalization to connect with the larger world. To the contrary. If you know how to read the story that is preserved in the multilingual shop windows of its neighborhoods, you will recognize that had Chicago's early movers and shakers not sensed that it needed to become what we now call a global city, it would not have been a city at all. Save for their foresight, Chicago likely would have remained pretty much as it began, a motley collection of marginal traders eking out a living along the banks of an obscure and sluggish river on the frontier of American society.

It is too early to say what Chicago's role in the globalization of commerce and industry will be in, say, a decade or so. But history—the kind whose raw data is preserved in the shop signs of neighborhoods like Albany Park—makes this much crystal clear: With respect to the single most indispensable raw material of a city, the people who occupy it, Chicago's fortunes have always depended upon establishing and maintaining connections with lands and peoples across the seas.

Already in the middle years of the nineteenth century, for instance, the *Chicago Tribune* editorialized that immigration was so vital to the city's prosperity that, if necessary, the federal government ought to assist foreigners to come here. So too did the Chicago Lyceum, a civic body of the day.

The realization that Chicago's fortunes were tied to those of other nations was sustained even in the period between the World Wars, when the Middle West was famously the home of isolationism. Isolation might have been the ruling concept at the weekly luncheons of Rotary Clubs elsewhere in the nation's heartland, but Chicago's city fathers were skeptical in the extreme of the idea that the United States could cut itself off from Europe and live secure behind the barriers of its two great oceans.

In 1922, the British statesman Sir Charles Cheers Wakefield, visiting Chicago, was impressed to find that his host, the Chicago Association of Commerce, had published a pamphlet titled *What Shall Our Foreign Policy Be?* "It was clear that the trend of thought was very much towards a realization that the world is an economic unit," he reported in his book *America To-day and To-morrow.*

Yet though Chicago's leaders clearly sensed their dependence upon the larger world, they did not have a conviction that the city was called upon to blaze a trail toward globalization. Their vision was not moral, but practical. They could see that their city's situation was unique, and that its success was dependent upon forging a civic strategy appropriate to that uniqueness.

City in Motion

Other cities have perpetuated themselves largely by the natural growth of their base population, as one generation of inhabitants begets the next. That has not been the way it worked in Chicago. There is a good reason why Chicago's population growth did not build upon the fecundity of its older settlers: they rarely stayed around long enough.

Instead, Chicago has always been a city of newcomers, making it not just a place, but a process as well. For almost two hundred years, immigrants have come to Chicago seeking opportunities denied them in their homelands. The city's neighborhoods have provided an opportunity to get a foothold in their adopted homeland. Having served that urban apprenticeship, they have moved on to suburbia and the middle class, leaving behind them the city's tenements and storefronts for the next generation of immigrants.

Look closely at some plate-glass windows in Albany Park and you can still see where yesterday's Yiddish and Hebrew lettering has been scraped off, making room for signs in languages that, until recently, were not heard in the city's streets: Assyrian and Korean, Pashtu and Hmong.

Not long ago, the principal of one North Side grade school, aptly named the Albany Park Multicultural Academy, calculated that thirty languages were represented in its student body. The school's newspaper publishes in three languages: English, Spanish, and Urdu. Return to that same school a decade hence, and a new generation of students might be bringing the same number of languages from home to school, but they are likely to be different languages.

Today, Chicago's 911 Emergency Center responds to calls in 150 languages, of which the most frequently needed are Spanish, Polish, Russian, Mandarin, Korean, Turkish, Cantonese, Arabic, Vietnamese, Italian, and Lithuanian.

In recent years, politicians and the media have been hypersensitive to the issue of immigration. Looking at the faces of today's newest arrivals and comparing them with yesterday's, the news weeklies have done story after story on the "New Immigrants." So, too, has television.

But in Chicago, the new immigrant is an old story. It has perennially been a city of new immigrants. It has always been a place where, as one generation of immigrants gets ready to move on, it stakes its claim to a place in the mainstream by loudly proclaiming its disdain for the latest newcomers. Ethnic groups who only recently had to bear the pejorative label "greenhorns" are quick to bestow that characterization on their successors in the tenements of the city's immigrant neighborhoods.

"It isn't so much a city," the novelist Nelson Algren observed of Chicago, "as it is a vast way station." This connects to the unusual way that the Industrial Revolution played out along the southwestern shores of Lake Michigan. Before industrialization in the eighteenth century, of course, the vast majority of the human race was rural. The principal wealth in most societies derived from the fertility of the soil, and the rhythms of daily life were closely tied to the agricultural calendar. Our public schools still go into extended recess during the summer months, even though it has been decades since American children were needed as laborers on their families' farms during the height of the growing season.

Industrialization caused a dramatic shift in those age-old patterns. Beginning in England in the eighteenth century, a new system of factory production spread to Europe and North America. Factories need factory hands, which required large assemblies of workers. Since transportation was rudimentary, workers had to live within walking distance of the mill or factory where they worked. People had to be induced, cajoled, or forced to leave the countryside to live in emerging cities of industrializing nations.

Going from rural to city dwellers put tremendous strains on family life. Living conditions in rapidly growing industrial cities often were deplorable. The works of Charles Dickens offer a bookshelf's worth of testimony to the suffering that accompanied the formation of England's new class of urban-dwelling factory workers.

In the United States, the process had a complicating twist. Whereas in

England it was English peasants who became England's mill hands, and the same pattern applied in Germany and the other continental countries, pioneering entrepreneurs here found that it was virtually impossible to attract America's rural dwellers to the cities. In the nineteenth century, the United States was a thinly settled nation with vast stretches of underpopulated land, especially on the western frontier, which then began not far from Chicago. Much of this land was available practically for the taking, especially after Congress passed the Homestead Act in 1862. That legislation made it possible for landless Americans to become property owners. With that opportunity available, there was little incentive for those who lived in rural areas or small towns to move into a city like Chicago.

Imported Labor for Growing Industries

When the Chicago magnates Cyrus McCormick and George Pullman began building, respectively, the plows and railroad cars that would transform agriculture and transportation, they could not persuade large enough numbers of farm families from Wisconsin and Indiana to come to Chicago and staff their factories. Instead, they and others had to import their labor force, much as entrepreneurs in other countries might have to import raw materials. Chicago's industrialists dispatched agents to Europe to advertise that this was a city where anyone willing to work would never be out of a job. The message was especially carried to the underdeveloped nations of eastern and southern Europe, where the peasantry didn't have a nearby alternative to poverty.

The response was staggering. Each year, tens of thousands came to Chicago. From County Mayo and County Cork, they set out in hopes of finding a better life in Bridgeport and Back of the Yards. So, too, did pious Jews in frock coats and beaver hats, fleeing the pogroms of czarist Russia, and Poles escaping the anti-Catholic persecutions of their divided nation's foreign masters. Sicilians and Calabrese left their impoverished villages for Taylor Street and Grand Avenue.

All of those new arrivals, of course, brought with them their ancestral languages. So as Chicago's factories expanded and the city grew from a frontier settlement into a sprawling metropolis, it was less and less an English-speaking city. Instead, Chicago became the transplanted home to dozens of immigrant cultures. By 1850, less than two decades after Chicago's incorporation, half its population was foreign born. By 1890, 77.9 percent of Chicagoans were either immigrants or children of immigrants. It was precisely that aspect of Chicago that impressed visitors from abroad, among them Monsignor Count Vay de Vaya and Luskod, a Hungarian prelate who reported on his 1905 visit to Chicago in *The Inner Life of the United States.*

"It would seem as if all the millions of human beings disembarking year by year upon the shores of the United States were unconsciously drawn to make this place their headquarters," he observed of Chicago. "Nowhere else has immigration assumed such huge proportions, and nowhere else does the immigration question so seriously affect the local administration and development."

Four years after the monsignor's visit, Chicago's Association of Commerce was taking perverse pride in the fact that the city's "confusion of tongues is the worst since Babel!" Its official *Guide Book* noted that Chicago's neighborhoods were "really little cities within the metropolis, each speaking its own language, clinging to its hereditary customs, and in large part governing itself." At the height of that immigrant flood, Chicago was the largest Lithuanian-speaking city in the world. There were more Czech-speakers in Chicago than any place else, save for Prague. The only city with more Polish-speakers was Warsaw. It was the third-largest Irish, Swedish, and Jewish city on the face of the earth.

Those non-English linguistic concentrations in the city's neighborhoods gave Chicago a unique flavor among American cities. The older cities of the East Coast, such as Boston, Philadelphia, and even New York, had developed their civic characteristics before the great age of immigration. They retained a cultural orientation given them by their Yankee-stock early settlers. The cities of the Far West, being newer, would develop along other lines.

But Chicago was a creation of the immigrant. It was already a product of a local version of globalization a century before that term entered the modern political vocabulary. In the early part of the twentieth century, those immigrants were joined by another wave of newcomers from the American South. Two factors made Chicago a magnet for African Americans: the Illinois Central Railroad, whose tracks ran from the city to the southern states where most blacks then lived, and the *Chicago Defender* newspaper. In 1917, Robert Abbot, the paper's founder, editorially called for "a great northern drive," arguing that in the northern cities, blacks would find jobs and refuge from Jim Crow segregation.

That message was carried south by Pullman car porters who often clandestinely dropped off bundles of the newspaper in Mississippi towns. Southern sheriffs tried confiscating the *Defender,* the plantation owners being anxious not to lose their cheap labor force. But the Great Migration, as it came to be known, became virtually a religious cause. Championing it made the *Chicago Defender* the country's largest black newspaper. Between 1910 and 1930, Chicago's black population grew more than fivefold, from 44,000 to 234,000.

Many settled on the South Side, often bringing with them institutions from their older homes. The Hattiesburg Barber Shop, for instance, was transplanted from the Mississippi town of that name to Thirty-fifth and Rhodes. Its former home had been a social center, where people gathered to read the *Chicago Defender*'s weekly accounts of a better life in Chicago. Catching the migration fever, the owner and forty others formed an association to buy discounted tickets on the Illinois Central in 1917. Reestablished here, the barbershop became an unofficial settlement house during the formative years of Chicago's black community.

Immigrants from the European continents settled in the city as well. "The old West Side was all movement," noted the housing reformer Edith Abbott in her 1936 study *The Tenements of Chicago*. "Everyone had just come from somewhere—usually from across the ocean—and all the world was going somewhere else. Here were the most foreign newspapers, the foreign banks . . . the churches representing various nationalistic groups, that made these areas not unlike a series of foreign cities brought together within the metropolitan area."

That formative period in the city's history was brought to a close by a wave of anti-immigrant sentiment that captured the larger nation just after World War I. In 1924, the federal government imposed sharp, new limitations on immigration. Yearly quotas were pegged to the percentage of various nationalities in the country at a date before the great waves of late nineteenth-century immigration. In effect, that cut Chicago off from the countries of eastern and southern Europe, from which it had been drawing the great bulk of its populace. When those new quotas went into effect, 27 percent of Chicagoans were European born. By 1950, that figure had dropped to 20 percent. It fell again, to 15 percent, by 1960. And by 1970, it was less than 10 percent. Poland had been a major source of new Chicagoans. Whole neighborhoods along Division Street and Milwaukee Avenue could more easily be navigated in Polish than English. In 1920, 137,611 Chicagoans had been born in Poland. By 1970, their number had fallen to 55,711.

In 1970, the median age of European-born Chicagoans was sixty-two. Chicago's immigrant stock was rapidly aging, and it thus seemed as if the city's career as a home-away-from-home for foreign cultures might soon be over.

Recent Years: The Second Wave

Not long after this, Chicago experienced a new, second wave of immigration. The economic logic was the same as it always had been. Chicago's industrial plants and its service industries needed workers, and it was not possible to draw them from the ranks of the old settlers. A century earlier, the American born could not be induced to work in the city's factories because of the land-owning opportunity offered by the Homestead Act. In the 1980s and 90s, the native born—whose ranks now included considerable numbers of the children and grandchildren of immigrants—had a new alternative to blue-collar jobs. The tremendous expansion of higher education in the United States made it possible for those who came through Ellis Island to send their offspring to college. That development began with the GI Bill immediately after World War II and was quickened by the rush to expand universities after the Soviets launched Sputnik in 1957. Far more Americans were able to get university training than ever before and were thereby removed from the unskilled labor force.

Meanwhile, Chicago continued to be a magnet in parts of the world where people's life opportunities were limited. In recent decades, it has been fashionable to talk about a "postindustrial" economy, and Chicago certainly lost factory jobs, as other American cities did. But not all of those companies that abandoned their plants in the city moved overseas. Many set up shop in the city's suburbs, where they still needed someone to work their assembly lines. And in a refugee camp in Southeast Asia or a poverty-stricken village in Mexico, Chicago was still very much of a beacon. To thousands of families, it seemed better to go there than to stay at home.

The combination of people in foreign lands desperate for opportunities and a blue-collar labor shortage in Chicago made the metropolis's factories again what they had been a century earlier: assembly-line outposts of dozens of newly transplanted cultures.

In 1998, Sure Electronics estimated that 90 percent of the production workers at its Buffalo Grove plant were immigrants. Switchcraft, Inc., on Chicago's Northwest Side, reported that 70 percent of its six hundred workers were foreign born. At Beltone Electronics, at the city's far northwest edge, 75 percent of the workforce was foreign born. Beltone officials considered immigrants so vital to the company that they developed an extensive network of translators so that no one in its plant would be linguistically isolated.

Accordingly, even as the city was losing its older immigrants, Chicago's streets were beginning to resound with new languages. Chicago's Spanish-speaking population doubled in the 1960s, then doubled again in the 1970s. By 1980, Spanish-speakers accounted for 14 percent of the city's total population. Early estimates of the 2000 census put that figure at 26 percent, making it the city's fastest-growing community.

Most of Chicago's newest immigrants are not European stock like their predecessors. The Spanish-speakers come not from Spain but from Latin America—especially from Mexico, Puerto Rico, and Cuba. The 2000 census shows that, of the city's foreign-born inhabitants, 23 percent came from Europe, while 74 percent were born in Latin America or Asia. These recent immigrants have returned Chicago to its roots as a multicultural city. Of its estimated 2,895,964 current inhabitants, 628,903 were born in another country. In the 1890s, at the height of the old immigration, 408,666 Chicagoans were foreign born. (Of course, Chicago was a smaller city then, so the percentage of foreign-born at the time—32 percent—was greater than today's 22 percent.)

Yet raw statistics don't always capture the whole story of a city's fate. So consider the following meta-analysis, as it were, of the numbers.

In 1890, the city's African American community was tiny. Only 14,271 Chicagoans, or 1 percent of the total population, were black. Now, black Chicagoans number 1,005,522, or 36 percent of the city's population. Because of slavery, which ripped their ancestors out of their African cultures, the mother tongue of the overwhelming majority of black Chicagoans could only be English. (Though it should be noted that the city also now has an estimated 23,132 residents who recently came from sub-Saharan Africa.)

Mentally set aside those whose home language thus could only be English and the percentage of Chicagoans who speak a foreign tongue at home rises to 51 percent. Which means that, if you live in Chicago and are not black, the chances are one in two that you speak a non-English language at home. Moreover, those odds have been rising recently.

New Immigrant Patterns

In 1990, 9,902 Chicagoans reported themselves to the census takers as Arabic-speakers. Data from the 2000 census shows the number of people of Arab ancestry rising to 14,971. In addition, there are large concentrations of people of Arab ancestry just across the city's borders, in suburbs like Oak Lawn. In the Chicago-Indiana urbanized area, a total of 45,546 people listed themselves as being of Arab ancestry in the 2000 census. Those suburbanized

Arabic-speakers reflect a phenomenon of the new immigrants. Some of them move into the middle class and out of the city earlier in their New World careers than did their predecessors in the great age of European immigration. These immigrants largely are not peasants like their nineteenth-century counterparts; they arrive here with professional skills, and thus they are middle class almost from the beginning.

Chicago's new East Indian community contains large numbers of health professionals, engineers, and other technicians. Accordingly, many have been able to move into suburbia almost as soon as they arrived in the Chicago area. They have done so in such numbers that Oakbrook Terrace, long a WASP-ish community, became overnight a kind of "Little India," the contemporary analogue of those "Little Italy's" and "Polonias" that used to characterize the city's neighborhoods.

But Not Everyone Is Pleased

Of course, now as then, not all Chicagoans have been pleased with the city's rainbow of foreign cultures, the cacophony of foreign tongues that echo along its streets.

A walk down Devon Avenue is a rich experience for anthropologists, professional or amateur. There for the hearing are exotic languages like Aramaic, the language of Jesus. Indian women wrapped in brightly colored saris share the sidewalk with pious Jews, the style of their frock coats and fur hats signaling their Hasidic subsect. That Far North Side street is a gustatory paradise for those whose digestive juices are stimulated by the sights and smells of foods from faraway places.

But there have always been Americans who are made uneasy by the very same sights, sounds, and smells—in short, by anything different. Before the first great wave of immigration in the nineteenth century, most Americans were British by descent, Protestant by religion, and English-speaking. The vast majority of the first immigrants were Catholic, Jewish, or members of the various Orthodox Christian churches. As immigrants poured into the city, the descendants of Chicago's Yankee founders saw their population share shrink to less than 15 percent.

In the suburban ring around the city, however, those proportions were reversed. Old-line Americans dominated the population. That contrast between an immigrant city and its Yankee hinterland set into motion the kind of two-culture problem that has bedeviled American society ever since. To Yankee Americans, immigrant cultures have seemed to threaten what they see as the real American values. To immigrants, the cultural snubs of older America have sounded a clear warning: newcomers are welcome here for their strong arms and backs, but they are expected to remain quiet politically and defer to their predecessors.

In 1920, a writer in the *Saturday Evening Post*, the bible of Yankee-stock, small-town America, thundered: "If the United States is the melting pot something is wrong with the heating system; for an inconveniently large portion of the new immigration floats round in unsightly indigestible lumps." Chicago, the preeminent immigrant city, has always found itself right in the midst of that clash of cultures.

In 1855, the city's administration was captured by the Know Nothing Party, a political faction dedicated to keeping immigrants in their place. The new mayor, Levi Boone, decreed that taverns that served beer (the German newcomers' beverage of choice) would have to close on Sundays. Taverns serving whiskey (favored by Yankees) could remain open. When a group of tavern owners on the largely German North Side organized a protest march, Boone had a cannon mounted in front of city hall. Twenty protesters were wounded and one was killed in the melee that followed, which went into the history books as the Beer Riots.

Politically, that cultural split has been played out by the traditional division of local politics between a city dominated by the Democratic Party and its suburbs, where the Republicans were supreme. The famed Chicago "machine" was built on immigrant votes, once the city had a sufficient base of newcomers who had become citizens. The machine's founder, Mayor Anton Cermak, was Bohemian. His successors were Jewish (Jake Arvey) and Irish (Ed Kelley).

The Mexican Model

Chicago's Mexican community offers a cross-generational example of how the city's fortunes have been tied to globalization, at least the human-capital variety. Mexicans took part in both great waves of immigration to Chicago. A small community was already established here in the early years of the twentieth century, when it formed an exception to the rule that the city's immigrant neighborhoods were populated by the European born. Now, with non-Europeans the dominant source of new Chicagoans, Mexicans form the largest single group among them.

The Mexican experience in Chicago has a unique aspect. Because their homeland was, relatively speaking, closer, the city's Mexicans have had the opportunity to return there or commute, thus maintaining a connection with their mother country that other immigrants, both European and non-European, did not enjoy.

The history of Chicago's Mexican community also nicely illustrates America's contradictory set of attitudes toward immigrants, welcoming them in one era, only to reject them scarcely a decade later.

Mexicans first came to Chicago for the same reason that European immigrants did. In 1916, needing track workers, the railroads began recruiting at the border between Texas and Mexico. Chicago, the hub of the nation's rail system, was a natural destination for those recruits, and 206 were sent there that year. When the United States entered World War I, other Chicago industries found themselves in a pinch as their older workers were called into military service. Accordingly, representatives of the steel mills and packinghouses followed the footsteps of the railroads' officials to those recruiting grounds along the border.

In 1919 there was a vast strike in the steel industry. Mexican workers were brought in to replace those on the picket lines thrown up around Chicago's plants. At Inland Steel alone, the number of Mexican workers escalated from 90 in 1918 to 945 a year later. The episode proved a mixed blessing for Chicago's nascent Mexican community. For years to come, older European-stock workers looked down on Mexicans working alongside them as potential strikebreakers, aliens who might put their employment in jeopardy. The feelings followed Chicago's Mexicans even after their enthusiastic participation in the great wave of union organizing in the 1930s.

By 1920, the census counted 1,200 Mexicans in Chicago. By 1930 that number had risen to 20,000, but these newcomers did not yet constitute a community in the same sense as other immigrant groups. At the beginning of the 1920s, most were young males, either single or with families back in Mexico. Expecting to return home at some point, few applied for citizenship. They saw themselves not as Americans-to-be, but as Mexicans living temporarily in an alien culture whose mysterious ways they had little interest in penetrating. By the end of the decade, however, a third of the community were women and children, indicating that some Mexicans were beginning to think of Chicago not as a transient home but a place to put down roots and raise families.

Yet during the thirties, many of Chicago's Mexicans did return home, a lot more quickly than they had expected. With the Great Depression sending the unemployment figures soaring, pressure was brought upon the government to send immigrants packing. The argument was remarkably similar to that of present-day advocates of immigration restrictions: Why should foreigners take jobs away from American citizens?

Many other immigrants who had not yet obtained citizenship were affected by the federal government's "repatriation program." Thousand of Poles and Italians were sent back to their homelands. But proportional to their numbers, still more Mexicans were sent home. By the end of the 1930s, the Chicago Mexican colony had shrunk to 14,000.

When the Second World War began, the repatriation program was not just suspended but reversed. As had happened earlier, the draft led to a labor shortage. In response, the United States entered into an agreement with Mexico by which that nation agreed that its share in the struggle against the Axis would be to send workers north. Between 1930 and 1945, 15,000 railroad workers were brought to Chicago. Private industry also looked to Mexicans to flesh out its wartime workforce. Sears, Roebuck and Company, desperate for garment workers, distributed circulars in Dallas and Fort Worth, hoping to persuade Mexicans living there to come to Chicago.

Under the terms of the government's so-called "bracero program," it was expected that those war-workers would return to Mexico at the conflict's end. Yet, patently, many either did not or shortly doubled back. By 1950, the city's Mexican population had more than made up for its depression-era losses and stood at 24,000. In 1953, the director of the Chicago office of the U.S. Immigration and Naturalization Service said that no matter what the census showed, he was convinced there were 100,000 Mexicans in Chicago—which he clearly saw as a problem, witness his referring to them by the unlovely term "wetbacks."

The word had gone out to the villages of Mexico, as it had earlier to those of eastern and southern Europe, that there was a good living to be made in Chicago. In 1975, the Reverend J. McPolin, a Catholic prelate who had watched the process, delivered a lecture entitled "Mexicans in Chicago." "Letters began to make their way back into the homes of those families whose relatives or friends have gone to the United States, and they told of a land of peace and plenty," he said. "Often the marvelous character of the story grew as it was repeated and people came in ever-increasing numbers."

As the immigrants came north, Chicago neighborhoods were remade ethnically. On the Near Southwest Side, the Bohemian Settlement House had been founded in 1896 to serve European newcomers. With the descendants of those Europeans moving on to suburbs like Cicero and Riverside, the Bohemian Settlement House was transformed into Casa Azlan, a social-service center for Mexican newcomers.

The Near Southwest community was still overwhelmingly blue-collar. In 1953, a Chicago newspaper reporter could find only seven Mexican nurses, five schoolteachers, one dentist, and one Mexican policeman. Nonetheless, when Halsted Street, just west of the Loop, was bulldozed to make room for a new campus for the University of Illinois, its Mexican and Mexican American inhabitants followed their Slavic predecessors south and west to Pilsen, along Eighteenth and Twenty-second Streets. From there, as they prospered, they bought property in Little Village along Twenty-sixth Street west of California Avenue, again often from Slavic families.

By the 1960s, Joseph Gardunio, who had come to Chicago from Mexico as a factory worker a decade earlier, sensed that this volume was only going to increase and persuaded the Greyhound company to make the experiment of sending a bus from a storefront station he opened on South Damen Avenue, in a neighborhood that was just then becoming Spanish-speaking. Gardunio and Greyhound were soon dispatching six buses daily to the Mexican border, not from the huge downtown terminal, but from a Spanish-speaking outpost in an immigrant neighborhood.

During the years of World War II, a federal agency, reflecting the trepidation with which older Americans have always viewed immigrants, made a grant to a local organization, the Chicago Area Project, intended to speed up "the full integration of Mexicans into our national life." That is to say, they were to be stripped, as rapidly as possible, of their homeland's culture.

But by the time Gardunio established his busline connection between the Southwest Side and Mexico, it was apparent that something quite different had taken place. In Pilsen and Little Village and around the steel mills of South Chicago, Mexicans, like others before them, had transformed Chicago neighborhoods into still another outpost of a foreign culture. Currently, that same process is taking place beyond the city's borders. The 2000 census found that Mexicans and Mexican Americans are now 74.4 percent of the population in Cicero, long a preserve of European immigrant stocks. And Spanish-speakers, predominantly people of Mexican origin, constitute 53.9 percent of the population of Melrose Park and 79.1 percent of the population of nearby Stone Park.

Mexican Americans have also begun to move up the economic ladder and into positions of authority. For decades, their political progress was slowed by the high percentage of noncitizens, and thus nonvoters, in the Mexican community. But beginning with the election of the reform-minded Mayor Harold Washington, Mexicans and Mexican Americans have become a part of the ethnic mix that determines the city's political course. Their rewards have been proportional. In recent years, Raymond Orozco was the first Mexican American to serve as Chicago's fire commissioner. Matt Rodriguez, half-Mexican and half-Polish, headed the Chicago Police Department from 1992 to 1997.

In his memoir, *Harvest of Hope*, the physician Jorge Prieto recalls his own part in that slow climb of the Mexican community from the status of tolerated but resented newcomers to a constituent part of the local establishment. In 1950, Prieto came from Mexico to do an internship at Chicago's Columbus Hospital, where, except for a couple of Cuban doctors, he was the only Spanish-speaker. Subsequently, he set up practice in the nascent Mexican community on the Southwest Side. By the 1970s, he had become the head of a medical section at Cook County Hospital. A decade and a half later, Mayor Harold Washington appointed Prieto as president of the Board of Health. "I had come to Chicago hoping to become a reasonably good physician to one neighborhood," Prieto wrote. "Now I was hearing the Mayor of this huge city offering to make me responsible for the public health of all of its neighborhoods. My life had come full circle."

Mexican immigrants have begun wielding influence not just in Chicago but in Mexico as well. Immigrants routinely send money to relatives that remain in their home countries, and Mexican immigrants have been no exception. Moreover, they have gone a step beyond helping individual family members: through hometown associations, they are raising funds for infrastructure and cultural projects in Mexico.

There are an estimated 190 hometown associations in the Chicago area and membership is based on the town or village of origin. In 1995, the Federación de Clubes Unidos Zacatecanos en Illinois, the umbrella group for hometown associations for the state of Zacatecas, organized a matching-fund program for public works and infrastructure projects. Through the program, the Mexican federal government, the state of Zacatecas, and municipal government bodies matched the funds raised by the Federación. Since then, other hometown associations have adopted similar programs, and millions of dollars from the Chicago area have been matched by local, state, and federal funds and have brought much-needed public works improvements to several states in Mexico. These connections have created a base of power from which Mexican immigrants can have a say in the government policies in their country of origin.

The Transnationals

Recently, sociologists and political scientists have adopted the term "transnational communities" to describe the situation of the increasing numbers of groups like Chicago's Mexicans who live in one country but maintain strong ties to another. In fact, the phenomenon can be traced to the earliest days of immigration to Chicago. Almost all new immigrant groups have been anxious to retain links to their old homeland. (The one exception was Jews fleeing Russia, where the czarist regime was an official sponsor of anti-Semitic repression and pogroms.) Immigrants' letters collected by Florian Znaniecki for his classic study *The Polish Peasant in Europe and America* eloquently testify to the efforts of early Polish immigrants to keep in touch with relatives back home.

Yet until recently, the means to maintain those ties were limited. Letters had to go back and forth by ship. Even when telephones became common in blue-collar homes, the cost of a trans-Atlantic call was prohibitive for all but the most urgent messages: announcement of deaths, maybe marriages and births.

Most of the earlier immigrants had little hope of influencing events in their old homelands. They had come from countries like Russia, Germany, and Austria-Hungary with autocratic governments unwilling to accept political advice at home, let alone from abroad. Indeed, many German immigrants came to the Midwest after taking part in an unsuccessful attempt in 1848 to transform Germany along democratic lines.

For decades afterwards, the only immigrant groups even to dream of having a political impact at home were self-proclaimed revolutionaries. Chicago, with its massive base of the foreign born, was the effective capital of radical politics in America. The Socialist Party, the Industrial Workers of the World, and the Communist Party each held formative conventions in Chicago. Each had a base of immigrant political activists.

Closer to Home

Technology has effectively shortened the distance between Chicago's immigrant communities and their old homelands. Long-distance phone calls halfway around the world have become affordable to even the newest arrival. Cell phones, once a mark of the upper class, are now ubiquitous. The court-ordered breakup of AT&T was followed by fierce competition among successor companies, and the local consequences can be seen along Lawrence Avenue, the new immigrants' shopping rialto. One shop alone, Tasnim Enterprises, stocks cut-rate phone cards with which immigrants from almost two hundred countries can keep in touch with relatives and friends back home. Recently, Tasnim and rivals have been engaged in a fierce battle for the patronage of an immigrant group that even trained sociologists might have missed as part of the Chicago mix. Shop windows carry hastily scribbled signs promising to beat the competition's price for phone cards for Mongolia.

In similar fashion, intercontinental airline fares are now cheap enough that relatively recent immigrants can afford a visit home and even bring relatives over to visit Chicago. The steamship of a century ago was so expensive it took years to save enough money for a trip. New arrivals worked for years in Chicago's factories before they could buy the additional tickets to bring wives and children over.

The Koreans

Those changed circumstances are clearly reflected in the experience of Chicago's Korean community. Koreans were rare in Chicago before the 1960s, their tiny settlement then lying along Clark Street near Wrigley Field. But in the seventies and eighties, the number of Korean immigrants increased, owing to an unusual combination of circumstances in their homeland. Korea's universities began to produce a significant new professional class, especially lawyers and engineers, but the country's underdeveloped economy made it difficult for many to establish careers at home. Additionally, the authoritarian South Korean regime tolerated no political dissent. Therefore, younger, educated Koreans were inspired to seek opportunities abroad.

Los Angeles, being relatively close to their home country, received the greatest number of Korean immigrants, but Chicago also drew considerable numbers. The reason for this is curious, says Kwang Dong Jo, editor of the daily *Korean Times,* published in the Albany Park neighborhood. Avid moviegoers, Koreans were familiar with Chicago through the Mafia-themed movies that have made the city known around the world as Al Capone's town. But in the background of those same mob movies, Jo notes, Koreans could see Chicago's factories. So like others before them, they realized there were jobs to be had here.

Because they were educated, many Korean immigrants could quickly move up from punching a time clock. But lacking English-language skills, they had little hope of reestablishing themselves as professionals. Instead, they opened small shops along Lawrence Avenue, transforming Albany Park into a new "Little Korea." The profits have allowed immigrant parents to send their children to American universities, thus returning families to the professional class to which they belonged in the old country.

In the last six years, Korean families increasingly have moved out of the city, following the path of their Jewish predecessors from the Northwest Side to Skokie. By now a second shopping area has developed, as Korean businesses have followed their customers north to the vicinity of Milwaukee Avenue and Golf Road, where suburban shopping malls have been transformed into a second-generation "Little Korea."

Through all those developments, Koreans have maintained homeland ties of an immediacy that would have been impossible only a short while ago. According to Jo, the first generation of Korean immigrants kept in close touch with political developments in the homeland. Their hope was to quicken the transformation of Korea into a democracy. More recently, economic developments back home have interested Chicago's Korean community. Korea's economy developed so rapidly that the country began to challenge Japan as the industrial leader of East Asia. With so many Korean immigrants having established themselves as small business owners in Chicago, Jo observes, they are forging commercial links with Korea. Their vision is quintessentially global: to exploit the productive capacity of their old homeland and the market potential of their adoptive homeland by becoming Chicago-based importers of Korean goods for distribution throughout the United States.

As other countries similarly industrialize, their expatriate communities in Chicago will be naturally tempted to forge similar transnational links.

Chicago's Koreans have also established a new, human linkage with their older homeland. Jo notes that the community here is at a transition point. Its pioneers are aging, and a second generation is concerned lest its children be stripped of their ancestral culture by the dominant youth culture of America. Accordingly, Korean families are sending children back to Korea during summer school holidays. He estimates that between one thousand and two thousand young Korean Americans currently fly back to Korea each summer from Chicago.

Transnational Politics

Mexican immigrants have taken the lead in establishing political links across the borders. Previously, some older immigrant groups had begun to play a small but significant long-distance role in the political life of their homelands. Greek political parties have opened temporary offices in Chicago, hoping that Chicago's Greek Americans would urge relatives back home to vote in that country's always hotly contested elections.

But Mexican immigrants have taken that process a step further, according to Luis E. Pelayo, president of the Hispanic Council. He thinks that the experience of living in the United States has enabled Mexican Americans to persuade family members back home that there can be an alternative to Mexico's traditional politics of cronyism and corruption.

Because of the relatively short distance from Chicago to Mexico, Mexican political parties have been active in this city since the 1980s. During national elections, they have maintained campaign offices in Mexican neighborhoods, which seemed to have played a critical role in the Mexican presidential election of 2000. According to Pelayo, the phone calls back home stimulated by campaign offices here may well have saved Mexico from turmoil.

In recent years, he explains, Mexico has been rocked by a series of political scandals involving prominent members of that country's ruling Institutional Revolutionary Party, or PRI. In power since the Mexican revolution of 1911, the PRI had essentially transformed the country into a one-party state, for all its democratic constitution. Nomination by the PRI was tantamount to election, especially in national races. That provided a measure of stability from one administration to the next, but it also made it difficult to institute necessary reforms. By the time a politician had reached the point of being a candidate for the PRI's nomination, he or she would be well socialized into the don't-rock-the-boat ethic natural to an unchallenged political faction.

By the end of the 1990s, that system seemed ossified to Mexicans, who saw their government unable to cope with financial irregularities by the establishment and a sagging economy. Against that background, an immigrant organization, Mexican Migrants for Change, established itself in Chicago's Spanish-speaking neighborhoods. When Mexican president Vicente Fox was a candidate of the National Action Party, he took time out from his campaign stops in Mexico to visit Chicago. The daughter of his rival, the PRI's candidate, made a campaign tour of Cicero, courting the support of its sizable Mexican community.

Fox won, ending seventy-one years of PRI dominance. According to Pelayo, the reformer's victory was partially due to the fact that his supporters in Chicago (and elsewhere in the United States) were able to convince voters back home that peaceful change through democratic means was possible. It was, Pelayo says, a lesson learned by living in the United States and exported home. "Without those phone calls home, saying: 'Vote, don't give up on the process,'" Pelayo argues, "Mexico could have slid into revolution."

In recognition of the role of Mexican Americans in his victory, President Fox has promised to work for new election laws that would allow Mexicans living abroad to vote in their homeland's elections via absentee ballots. He made sure to repeat that promise during a victory tour of Chicago's Mexican community in July 2001.

As more Third World countries move toward democratic constitutions, it seems probable that their cultural outposts in Chicago's immigrant neighborhoods will begin to play a similar role in those nations' political lives.

That assumes, of course, that Chicago will continue to be a first home to new arrivals. To judge by history and economics, that should be the case in this new age of globalization. Both the "push"—what impels other peoples to leave home—and the "pull"—what attracts them to Chicago—are as real as they were in the past.

Patrick Durkin is principal of the William Goudy Elementary School in Uptown, once a fashionable North Side neighborhood and now a landing place for new arrivals in Chicago. In recent years, he has witnessed refugees from the world's hot spots registering their children for school: families that have fled the bloodletting in the former Yugoslavia, others who escaped poverty and civil wars in Africa and Southeast Asia.

Durkin has developed a rule of thumb for predicting where his next year's students will come from. So far it has not failed him. "I read the papers and see where they are shooting at each other today," he says. "I know that those kids will be the next to show up at Goudy." Chicago, meanwhile, needs new arrivals even more than it did their predecessors.

Imported Brainpower

During the great age of immigration in the nineteenth and early twentieth centuries, newcomers provided the muscle for the city's industries, and native-born Americans supplied the brainpower. The engineers who designed the assembly lines were largely Yankee-stock old settlers, as were the doctors who took care of old-line Americans and immigrants alike.

Chicago's needs had not changed much by the 1960s, when Korean professionals began arriving here. Hospitals and engineering firms did not need new arrivals handicapped by poor or nonexistent English-language skills. With the arrival of the offspring of an earlier generation of immigrants on campus, America's universities were still turning out a sufficient supply of professionals to meet the needs of a city like Chicago.

That is no longer true. As the American economy has moved through a second industrial revolution, entering the much-celebrated information age, our supply of university graduates trained to staff a high-tech economy has been stretched increasingly thin. Where engineering and other technical fields used to be the concentration of choice for those who were the first in their families to go to college, changes in the curriculum (and the ethos) of America's high schools have resulted in fewer graduates with the desire or capacity to study scientific subjects in college. Indeed, if they had only the native born to draw from, American universities would be hard pressed to enroll enough students in their science courses to justify the expense of maintaining their laboratories.

In 2002, 646 of the 1,041 graduate students in engineering at the University of Illinois at Chicago were foreign born. At Fermi National Accelerator Laboratory, located in Batavia, in the much-touted high-tech corridor to the west, the number was 1,400 out of 2,600 scientists. Those figures accord with national estimates that half of all graduate students in computer science and engineering at American universities are foreign born.

Much the same is true of American medicine. U.S. medical schools do not graduate enough doctors to maintain the country's health care system. Dr. Pradeep Thapar came to Chicago with a medical degree from an Indian university in 1984. He practices child psychiatry in south-suburban Flossmoor and notes that he is the only doctor in the immediate area with specialty training in that medical subspecialty. "Go to any hospital in the United States," he said, "and you'll find Indian doctors on the staff."

Indeed, Chicago's medical community has a new sociological profile. Research and university hospitals have mixed staffs, with some doctors native born and others foreign born or trained. Outlying and community hospitals have become largely the preserve of foreign-born physicians.

The need for immigrants with higher skills than their predecessors has made the fortunes of Chicago's new East Indian community. Ninety percent of Indian immigrants are English-speaking, so they are prepared to go to work in high-skilled jobs the moment they arrive in Chicago. And over 60 percent of Indian immigrants are trained professionals, filling the technological employment void left by America's universities.

For the members of Chicago's Indian immigrant community, that combination of their skills and the city's needs has meant an unprecedented rate of social advancement. Most have not put in the urban season of their European predecessors: by a three-to-one ratio, new arrivals have gone directly to the suburbs. Currently, four out of five Indian immigrants in the Chicago area live in the suburbs. Many have settled around the high-tech plants where they work, such as Motorola's facility in Schaumburg, and Lucent Technologies in Lisle. Between 600 and 700 Indians work at Lucent, where they have organized themselves into an Indian Cultural Association. Naperville, the epicenter of the Chicago area's high-tech corridor, has an Indian population of 5,000.

Reflecting the increasing dependence on high-tech immigrants, the Chicago area's Indian population doubled between the censuses of 1990 and 2000. It now stands at 124,723. Those numbers strongly suggest that Chicago would have as difficult a time participating in the new globalized economy without a continuing flow of immigrants as it would have in the smokestack economy of a century ago.

Meanwhile, Chicago's dependence upon immigrants at the blue-collar level of its workforce has a new dimension. In recent years, as we are incessantly told, America has been passing into a service economy, and Chicago's share of that postindustrial economy is largely manned by newcomers.

Kitchen work in Chicago's restaurants has become a near monopoly of immigrants. Whatever the ethnicity proclaimed on its marquee, back in the kitchen, save for the occasional celebrity chef, it is likely that the cooking is being done by Mexicans. Officials of Chicago's taxi industry estimate that 80 percent of the city's cab drivers are immigrants. And Leon Bobola, an executive with Lakeside Building Maintenance, himself born in Poland, says that 95 percent of the workers who clean the Loop's offices are foreign born.

The Immigrant Future?

With Chicago dependent upon immigrants at both ends of its social scale, logic dictates that the city's future replicate its past. It should continue to be a place where newcomers find a foothold in their adopted homeland while making a critical contribution to the local economy. Yet, as the history of Chicago's Mexican community demonstrates, national policy with respect to immigration is debated with as much passion as reason. In the wake of September 11, 2001, the image of the immigrant has been shifting from a welcome addition to the American family to a potentially dangerous threat to the country's security.

On the very morning when hijacked airplanes flew into the World Trade

Center and the Pentagon, the U.S. House of Representatives was set to debate extending a program allowing foreigners living in the United States to apply for resident visas without having to first return to their home country. That question was set aside in favor of the new agenda of somehow making our borders effective barriers against foreign-born terrorists. The Immigration Reform Caucus, an unabashedly anti-immigrant group in Congress, quickly doubled its membership to thirty senators and representatives. A survey made shortly after September 11 showed that two-thirds of Americans felt that lax enforcement of the nation's immigration regulations had contributed to our vulnerability to terrorism.

Ironically, until September 11, popular sentiment had been shifting in favor of immigrants. During his quadrennial campaigns for the Republican nomination for president, Pat Buchanan has made anti-immigrant legislative proposals a centerpiece of his message to the electorate, and in 1995, California's Governor Pete Wilson railed about the porous border with Mexico.

But these positions did not meet with much sympathy. A booming economy had made Americans more tolerant of newcomers. The nation seemed to have set aside the anger that had inspired, in 1996, new restrictions placed upon legal immigrants' applying for governmentally funded social services as part of welfare reform. A year later Congress began restoring such benefits as food stamps to legal immigrants. Conservative business owners spoke out as advocates of immigration as a necessary lubricant of the country's economy. A pro-business organization, the Essential Worker Immigration Coalition, was pushing Congress for legislation to increase the numbers of immigrants allowed into the country under the so-called H-1B visa, which grants foreigners with special high-tech skills quicker entry. The restaurant industry was simultaneously lobbying for increased immigration quotas for the low-skilled workers necessary to keep its kitchens functioning.

So it might be that once the shock of September 11 is sufficiently behind us, the country will forget its current preoccupation with "aliens" and return to seeing immigrants in a positive light. On the other hand, it might not. And that would be a problem for Chicago. The city could be cut off from the flow of newcomers upon which its fortunes have always depended.

This would not be a death warrant, however. It would simply mean that, ironically, Chicago would enter the age of self-conscious globalization stripped of the global human capital with which it developed. More probably, though, the city's future will look like its past.

Indeed, it is likely that even now young people are walking the streets of Chicago's immigrant neighborhoods seeking an evening's respite from adults, as adolescents always do. Life, no doubt, will carry many of them away from the neighborhoods of their youth, just as it did the former inhabitants. Should any return on a sentimental journey decades from now, they will find shop windows relettered in a newer set of immigrant languages. Yet in them, those visitors will still recognize something familiar as well as something different.

For though it is told in many chapters, each in a different tongue, Chicago's story has always been remarkably the same: a city indebted to globalization, a hundred years before the word entered the lexicon of professors and government leaders.

5 Human Rights Legacy

STEPHEN FRANKLIN

THE CHALLENGES were heartbreaking. Stirred by the brutality and mayhem that afflicted the former Yugoslavia, the United Nations took a monumental step forward on behalf of human rights. It committed itself to go beyond just bringing peace. It vowed not just to carry out "victor's justice," but to set a global agenda and a warning for future human rights violators. It would track down those who had carried out systematic abuses in the conflict that had swallowed up Serbs, Croats, and Bosnians and prosecute those who had violated basic human rights in a newly established forum, the International Criminal Tribunal for the former Yugoslavia (ICTY).

The human rights revolution in international law began in earnest with the adoption by the UN of the Declaration of Human Rights in 1948, extending core concepts recognized in the law of war by the beginning of the twentieth century. Human rights became the vision that undermined the Soviet Union in the 1980s and the rallying cry that justified international intervention in Croatia, Bosnia, and Kosovo in the 1990s. But the novelty of establishing and administering such a court raised major problems, the most significant of which was the absence of any plan for how to proceed. Months went by before the UN finally agreed to provide funding, and even then the amount was unusually meager, only $900,000. On top of that, a vast terrain had to be covered in the criminal investigation. The region was dangerous. Members of hostile militias were still at hand. Witnesses were scattered, and those who could be found were terrified about recounting the tragedies they had endured.

Several European governments were cool to the idea of such an investigation, fearing that it would churn up emotions that would jeopardize the already fragile peace talks then under way. Yet against all odds, the investigation was carried out. Had it not been for work begun thousands of miles away in Chicago, this precedent-setting expansion of the jurisdiction of human rights might never have taken place.

Starting with DePaul

It was a team at the International Human Rights Law Institute at DePaul University Law School, under the leadership of M. Cherif Bassiouni, an Egyptian-born professor of international law, that conceived and developed the investigation strategy, racing against time for fear that evidence and witnesses would vanish. "It was an unparalleled investigation," Bassiouni said. "We had a war going on, and the UN bureaucracy was not too happy to see us go in there."

The evidence was overwhelming and confusing. Military consultants were hired to figure out what armed units had served where, and when. Lists were compiled giving the names of police and where they had served. From maps and other sources, the researchers were able to identify 151 mass graves and 800 places of detention. Narrowing the search further, the probe focused on survivors who could describe the torture that took place in the prison camps and the attacks on women that were carried out in communities during the fighting. Out of nearly 8,000 allegations of abuse, the investigation culled 600 of the most credible and gathered hundreds of affidavits in those cases.

A significant picture began to emerge from interviews with survivors still living in refugee camps in Croatia and Bosnia. In most rape cases, it is rare for the victim to know the attacker, but the investigators realized that was not the case in the fighting in the former Yugoslavia. As teams of interviewers quickly learned, many of the attackers were from the same communities as the victims. They had either been encouraged to take part in the attacks or had led them. Putting their material together, the investigators reached a conclusion: the rapes were part of a carefully planned program, a concentrated effort, and were not the random acts of madness during a war.

Eighteen months after beginning its work, the investigations commission turned in its final report, detailing the ethnic cleansing, rapes and assaults, and prison camp cruelties, based on 65,000 pages of documents, 300 hours of videotapes, maps, pictures, and affidavits by over 500 victims and witnesses of rape. DePaul's work totaled 3,500 pages. The commission's final report tallied 50,000 persons tortured and 20,000 raped, 187 mass graves, and 962 prison camps where over half a million people had been held. It put the number of people who fled their homes at 3 million.

After some delay, ICTY began its assignment of prosecuting the ones whose deeds had been scrupulously detailed in the investigation. It was a paper trail compiled far away in Chicago that had guaranteed that the crimes would not be forgotten.

Chicago institutions and individuals have been pioneers in turning aspirations to human rights accountability into actions. DePaul's Bassiouni circumvented roadblocks to the initial establishment of the ICTY by actually starting work before the UN got its act together to fund the court. Another law professor, Douglass W. Cassel, now at Northwestern University, regularly contributed to the development of intellectual capital and public understanding pertaining to human rights. The Illinois Institute of Technology's Chicago-Kent College of Law, under the leadership of Professor Henry H. Perritt, developed a "war crimes database" to assist the American Bar Association, the ICTY, the Red Cross, and other organizations to assemble evidence after the Kosovo crisis. Chicago-Kent's Bartram Brown served with the ICTY and also served as a member of the UN's Commission on Human Rights. All of these institutions assisted in the conceptual development and realization of the International Criminal Court (ICC), an organization that the United States refused to ratify.

Chicago was showing itself once again to be a place where people were willing to shoulder the burden of protecting human rights.

A Typical Chicago Response

Chicago does not have a finely tuned, well-orchestrated human rights network, but over the years it has always had individuals and organizations that have cared greatly about human rights. Their efforts have often been helter-skelter, individualistic, and passionate, some driven by organizations with long-established community ties, others with new names, new concerns, new faces—often many of them the faces of Chicago's recently arrived immigrant groups. This tradition reaches back into Chicago history.

One of the roots of this tradition is in Chicago's civic life. Activists such as Jane Addams set a precedent for extending concern about social problems beyond Chicago's city limits. Addams's work left behind an institutionalized consciousness among organizations and individuals about both injustice

Chicago-Kent College of Law at the Illinois Institute of Technology implemented Project Bosnia and Operation Kosovo, connecting the Bosnian Constitutional Court, its ombudsman, and the International Media Center in Banja Luka, Bosnia, to the Internet. These projects

—developed and deployed a mobile, Internet-connected database to help track refugees and to collect evidence of war crimes in Kosovo and surrounding countries;
—developed a plan for effective use of information technology to make legal information available to legal professionals and to the public;
—developed and implemented practical, practice-oriented legal education at the University of Pristina Law Faculty, including twenty "externships" for Kosovar law students to work in Kosovar legal institutions while in law school;
—provided technical assistance to the Kosovo Chamber of Commerce and the Ministry of Trade and Industry in developing plans for small-business assistance clinics and the promotion of investment opportunities in Kosovo; and assisted the UN Mission in Kosovo and the Kosovo Trust Agency.

suffered at home and injustice suffered abroad, and Chicago's many immigrant populations have sharpened the focus. As the twenty-first century began, many people in Chicago were caring about the fate of relatives in Latin America, Asia, Africa, and the Middle East, joined by others whose careers in law, global businesses, or overseas religious work led them to speak up about the rights problems in these places.

But some of the recent concern for global human rights in Chicago seems to come from a relatively new thirst for global justice. While the pains of the Holocaust or Central America's serial bloodbaths are never more than a moment away for some, for others, the idea of caring intensely about the fate of people far away is new. CNN led the way, and hosts of other television stations, broadcasting in numerous languages, followed suit in waking up Americans' conscience. Their instant replay of warfare and oppression in places rarely visited before made the world seem smaller and certain regions more immediate. This revolution in global broadcasting opened Chicagoans and others to the despair felt in such distant places as Afghanistan and such relatively close places as Mexico's Chiapas state.

Those interested in global human rights believe that Chicago's landlocked nature adds to its significance as a place to espouse these concerns. The thinking goes this way: Chicago stands for the heartland, Midwest values, a place where extremism is moderated and moderation is exalted, where what is considered average American is really average midwestern, where what plays wells in Peoria really plays well in heartland America. And if human rights issues are going to matter in the United States, they must matter in the heartland.

By the very nature of the city's metropolitan sprawl and ethnic diversity, it makes sense that Chicagoans would be eager to voice their opinions on a global stew of topics ranging from illegal executions in Guatemala to the abuse of religious rights in Iran. From immigrant groups to academic institutions to charitable organizations to social service organizations like the YMCA and Rotary International (founded in Chicago in 1905), and religious groups like the Baha'i, which has its North American headquarters in Chicago, there are many whose natural focus is the world and human rights. Few U.S. cities can claim a concentration of as many major academic programs focused on human rights issues as does Chicago, with ongoing research and advocacy efforts at DePaul, Northwestern, the University of Chicago, and the Chicago-Kent College of Law.

Chicago's place in the world's memory as a locus of the battle for human rights has been earned time and again, but one event stands out. The call for a shorter workday and less brutal labor-management relations had been championed for years by workers in Chicago. A union movement took hold at the end of the nineteenth century, and Chicago was a bastion of union organizing. But in 1886 these efforts took on a new meaning. When workers rallied on May 4, 1886, in Chicago's Haymarket area on behalf of the shorter workday and to protest the deaths of two workers in a clash with police at a locked-out South Side factory, someone threw a powerful bomb and chaos ensued. Four workers and eight policemen died, and dozens more were injured. Officials blamed the bloody confrontation on anarchists.

Within days, dozens of political radicals were swept up by police, and eight anarchists who were linked by authorities to the dispute were found guilty of murder. Four were hung, one committed suicide the day before his death sentence was to be carried out, and two others had their sentences commuted by Governor Peter Altgeld—whose political career was ended because of his repudiation of the injustices that took place at the trial. The eighth defendant was given a sentence of fifteen years of hard labor. The Haymarket incident inspired unions everywhere in the world (except in the United States) to set aside May 1—May Day—as the day to commemorate labor's struggles.

Globalizing Human Rights

Globalization kicked concerns about human rights into high gear. "Globalization, like any wind of change, blows equally at each door and window and sends the same waves crashing against coasts," wrote Richard C. Longworth in his book *Global Squeeze*. As the huge new global corporations ranged from one continent to another seeking out new markets and facilities, they became mired in a swamp of global injustices. Should they uphold the values of the world's developed nations or face fines and sanctions by doing business in places like South Africa under apartheid? Business took the corporations to places where the bitter fruits of war still lingered, and in Central America's work-hungry nations, where these corporations discovered cheap labor, they found themselves face to face with repressive regimes.

As these global companies spread their investments and operations, their shareholders and others asked what roles they played in countries where respect for human rights was negligible. Global commerce nurtured global awareness. If giant corporations could learn to travel the globe with ease, so could tourists, who ventured into places rarely explored before. Refugees could seek haven in countries once considered impossible to reach. Upheavals in Africa, Latin America, and the Middle East set their citizens adrift in search of new homes. Afghans, some of whom had never seen their own capital, took escape routes through Iran and Turkey on their way to Europe. Guatemalans and El Salvadorans flooded through Mexico on the way to the United States, fleeing years of warfare in their poverty-stricken countries.

In the twentieth century, as desperate refugees crossed borders in ever growing waves, right-wing groups across the developed world raised howls of protest over the presence of illegal immigrants on their soils. In the first years of the twenty-first century, over one million illegal refugees flooded into Greece. France counted over 300,000 illegal refugees. The global trafficking in human beings began to parallel global drug trafficking—except that it was far less risky for the traffickers. As the Swiss-based International Organization for Migration pointed out in an April 2001 report, few nations had laws against human traffickers, and when they did, the fines and penalties were few.

And so women and children were bought and sold across borders. Women were trafficked for forced labor or for work in the sex industry. Sexual tourism found a niche among world travelers. According to a 1998 report issued by the U.S. Department of State, between 700,000 and two million women and children are trafficked globally. In 2001, a handful of immigrant-resettlement organizations and other social-work agencies met to talk about how they would cope with what appeared to be Chicago's inclusion on the global track of female trafficking.

As global justice went from being the topic of graduate school seminars and inscrutable legal treatises to something on the evening news, religious, labor, and social groups found themselves caught up in the affairs of places they had never considered before. Faced with the impending shutdown of a longtime Chicago institution by its Swiss-based owners, union leaders traveled to Argentina in 2001 to plead with workers there not to accept the transfer of jobs to Chicago. Events of the twentieth century did much to open the world's eyes to what had lingered in the darkness for years. As the media focus shifted from one tragedy to another, from Indochina to Africa to the Middle East, some people complained of "global misery overload" and found the world's despair too emotionally exhausting. Some of the blinds went down and the shutters went up.

But the conversation had changed forever, and the message has been amplified around the world. Speaking up for the human rights of Iraqi Kurds or the citizens of East Timor or the Afghan victims of the ruling Taliban was no longer the sole responsibility of small, zealous groups. The expansion of the world through communications and travel added new energy to the quest for human rights. "The most significant change in the human rights movement as it goes into the 21st century is that it will go on the offensive," wrote Geoffrey Robertson, a British barrister and activist for global justice.

Chicago Changes, Too

As the world changed, so did Chicago. Ironically, for a city so proud of its broad immigrant shoulders, Chicago has been inclined to downplay international matters and to focus on things at home. "At home" means the United States—but up close and under a microscope it really refers to the heartland, the American Midwest. Yet Chicago is more than a provincial center. It is the loudest, largest, and most diverse city in the Midwest. It is the Midwest's capital. In that role it has given shelter to the political conservatism and isolationism that has coursed through the region. Although the isolationist impulse has perhaps been less strong here than elsewhere in the heartland, it found a home in Chicago.

Colonel Robert R. McCormick made sure of that. The longtime editor and publisher of the *Chicago Tribune* in the first half of the twentieth century, he was a champion of heartland values, and his publication was a beacon for the isolationism that he heartily embraced. Coming from a paper of the *Tribune*'s stature in what was at the time the nation's second-largest city, the colonel's voice could not be ignored. McCormick firmly believed that the vast midwestern region reached by the *Tribune* was the "vital center of America." In comparison, New York was a "Sodom and Gomorrah of sin." In the days leading up to World War II, McCormick was an unrelenting opponent of America's involvement in the war.

While others in Chicago urged Americans to respond to the Nazis' disregard of borders and rights, the *Tribune* urged restraint and a distancing from the disorder in Europe. McCormick's own newspaper's revelations of concentration camps and the systematic murder of Jews did nothing to change the colonel's beliefs. "No arguments of sentiment or self-interest could shake his belief in American isolation," wrote Richard Norton Smith in his biography of the influential publisher.

Chicago's geography has had other effects on the city's thinking. It has nurtured an uneasy feeling of "middleness"—being neither New York nor Los Angeles. Because it sits in the nation's middle, a place to pass over on the way to either coast, Chicago has cast many an insecure glance over its shoulder, however broad, at its coastal competitors, wishing it had what they seemed to have. But the city has also benefited from being somewhat out of the flight path. Not being on the spot where important organizations are located, official contacts are made and nourished, or foreign diplomats mix with U.S. policy makers, Chicago may feel a sense of inferiority. But not being anywhere else has worked to the advantages of those concerned about human rights issues in Chicago. Rights activists have not had to worry about stepping on the toes of large, well-established human rights organizations in New York or Washington. Rather than bumping up against the bailiwicks of veteran human rights organizations, or having to defer to their long histories of human rights work overseas, Chicago's groups have plunged ahead on their own. They have had the freedom to chart their way and to pick their own causes and battles.

Chicago, in short, is a warehouse of contradictions. Studs Terkel, Chicago's much-loved, gravel-voiced storyteller, wrote in *Chicago,* his rhapsodic tone poem to the city: "Our double-vision, double-standard, double-value and double-cross have been patent ever since—at least, since the earliest of our city fathers took the Pottawatomies for all they had." Nelson Algren, one of Terkel's heroes, was also a true believer in Chicago's doubleness. "Chicago . . . forever keeps two faces, one for winners and one for losers; one for hustlers and one for squares. . . . One for Go-Getters and one for Go-Get It Yourselfers. . . . One for early risers and one for evening hiders," Algren wrote in *Chicago: City on the Make,* his examination of the city's soul.

The city cares about the world but sometimes doesn't care about its own. It turned its back for years on the racial isolation and segregation of Chicago's African Americans. Chicago reaches out to disenfranchised workers around the globe, but it ignores newly arrived immigrants who often labor in grim conditions bereft of dignity and respect. Union and community groups have documented how many immigrants toil in modern-day sweatshop conditions, where time clocks do not matter, on-the-job injuries are downplayed, and basic workers' rights barely exist.

Chicago frets about lawlessness that crushes the hopes of the world's poor and disadvantaged, but the poor in Chicago also suffer from injustices and inequities that fill its courts and send its residents to state prisons.

Chicago works. But Chicago doesn't always work when it comes to human rights below its heartland horizons here at home. There's a disinclination in Chicago to set up organizations that might channel communal energies, a frustrating fact of life for those who know the strength that comes from working together. Yet not everyone agrees with the idea that better coordination will make much of a difference among those concerned about human rights in Chicago. "I'm not sold, at least in human rights work, on the idea that we have to spend a lot of energy coordinating. When there is a common interest in a project, we find it," said Douglass W. Cassel, the law professor who helped set up the International Human Rights Law Institute at DePaul University and later founded a similar organization at the Northwestern University Law School.

Why does Chicago care about human rights? Partly this can be understood by looking at the institutions and people caught up in these efforts. But some of the concerns don't easily fit any formulas. Rather, as Cassel suggests, a serendipitous coming together of people and organizations has taken place. One program, sometimes just one individual, has spurred others to take a step down a road they might not have yet tried. As a result of an unusual pool of grit, talent, and concern, the good work on good causes has, indeed, gotten done.

To understand where this energy comes from, you have to peel back layers of the city's history, going back to people and organizations that have left a mark on Chicago's collective consciousness. Chicago has a long legacy of social activism that typically begins in the city, soon turns its focus outward toward the rest of the nation, and eventually fixes on the world beyond.

From a Base of Social Activism

Jane Addams

When Jane Addams arrived in Chicago near the end of the nineteenth century from a small Illinois town, she brought with her the somewhat naive views of the well-to-do about how to boost the poor and immigrant classes up to a higher way of life. Her genius was to create Hull-House, a working experiment in urban reform. It was not the nation's first settlement house, but it became the model, the most famous of its kind in the United States. Chicago's first day-care center, public playground, kindergarten, and free health-care clinic all were born at Hull-House. To celebrate immigrants' contributions to working America, Addams established a labor museum.

"We based the value of our efforts not upon any special training, but upon the old belief that he who lives near the life of the poor, he who knows the devastating effects of disease and vice, has at least an unrivaled opportunity to make a genuine contribution to their understanding," she wrote in *The Second Twenty Years at Hull-House*.

But her gaze eventually turned away from Chicago toward reforming the rest of the world in the way she had helped Chicago's poor. Her influence was widespread. She was one of the early supporters of the National Association for the Advancement of Colored People (NAACP) in the early years of the twentieth century. She spoke out against lynchings in the South long before such cries were commonly heard. Women's rights became a major rallying issue for her. Fair treatment for immigrants and tolerance for those whose politics didn't fit into the mainstream loomed large on her agenda of concerns. One of her students in grassroots politics was Sidney Hillman, an apprentice cutter at a large garment house in Chicago.

His dealing with a garment workers' strike in 1910 catapulted him to the attention of Addams and others who helped workers and immigrants find their own voices. The young Russian immigrant went on to help found the Amalgamated Clothing Workers Union of America in Chicago in 1914 and then to serve as the president of the politically influential union for years.

From 1915 onward, Addams's major vehicle was the Women's International League for Peace and Freedom. Her pacifism during World War I and her involvement afterwards in defending radicals and immigrants cost her dearly in the public's esteem. "Addams Favors Reds" was a *Chicago Tribune* headline that expressed the resentment she typically faced for speaking out about war.

Even though she won the Nobel Peace Prize in 1931 for her efforts on behalf of world peace, she never regained the admiration of the American public.

Her progression from settlement social worker to pacifist had its underpinnings in an era that encouraged people to look for ways to speak out about people's human rights. From the stockyards to the sweatshops to the airless, densely crowded slums, progressives and reformers went about pointing their fingers at abuses and offering solutions. One of those in the social orbit of Hull-House was the Chicago attorney Clarence Darrow, whose fabled career was marked by his defense of blacks and union members.

Dwight Moody

In Chicago's religious community, activism has often extended outward. One of the best examples is the career of Dwight Lyman Moody, founder of the Moody Bible School in Chicago. A successful businessman turned Christian evangelist during the latter part of the nineteenth century, he was a high-ranking official with the Young Men's Christian Association in Chicago and nationally. After taking his message across the United States, Moody was convinced that the same work had to be done overseas. His conviction was critical in the YMCA's efforts to expand its foreign work to its overseas branches.

Saul Alinsky

If Jane Addams's commitment to world peace led to her downfall in the eyes of the American public, then Saul Alinsky's sometimes outlandish deeds made him a hero to those he championed. He was a social activist, community organizer, troublemaker, and innovator who opened new vistas for Chicago-trained activists for years to come. He largely stayed home, but his teachings traveled. More often despised by those he hounded, Alinsky had endeared himself to those whom he cared about. He came from Chicago's West Side, the son of Russian Jewish immigrants. After graduating from the University of Chicago, he became a sociologist for the Illinois prisons, but in time he found his voice and vision in working with youth gangs. Taking a lesson from union organizers, he set about organizing in the neighborhoods where he worked. He helped form the Back of the Yards Council, which marched and shouted its way to recognition of its needs by city officials—a victory for Chicago residents who had long felt shunted aside. Alinsky was able to bring blacks and whites, Jews and Christians, business people and union diehards together in the gritty blue-collar neighborhood where many had once worked in the stockyards.

Over the years, he took his community organizing efforts around the country. With support from religious leaders, he founded the Industrial Areas Foundation, which became the breeding ground for community organizers for years to come. (Cesar Chavez, the inspirational hero of the nation's farmworkers, was one of those who benefited from Alinsky's teachings.) Out of Alinsky's efforts came Chicago's Woodlawn Organization, the nation's first black urban community organization.

His teachings were passed on to generations of social workers and community organizers and have traveled the world to the places where U.S. Peace Corps volunteers and others have tried to instill a sense of community cohesion.

Julius Rosenwald

A similar passion about social and racial justice drove Julius Rosenwald, president of the Chicago-based Sears, Roebuck and Company. Realizing the terrible injustices done to black Americans, Rosenwald, a philanthropist, provided financial support for the Urban League, schools across the South designed to raise the education levels of blacks, and YMCAs that served only blacks. He supported fair and decent housing for blacks, whose pleas for humane accommodations had repeatedly been denied by city officials and charities. Rosenwald was a member of Chicago's Commission on Race Relations, whose lengthy report on the 1919 race riot was a portent to the city of the corrosive racial divide within its borders and the tragedies that lay ahead.

Thirty-eight persons—twenty-three blacks and fifteen whites—lost their lives in the 1919 confrontation, the first major display of racial outrage in Chicago. A clash at a South Side beach set off the violence. But the seeds had been planted long before. As Chicago's industries expanded in the early years of the twentieth century, blacks were welcomed as desperately needed workers. But they were frequently called upon to be strike breakers, and they were the ones who took on the toughest, least wanted jobs. They faced resistance from unions that upheld racial barriers not unlike the ones that they had fled in the South. Nonetheless, answering the call from the *Chicago Defender,* once the nation's most vibrant black newspaper, blacks continually left the South for Chicago. There they began escaping segregated areas, moving into once strictly white neighborhoods. Their homes were bombed, or bombs were used against real-estate agents who had led their way. White hooligans preyed on blacks who lived on the edge where the two communities intersected. Fleeing lynching in the South, blacks came face to face with racial bigotry in the Midwest.

What provoked whites and blacks in 1919 boiled to the surface again and again. Whites persisted in holding the line against black neighbors, so much so that the historian Arnold Hirsch called the community disputes that occurred in the 1940s "hidden violence and guerrilla warfare." Richard Wright described the path that the black community found itself locked into in Chicago. "Many migrants like us were driven and pursued, in the manner of characters in a Greek play, down the paths of defeats; but luck must have been with us, for we somehow survived," he wrote.

When Martin Luther King Jr. brought his civil rights movement to Chicago, he described the city as the "Birmingham of the North." If the struggle for civil rights could succeed in Chicago, King predicted, then it could win "anywhere in the country." But he did not underestimate the threat that blacks faced in seeking their rights in Chicago. In August 1966 he led a march through a nearly all-white enclave on Chicago's South Side. Thousands of furious white demonstrators lined the march route. Afterwards King summed up the situation: "I have seen many demonstrations in the South, but I have never seen anything so hostile and so hateful as I have today."

Labeled by the U.S. Commission on Civil Rights in 1959 as "the most residentially segregated large city in the nation," Chicago held that title for years, and city officials did little to change that truth. They fought the civil rights movement because it threatened to change the racial status quo, and they resisted the government-sponsored antipoverty movement in the 1960s because it initially threatened to take away power from city hall.

An enlightened view about public housing saw integration as a goal. But that idea evaporated over the years as high-rise housing projects meant to bring new life and services to impoverished communities became segregated fortresses of despair. The projects compounded Chicago's segregation. Only in the last years of the twentieth century did Chicago's leaders begin to undo the problems created by these lofty compounds. The answer was to tear down the high-rises and put the residents in affordable low-rise housing distributed throughout the city.

Still, Chicago's efforts to overcome generations of racial and economic segregation were stymied by the failure of city officials to find a resolution beyond Chicago's borders. The solution to housing integration for poor minorities, as other cities have learned, is to open up housing in the mostly white suburbs. But that was a step Chicago was not able to take. Just as the city began confronting the bitter legacy of its segregated housing for poor minorities, it began to deal with another offshoot of the city's racial isolation of low-income blacks and Latinos. The city began holding its schools accountable for the education they provided, and in many neighborhoods where poor black and Latino families predominated, the classroom results were dismal.

Immigrant Activists

Chicago, the city of tongues, was a place where immigrants from many countries flourished despite the brutalities of the slaughterhouse and the steel mill, and where their rights and needs called out for attention. In his famous muckraking novel *The Jungle,* Upton Sinclair wrote about conditions in Chicago's meat-packing houses and awakened the nation to the manufacturing practices of that industry. The book was also a plea for compassion for the mostly Eastern European immigrants who were locked into cruel lives on the packing house floor, but that plea was overlooked.

The workers were not silent, however. Immigrants brought a political awareness with them that stoked the union drive in Chicago and across the United States. Much of this energy in Chicago came from German immigrants, who were the largest single ethnic group in the city at the end of the nineteenth century. They carried with them a faith in unions, radicalism, and anarchism. Across the United States, workers calling for an eight-hour day were echoing a cry from Chicago.

Chicago was the linchpin in the battle for workers' rights at the end of the nineteenth century. A clash of workers at the Pullman Palace Car Company soon escalated into a nationwide transit crisis when the workers won the support of the American Railway Union. Workers and unions were galvanized by the effort, but the federal government and the railroad companies used their might to put down the railway workers' strike. The result of the workers' crushing defeat made the union's president, Eugene V. Debs, determined to find a more effective way to fight capitalism. The founding of the Socialist Party in the United States with Debs as its leader followed soon after. Likewise, radical union members found Chicago the place to meet and form the Industrial Workers of the World (IWW) in the city in 1905. As immigrants had brought the passion for workers' rights to Chicago, so Chicago sent it back out to the world.

Hearing Cries for Help

As the twentieth century proceeded, a seemingly endless series of revelations of disregard for human rights emerged. Religious and immigrant groups in Chicago responded to calls for help. The large Polish community in Chicago became a voice for Poles under Communism at home and then an advocate for an independent Poland. Chicago's Assyrians, who form one of the largest communities of the kind in the United States, supported their fellow Iraqi Christians throughout Iraq's tormented history under Saddam Hussein and his predecessors. Members of the Baha'i faith in the Chicago area—where the Baha'i temple established in suburban Wilmette in 1953 was the first founded in the West—have championed the cause of their coreligionists around the world.

Chicago's Jewish community is one of the nation's largest. It spoke out on behalf of Jews in the former Soviet Union and helped settle over thirty thousand Jews fleeing religious persecution under the Kremlin's rule. These émigrés have become the largest group of Soviet Jewish refugees resettled in the United States outside of New York City.

But the Jewish community has not helped only its own. The Jewish Federation of Metropolitan Chicago became the coordinator of the state's efforts to help resettle refugees of any religion, from anywhere around the world. The Hebrew Immigrant Aid Society (HIAS), the organization that helped immigrant Jews find a home in Chicago in the late nineteenth century, has taken up the same role for others. It helped Vietnamese settle in the Chicago area in the aftermath of the Vietnam War and shared in efforts with other agencies on behalf of Bosnians and Kosovar Muslims.

Chicago's Bosnians, one of the oldest Muslim communities in the metropolitan area, helped settle hundreds of refugees who needed medical care and a new home after chaos swept across their communities in the former Yugoslavia. As Muslim communities in the Chicago area grew in the last century, so did their charities, which benefit Muslims around the world. The oldest Palestinian charity in the United States, the United Holy Land Fund, was set up in 1968 in Chicago. Some years later, other Arab and Muslim charities took up similar roles as the population of Indians, Pakistanis, and Arabs swelled.

And when Muslims faced intolerance and hatred in the United States after the terrorist attacks in September 2001, Christian and Jewish groups in Chicago stepped forward to speak out on their behalf, in some cases forming human shields to protect them while they prayed in their mosques.

Chicago's African American community played a role in opposing apartheid in South Africa and, later, in urging that more attention be paid to the desperate conditions in many of Africa's floundering nations. Through his Chicago-based operations, the Reverend Jesse Jackson sought to link Africans with African Americans and to put African issues higher on the agenda in Washington and elsewhere.

Jackson operated for years as a diplomatic Lone Ranger, meeting with world leaders ranging from Fidel Castro to Yasser Arafat, campaigning on behalf of poor countries' needs and rescuing persons in harm's way. His efforts led to the release from Syria of a downed U.S. pilot in 1984 as well as freedom for hostages held in 1990 by the Iraqi leader Saddam Hussein.

But his most indelible efforts may have been in Africa. Named by President Bill Clinton as a special envoy to promote democracy in Africa, he met regularly with leaders and politicians across the continent. In 1999, he helped broker a cease-fire between the government and rebels in Sierra Leone. Likewise, he boosted economic ties with Africa through his organization, the Rainbow/PUSH Coalition. He became a larger-than-life figure in Africa, and at times during his trips, people ranging from high-ranking officials to average persons would rush up and embrace him in public.

The Chicago area's Mexican American community, one of the nation's largest, makes its voice clear on the rights and needs of Mexico in the world and vis-à-vis the United States. It has also spoken out on the economic rights of those who live in poverty in Mexico, whose first struggle is to stay alive. And whole communities in Mexico have benefited from the financial support channeled back from family members who, as workers and immigrants, have found new homes and livelihoods in Chicago.

Hundreds of Central Americans, often escaping mayhem, warfare, and organized cruelty, have found new homes in the Chicago area. Many were assisted by informal efforts to provide a haven for them at a time when the U.S. government would not extend an official welcome to these refugees. So great was the outcry for help in the 1980s that a number of Chicago-area churches and synagogues created an alliance to provide sanctuary for these people fleeing violent upheavals in Guatemala, Nicaragua, and El Salvador.

The Chicago Religious Leadership Network on Latin America

Out of such an effort came the Chicago Religious Leadership Network on Latin America. Its membership has stayed modest—about five hundred persons in different religious communities in the Chicago area—and its goals have been equally modest. It tries to inform Chicago-area religious leaders and groups about the critical issues in Latin America; writes letters on behalf of human rights victims; once a year sends a small group to visit a Latin American country where there are pressing matters involving peace, human rights, and justice; and at least once a year sends a delegation to Washington to meet with U.S. policy makers to discuss its concerns. On one level, it has not been difficult to find support for the organization's concerns in the Chicago area, according to its director, Gary Cozette, once a lay missionary in El Salvador. "There's an awareness in terms of torture and forced disappearances," he said. But violations of other rights such as the right to housing, education, and dignity on the job do not evoke the same keen concern among Chicagoans.

Fortunately, the organization does not exist in a vacuum in Chicago. At times, it has been able to rely on support from, for example, the international human rights program at Northwestern University's Law School. And once, when one of its delegations was visiting Guatemala, the Religious Leadership Network was able to aid another small human rights group in Chicago that has made labor rights its core concern. Fearful that a Guatemalan labor leader whose life was in danger would not be able to leave his country safely, a visiting group from the network provided twenty-four-hour protection for the union official until he was able to fly to the United States, where he sought asylum.

The U.S. Labor Education in the Americas Project

The small group mentioned above is the U.S. Labor Education in the Americas Project. A financially lean operation with only a few workers, it was first known as the U.S. Guatemala Labor Education Project when it was created in 1987 in New York. It changed its name in 1998 to reflect its expanded boundaries in Central and Latin America. It moved to Chicago in 1990, when Steve Coats, its founder, relocated to the city. The only independent agency of its kind in the United States, its goal is to advocate on behalf of workers' rights. But it often carries this out by negotiating directly with companies to get them to sign labor agreements and to accept outside monitoring of the conditions in their workplaces. Despite its minuscule size, it has had an impact. To push up the wages for low-paid coffee workers in Central America, for example, it conducted a campaign to get the giant Starbucks company to agree on a code of conduct for treatment of workers in the coffee plantations and to accept responsibility for the pay the workers receive from independent coffee suppliers. After some resistance, the Seattle-based company agreed, making it the first major U.S. coffee provider to have done so. The project also was able to persuade U.S.-based Chiquita Brands to accept responsibility for its independent suppliers' hiring and treatment of their workers.

A familiar pattern among organizations in Chicago is that of one group nurturing another. Steve Coats opened a door for Hannah Frisch to carry out human rights work similar to that of the Americas Project. Frisch had worked for the Central American labor effort as a volunteer. She and others saw a need for a program to support female workers there by developing bonds between themselves and women from Central America. In 1998, out of their efforts came STITCH, like its parent organization a tiny operation, with one full-time worker in Central America, one in Washington, D.C., and one in Chicago. It is the only program of its kind, run by a U.S.-based organization for the specific goal of helping female workers in Central American factories.

Besides helping female workers gain the right to organize in Central American factories, it runs a weeklong program that allows women from the United States to study Spanish in Guatemala as well as to meet human rights activists there. By linking women from the United States and Central America, the program creates a level of awareness and empathy that may not have existed before.

Opening the Door

The Heartland Alliance

The Heartland Alliance for Human Needs and Human Rights is an agency founded in Chicago more than one hundred years ago to help recently arrived foreigners. Moving from issue to issue, it has secured a place for itself as it deals with human rights at home and abroad. It began in 1888 at the height of the reform movement within the city and was known then as Travelers and Immigrants Aid. Over time its mission evolved to reach to the poor, the homeless, the mentally ill, victims of domestic abuse, and those suffering from AIDS. In 1988, because of the growing number of refugees from Cambodia and Central America who had escaped torture but had been mentally scarred by the torturers, the Heartland Alliance opened the Marjorie Kovler Center for the Treatment of Survivors of Torture, one of the nation's first centers for such treatment. More than two dozen facilities have since taken up this kind of work in the United States, where there are an estimated several hundred thousand victims of torture. But the caseload for the Kovler Center on Chicago's North Side is second in volume only to that of Bellevue Hospital in New York City. Its roll of clients has grown over the years. It has seen torture victims from more than forty countries and could serve more, but limited funds have forced it to impose a waiting list. Over the years, it has succeeded in stretching its services by relying on an expanded core of volunteers, ranging from clergy to psychologists, and with help from organizations such as Physicians for Human Rights. The Kovler Center operates as a training center for the volunteers and specialists from the United States and overseas.

Working with torture victims and those seeking asylum in the United States is only one way that the Heartland Alliance has expanded. Its Mexico–U.S. Advocates Network works with U.S. and Mexican officials to help set standards for treatment of migrants detained by either country. Its Midwest Immigrants and Human Rights Center was founded in 1985. It relies on pro bono attorneys and provides legal protection and guidance for immigrants. In an era of globalized criminality, it has worked on behalf of women and children who have been trafficked across international borders.

Along with others, the Heartland Alliance has broadened its scope over the years to make global human rights a high priority for its work in Chicago. "Why do we care about human rights?" asked Sid Mohn, the agency's president. "Because we can trace nearly all of the problems that wind up on our doorstep from somewhere in the world."

David Berten and Asylumlaw

David Berten is a Chicago lawyer who represents companies in patent disputes and other commercial litigation. His effort to help others around the world came out of his work as a volunteer with the Midwest Immigrants and Human Rights Center. Several years ago, while working on behalf of a woman from the Benadir tribe in Somalia who was seeking asylum, Berten found there were few documents to call upon to describe the conditions from which she had fled. During his interview with the woman, an interpreter mentioned by chance that he had some documents. One of them turned out to be a letter from the office of the United Nations High Commissioner for Refugees in Kenya to the U.S. embassy there, saying that because of the persecution faced by the Benadir in Somalia, they had to be resettled elsewhere for their safety. It urged U.S. officials to keep this in mind when considering asylum requests from members of the Benadir tribe. "It disturbed me that I got hold of it by happenstance," Berten recalled.

He resolved to find a solution for himself and others. The result is <www.asylumlaw.org>, a Web site set up in 1999. It has since established partnerships with an immigrant rights program in Canada and another in Australia. Its free services are open to anyone worldwide, and people can call upon the expertise of over two thousand attorneys and advocates. A lawyer anywhere in the world searching for guidance can seek out help. On an average day, the Web site carried the plea from an attorney for a Colombian woman who was seeking asylum in the United States because she had been threatened for blowing the whistle on government corruption; another from a lawyer seeking advice for an asylum case for a Turkish Christian hoping to find a home in the United States; and another from an attorney who was seeking background documents about human rights abuses in the former Soviet Union that could help with asylum cases.

A Law School Class on Prisoners' Rights in Peru

Sometimes the efforts to reach out are passing ones that do not take hold. Bartram Brown, a law professor at Chicago-Kent College of Law with extensive experience in international human rights, saw a need for an organization to bring together other interested lawyers in Chicago. He helped set up an organization known as Chicago Lawyers for Human Rights. The group took part in a visit to Haiti in 1994 and other trips overseas to bring Chicago attorneys face to face with human rights issues. But Brown's attempts to coordinate his group's efforts with those of others failed. The organization lost support, floundered, and merged with the Midwest Coalition for Human Rights. "Maybe it is a testament that all of these groups are so busy doing what they are doing that it is hard to find the energy to do the coordination," he said.

Ralph Ruebner, a professor at the John Marshall Law School, had no organization tugging at him, urging him to take part in an effort to bring some measure of justice to Peru. It was interest and curiosity that led Ruebner to take on the case of a young Illinois woman who had been arrested on drug trafficking charges in Peru. He was struck by the deplorable prison conditions in Peru and the profound slowness of the justice system there. There was no question about the woman's guilt; at issue was how she would be treated in the court and prisons.

Ruebner was teaching a human rights class at John Marshall at the time, and he and his sixteen law students took the opportunity to assist the young woman's family, from Danville, Illinois, with their legal struggle. After visiting their daughter and another young American arrested with her in prison in Lima, Ruebner, a veteran public defender in Chicago's courts, was convinced that their rights to decent care and justice were being ignored. When U.S. officials ignored the pleas for action filed by Ruebner and his students, Ruebner took the battle to a higher ground. He filed a lawsuit before the Inter-American Commission on Human Rights, an arm of the Organization of American States (OAS), based in Washington, D.C., in which he charged Peru with violating treaties guaranteeing decent conditions in its prisons. The added pressure worked. The two Americans, who were convicted on drug trafficking charges, were allowed to leave after three years and serve the remainder of their sentences on parole in the United States. As part of the deal for their release, the families agreed to drop the charges with the OAS. "The only reason they got out," Ruebner said, "was the dropping of the lawsuit. They [Peru] wanted the lawsuit dropped."

Scholars at Risk

In 1997, the University of Chicago followed DePaul University in setting up a human rights program with a similar focus on classroom teaching, research, and advocacy. But within a few years the University of Chicago Human Rights Program added an innovation not found anywhere else in the world, the Scholars at Risk program. The idea came from a point raised at a program conference: the University of Chicago had provided a safe haven for scholars fleeing oppression in Europe in the 1930s and 1940s. Why not do the same work today? That led to the creation in June 2000 of a small, sparsely funded effort to help scholars around the world whose rights are endangered. What is different about this program is that it not only provides moral support for academics under pressure, but also tries to remove them from harm's way by finding temporary teaching positions outside their own countries. Here and there, academics in the United States and overseas have set up programs to help those within their own professions or from their own country. "There is no other program in the world that addresses people from any discipline and any country," said Rob Quinn, an attorney with a background in international human rights work and director of the Scholars at Risk program.

Since the program's inception, only a few of the scholars seeking help have requested sanctuary in another country. These individuals have been placed in universities in the United States—one of them at the University of Chicago. Nearly seventy universities in the United States and Canada have offered their support for the program, and twelve have gone further, pledging to take in a scholar in need of sanctuary. The program has begun looking for ways to place some of these academics in teaching positions in countries closer to their homes, where they might continue their work in the same language, lessening the trauma of having to start over in English, a new language for many. The program has also initiated an effort to support student activists whose lives are similarly threatened by oppressive regimes.

Physicians Against Land Mines

Just as the Scholars at Risk program came from a legacy of caring, so too the Physicians Against Land Mines came from a deeply rooted base in Chicago's extensive medical community dedicated to dealing with disabilities and rehabilitation. Dr. William Kennedy Smith's personal concern about land mine victims began in 1991, when he worked at a clinic in Somalia run by the International Medical Corps. But the idea of creating an organization that would campaign against land mines as well as help victims came to life in Chicago, where he was doing his residency in rehabilitation medicine at Northwestern University Hospital. Realizing the depth and quality of expertise on hand at Northwestern as well as at the Rehabilitation Institute of Chicago, along with the resources of the Chicago-based American Medical Association, he sought out others who were similarly interested in combating the land mine problem. "I thought it was a natural progress. Chicago had world-class expertise. The question was how do you make these institutions related to one another," he said.

When the program began in 1996, its first goal was to encourage physicians to get involved in speaking out against the spread of land mines and in lobbying for better care of mine victims worldwide. Within two years, the young program took another of several steps to expand its work. With funding from the National Institute on Disability and Rehabilitation Research, it set up an Engineering Research Center to explore inexpensive and expeditious ways of making artificial limbs and wheelchairs. In much of the world, such items are simply beyond the reach of most victims of land mines and other weapons of destruction, and even for those who could afford them, the wait is lengthy.

The Center for International Rehabilitation

Out of the land mine effort came an even more ambitious and novel program—the Center for International Rehabilitation, founded in 1999. Not only would it advocate for the concerns of the disabled worldwide, but it would reach health care givers through online learning programs and conferences in low-income countries. So far, it has focused on Central America and the Balkans. It works in conjunction with the Department of Veterans Affairs Chicago Health Care System, Northwestern University Hospital's Prosthetic Orthotic Center, and the Rehabilitation Institute of Chicago. All three institutions are within easy reach of each other. But others have also supplied help. Leo Burnett Advertising, for example, provided an ad campaign on the problems of land mines on a pro bono basis. Chicago religious leaders supported an ecumenical day of prayer and reflection on the land mine problem. And the Rotary Club of Chicago lent its support to a joint effort to raise funds to deal with land mine problems and to help land mine victims.

Running such an internationally focused program in Chicago has had clear advantages, according to Dr. Smith. When it comes to international concerns, "there are less voices in Chicago and that means you have an opportunity to connect. . . . In Chicago, you can assume a place in the community and that would not be as easy in New York," he said.

Putting Law to Work

Douglass W. Cassel's career path had seemed quite clear. He had spent more than a decade and a half as general counsel of an organization called Business and Professional People for the Public Interest in Chicago. He was a middle-aged lawyer whose feet were firmly planted in something he cared about. What turned his interests outward was a series of overseas trips, beginning with China in 1976 and including a 1986 visit with a delegation of the National Lawyers Guild to Nicaragua to observe the drafting of a new constitution there. He returned to Central America a year later, going back to Nicaragua and later visiting Honduras with a delegation led by a Chicago-based religious group. When he returned home to Chicago from Central America, Cassel realized the trip had made a greater impact on him than he had realized. He was fascinated by the struggle for justice outside the United States and was moved especially by the daily battle to save lives.

Two years later, he had another chance to witness a human rights dilemma far from the United States when he visited the Israeli-occupied West Bank and the Gaza Strip at the invitation of the United Holy Land Fund, the Chicago-based charity supporting Palestinian interests. On the trip, he also visited Israel with the cooperation of the New Israel Fund, a small Israeli-American charity that backs progressive causes in Israel. "When I came back, I felt that was the final straw. This certainly was something I wanted to do, international human rights work," he recalls.

But Chicago offered no place where a lawyer could immerse himself in that kind of work. Cassel decided he would create an international human rights law center himself, linking up as many of Chicago's law schools as he could. But there was not much interest in a consortium. At DePaul University, however, he found a willing ear and, before long, an agreement to set up the International Human Rights Law Institute. The institute would both teach human rights law and take part in helping people fight for their rights. With support from a handful of foundations and DePaul, it got off the ground in 1990. Cassel was its executive director and Professor M. Cherif Bassiouni of the DePaul College of Law was president.

The institute was handed a monumental challenge when, in October 1992, the UN secretary general set up a five-person commission to investigate war crimes in the former Yugoslavia, and Bassiouni was one of the five. In no time, he threw the institute into a full-time investigation. Not since the Nuremberg trials and the trials in Japan after World War II had there been a world criminal court investigating crimes against humanity on such a scale as this effort launched by the UN.

Human Rights across the Seas

We are now back where we started, with Bassiouni and his DePaul colleagues and students working seven days a week, around the clock, digging for details about the fighting that claimed nearly two hundred thousand lives in the former Yugoslavia. Where the UN had failed to provide money at the start of the effort, the International Human Rights Law Institute sought the help of the Open Society Foundation of George Soros and the hometown John D. and Catherine T. MacArthur Foundation, which came to the rescue with funding until the UN kicked in.

Clearly, there are a number of shoulders in Chicago willing to share the burden of defending human rights around the world. The members of a community once known for its isolationism have refused over the years to be silent bystanders in the face of evil far away. Their ranks have grown as the world has become a smaller, more-connected place. They are human rights advocates, experts, and religious and community leaders. They are professionals committed to healing the emotional and physical wounds wrought by global injustices. They are people separated from the pain of global suffering by only a letter, telephone call, or live broadcast. Bringing these hearts and talents together is not an easy task.

But Chicago's challenge is not unique. Despite the explosion in attention to human rights abuses worldwide, Americans still search for the right measures of concern and commitment. They remain unsure whether distant problems born of wars, famine, and injustice are theirs. What stands out in Chicago, however, is a legacy of not turning one's face away.

Chicago has been a magnet for immigration for all of its history, creating a tapestry of nationalities and lifestyles, such as the one on display at Devon and Campbell Avenue. Photograph by Alex Garcia. Copyright 2003 by the *Chicago Tribune*.

Chicago's O'Hare has long been the world's busiest airport, the connection that links the city to the world and the engine for the region's global economic growth. Photograph by Jose More. Copyright 2003 by the *Chicago Tribune*.

As it always has been, politics is serious business in Chicago, a city that has learned to embrace diversity as a strength, particularly under Mayor Richard M. Daley. Photograph by Chuck Berman. Copyright 2003 by the *Chicago Tribune.*

At the city's heart rest architectural monuments that track its history and its purpose as a city always connected to the world and constantly transforming itself. The Wrigley Building is here viewed from the peak of the Tribune Tower. Photograph by Robert Murphy. Copyright 2003 by Robert Murphy. Courtesy of the Comer Archive of Chicago in the Year 2000, Richard J. Daley Library, University of Illinois at Chicago.

Home to more than two hundred theater groups, magnificent public works—this Picasso sculpture among them—and a vibrant music scene that covers everything from blues to opera, Chicago is recognized as a world-class cultural center. Photograph by Charles Osgood. Copyright 2003 by the *Chicago Tribune*.

Once known for its bloody stockyards and smoky steel mills, Chicago has blossomed into a service-industry center legendary for its architecture. This view looks west on the Chicago River toward the Merchandise Mart. Photograph by Robert Murphy. Copyright 2003 by Robert Murphy. Courtesy of the Comer Archive of Chicago in the Year 2000, Richard J. Daley Library, University of Illinois at Chicago.

Chicago presents an endless array of vistas that are aesthetically pleasing and revealing at the same time. Waterways and railroads connect within view of the
city's vibrant Loop. Photograph by Vaughn Wascovich. Copyright 2003 by Vaughn
Wascovich. Courtesy of the Comer Archive of Chicago in the Year 2000, Richard J.
Daley Library, University of Illinois at Chicago.

The diversity of Chicago's many ethnic groups helps to shape the city. A dramatic sand dragon is sculpted during the Korean Kite Festival at Montrose Beach. Photograph by Yvette Dostatni. Copyright 2003 by Yvette Dostatni. Courtesy of the Comer Archive of Chicago in the Year 2000, Richard J. Daley Library, University of Illinois at Chicago.

Having invented the derivatives market, Chicago is one of the world's largest financial markets. Floor traders are having a frantic day at the Board of Trade in the heart of Chicago's financial district. Photograph by Robert Davis. Copyright 2003 by Davis Designs Enterprises, Inc. Courtesy of the Comer Archive of Chicago in the Year 2000, Richard J. Daley Library, University of Illinois at Chicago.

Eliot Ness may have been the federal agent who finally caught Al Capone, whose name became welded to Chicago's tough image, but it was Michael Jordan who changed the world's perception of Chicago with stunning performances during his years with the world champion Chicago Bulls. Photograph by Phil Velasquez. Copyright 2003 by the *Chicago Tribune.*

Dancers in the Mexican Folkloric Ballet Company perform at California and Twenty-sixth in celebration of Mexican Independence Day. Photograph by John Booz. Copyright 2003 by John Booz. Courtesy of the Comer Archive of Chicago in the Year 2000, Richard J. Daley Library, University of Illinois at Chicago.

Global leaders meet in Chicago: in recognition of his dedicated service to mediate in conflict situations and to advocate on behalf of human rights for people all over the world, United Nations General Secretary Kofi Annan spoke with Rev. Jesse Jackson at Rainbow/PUSH Headquarters. Photograph by Milbert O. Brown. Copyright 2003 by the *Chicago Tribune*.

Chicago is a city where culture is rich and thriving: the Lyric Opera and the Chicago Symphony Orchestra are only two of the city's world-class cultural centers, which also include museums, theaters, dance venues, restaurants, and parks. Pictured is a scene from Lyric Opera's production of Mozart's *Marriage of Figaro:* left to right, Susan Graham as Cherubino, Hakan Hagegard as Count Almaviva, and Elizabeth Futral as Susanna. Photograph by Charles Osgood. Copyright 2003 by the *Chicago Tribune.*

Hardworking immigrants are vital to the economy of Chicago, but their life is far from easy. After working long hours at the factory and caring for a household, Remedios counts $4,500 to send to a "coyote" to pay for passage from Mexico for three adult family members. "Coyotes" charge anywhere from $700 to $2,500 to smuggle illegal immigrants across the border. They hold their human cargo hostage until the family pays the fees. Photograph by Jon Lowenstein. Copyright 2003 by Jon Lowenstein. Courtesy of the Comer Archive of Chicago in the Year 2000, Richard J. Daley Library, University of Illinois at Chicago.

Chicago is the largest intermodal hub in the Western Hemisphere, where cargo is transferred from planes, trains, trucks, and barges and transported throughout the Midwest, across all of the United States, and to all parts of the world. Photograph by Charles Osgood. Copyright 2003 by the *Chicago Tribune*.

6 City of Big Thinkers

CINDY SCHREUDER

CHICAGO, city of broad shoulders, is evolving into Chicago, city of broad bandwidth. This one-time hog-butchering capital of the world has morphed into a global metropolis. At a time when cell phones and Internet connections bring the world to even the most isolated community, a brawn-to-brains evolution must be undertaken by every aspirant to the title of a "global city." Intellectual capital drives the creation of a twenty-first-century global city and intellectual capital sustains it.

Each of the region's eight million people contributes, in some way, to this capital. But that capital is concentrated within the idea centers—including one hundred twenty-three colleges and universities, international companies, dozens of nongovernmental organizations, professional societies, libraries, newspapers, and magazines. Like synapses in the human brain, these idea centers branch out, reconnect, and shift in response to changing needs and new information. The way these institutions and the individuals within them connect—or miss connections—helps to determine Chicago's power on the world stage.

The global economy is reshaping the traditional banks of intellectual capital, that is, the universities, colleges, and professional schools. The clearest evidence of this is online or distance learning, programs many institutions—including the biggest schools in the region—are vigorously pursuing because it may be lucrative. It is too early to tell precisely how online education will reshape learning—whether enrollments at traditional bricks-and-mortar colleges will decline, for example. But how people pursue learning, and the extent to which they divorce it from traditional formal education, is changing.

Intellectual capital takes many forms. It includes the new technologies employed by a scholar at Northwestern University to digitize in three dimensions and open up, via the Internet, sacred Chinese cave-shrines closed for centuries. It takes in the Field Museum's Center for Cultural Understanding and Change, a partnership with at least eighteen other area museums and cultural institutions to examine cultural and ethnic diversity in the area. It includes Kartemquin Films, a Chicago-based, independent documentary film company. Kartemquin is telling the story of America's "New Immigrants," including a group of Ogoni people from Nigeria now living in Chicago, among them some family members of the writer and activist Ken Saro-Wiwa, who was executed in 1995. It includes the mental health clinic for refugee children established by the Heartland Alliance for Human Needs and Human Rights, a homegrown group. It encompasses all of these things, but is not limited to them, as there are literally hundreds upon hundreds of much-heralded as well as little-known connections.

A large and perhaps largely unacknowledged bank of intellectual capital includes two things that give Chicago in particular and the region in general a special identity. The first is the region's historic built environment—the downtown skyscrapers and historic buildings that gave birth to modern architecture, and the planned parks and public spaces that shaped urban design. The second is the agricultural knowledge cultivated through the generations in the rich prairie loam. This city-country dichotomy represents a deep base of intellectual capital in the elemental things that everyone, everywhere, needs: shelter and food.

In forward-thinking cities, intellectual capital is fostered from the beginning of life. That is true in Chicago. Infants who drool and coo are enrolled in foreign language programs by parents convinced their children's development will be enhanced, their lives made richer, and their place in the power structure secured by understanding a foreign tongue, the passport to a different culture.

But in this same region are public schools without any nonfiction books in their libraries. Children there who know a second language may find it is a detriment to their assimilation more than a credential fostering their success. Same standard metropolitan statistical area; different planet.

A global city increasingly requires its workers to cross from their specialty into others, to connect with people not normally encountered, to assemble old pieces into new shapes. That is why there are doctors who are lawyers, computer scientists with MBAs, world-renowned paleontologists who bring inner-city kids on fossil-hunting expeditions.

But missed connections abound alongside the many opportunities. This is true across the Chicago region, throughout the lifespan and to the detriment of the area. These failures occur for many reasons: inertia; the weight of history; a lack of knowledge about the work of others; competition for funding, students, prestige, and other resources; and a lack of time, energy, and priority.

Ferreting out the myriad international connections in this city and using them to strengthen existing ties as well as develop new ones can take time and energy. After all, even the most committed internationalist has but twenty-four hours in a day except, perhaps, upon crossing the international dateline.

Surveying the Landscape: Colleges and Universities

To understand how intellectual capital is grown alongside the corn that Illinois is famous for, a brief overview of higher education is in order. Colleges and universities are not the only places that intellectual capital is grown. Increasingly, companies, professional groups, and individuals cultivate that capital their entire lives and outside the borders of a college campus. But the universities, colleges, and professional schools are, historically, the way that capital was nurtured and are for many people still key points in the development of their knowledge and understanding of the world.

The state is home to 186 degree-granting institutions. Historically, public colleges and universities were created in rural areas while private institutions dominated in urban regions, a pattern that explains the dominance of private universities in the Chicago area. Just four of the state's twelve public universities—Chicago State, Governor's State, Northeastern Illinois, and the University of Illinois at Chicago—are in the Chicago area. (For the purposes of this discussion, Northern Illinois University in DeKalb is outside of the Chicago metropolitan region, although it draws many students and some faculty from the area.) Likewise, fewer than half—20 of 48—of the state's community colleges are in the Chicago area. But 97 of the 120 independent universities, colleges, and institutions, some nonprofit, others for-profit, call the region home.

Disparate histories, missions, and student and faculty interests and demographics result in widely varying degrees of engagement with global matters. These educational institutions can be broadly grouped into three categories: major players; institutions with targeted efforts; and small or specialized schools.

The Major Players

The major players are the three highest-profile universities. Like points on a compass, Northwestern University to the north, the University of Chicago to the south, and the University of Illinois at Chicago to the west occupy distinct positions in the city's intellectual grid.

The largest of these schools is also the youngest: the University of Illinois at Chicago, or UIC, part of the state land-grant university system. The university boasts of drawing students from 95 countries, all 50 states, and 3 U.S. territories, a diversity unmatched by most other colleges and universities in the country. Still, many of its nearly 25,000 students come from the Chicago area, and many of those students are the first in their family to attend college. The institution now offers 88 undergraduate majors, 86 master's degree fields, and 58 doctoral programs.

The University of Illinois's main campus is downstate, in Urbana-Champaign. But the UI also set up shop in Chicago on Navy Pier in 1946. Its initial scope was limited. But by 1965, when it was named the University of Illinois at Chicago Circle, that branch of the university began offering four-year programs. Seventeen years later, "it had grown to include eight academic colleges offering degree programs at both the graduate and undergraduate levels," according to the UIC undergraduate catalogue. Some of its international reach has been achieved because of strong, focused individuals, such as Virginia Ohlson, whose work in Japan after World War II shaped her thinking some years later as she developed a graduate program in public health. Other parts of UIC's growing international outlook come from informal contacts and opportunities, including a new master's degree in engineering, an online program developed in cooperation with several European universities.

"Just as our kids must know computers or they can't function, I think they've also got to know the international environment or they can't function," said Mary Niemiec, interim associate provost for external education and former interim director of the John Nuveen Center for International Affairs. "We're getting there. We're getting there. The awareness is there."

To the north lies the oldest of the three schools, Northwestern University. It was incorporated in 1851 after nine devout Methodists pledged a year earlier to create an institution of "the highest order of excellence" to serve people living in the original Northwest Territory (in other words, the residents of Ohio, Indiana, Illinois, Michigan, Wisconsin, and portions of Minnesota).

What began as a Methodist college of liberal arts by the lake has, particularly in recent years, shed its parochial beginnings, growing into an internationally known place of learning with a $3.7 billion endowment, about 13,600 students, and more than 2,000 faculty members. In 2002, the university's Kellogg Graduate School of Management was ranked the top business school in the world and in the United States by the Economist Intelligence Unit and *Business Week* magazine, respectively.

That transformation is continuing, said Lydia Villa-Komaroff, a Northwestern University vice president for research and a molecular biologist.

"I came to Northwestern from Harvard Medical School and spent a long time on the East Coast and in Boston. Those institutions are global enterprises," she said. "Northwestern was founded as a regional school. It's probably in the last decade that it has moved into a point where it now considers itself more than that and has joined the ranks of international and national schools." That assessment came belatedly, in part because Northwestern is clothed in 151 years of midwestern modesty.

"Chicago is a cosmopolitan city, but there is a sense in the population that we are comfortable with who we are in the Midwest and there's not a lot of feeling any pressure to make those [global] connections," Villa-Komaroff said. "The Midwest does not brag. It's not in the public eye as much as it could be and those characteristics of modesty and of feeling that it's not quite right to toot your own horn as much comes from the work ethic here."

But increasingly, the midwestern hubs of intellectual capital such as Northwestern are becoming global. Two forces are at work at Northwestern, Villa-Komaroff said. The first is the people themselves—starting at the top. President Henry S. Bienen is the former dean of the Woodrow Wilson School of Public and International Affairs at Princeton University. A political scientist whose interests include Africa, he has been a visiting professor in Nigeria, Uganda, and Kenya. That push creates ripples that extend across departments.

The other force, Villa-Komaroff said, is centered in business. She pointed out that "Chicago is a business hub. As the research enterprise grows at the university and becomes better it must make international connections."

To the south of Northwestern University lies the University of Chicago. At its founding in 1890 by the oil magnate John D. Rockefeller, it was the most comprehensive of what today are the three major universities. Like Northwestern, the University of Chicago has religious roots, though they lie not with the Methodists but with the Baptists. Propelled by the twin powers of Rockefeller money and an ambitious first president, William Rainey Harper, the University of Chicago from the start was the most wide-ranging of the big schools, combining the German model of graduate education with the English model of undergraduate education.

"Following the principle of trying to abolish evils by destroying them at the source, we felt that to aid colleges and universities, whose graduates would spread their culture far and wide, was the surest way to fight ignorance and promote the growth of useful knowledge," said Rockefeller.[1]

The University of Chicago was, for example, a center of Near Eastern studies from its founding. It created the first Egyptian studies teaching post in America and in 1896 founded the Haskell Oriental Museum, today the Oriental Institute. The media sought out the Oriental Institute's scholars to discuss the looting of Iraq's museums after U.S. forces entered Baghdad in April 2003. Since then, McGuire "Mac" Gibson, professor of Mesopotamian archaeology at the institute, has worked with UNESCO and other groups in helping the Baghdad Museum and its staff catalog and recover missing artifacts.

Worldwide engagement was perhaps most evident to outsiders during the 1940s. An international scientific team assembled at the University of Chicago and led by Enrico Fermi successfully set off the first self-sustaining nuclear reaction, a feat accomplished in laboratories under the university's football stands. More recently, economics professors and their students (several of whom have subsequently won the Nobel Prize in economics) developed a field of economics based on rational choice and free-market orientation and widely known as the Chicago School of Economics. Their colleagues at the University of Chicago Law School became advocates of a related field, an influential movement called Law and Economics, founded on the application of market-oriented economics to the law. Like Northwestern, the University of Chicago has a top-ranked business school that draws students from around the world. Today it has an endowment of about $3.5 billion, an enrollment of about 16,800, and more than 2,100 faculty—six of whom are Nobel laureates.

Schools That Pick Their Shots

Dozens of other universities, colleges, and professional schools in the region have thousands of notable international connections. These schools are not, by any means, "also-rans." But they may have a narrower international focus, a smaller enrollment, or a different mission and history than those of Northwestern, UIC, and the University of Chicago. Because these connec-

---

1. Quoted in *Titan: The Life of John D. Rockefeller, Sr.,* by Ron Chernow, New York: Random House, 1998.

tions are too numerous to recount individually, the focus here will be on three representative types. They are programs that are global from the start; programs whose international reach has grown as the subject area develops more global connections; and once narrowly focused schools that have recently developed international ties.

DePaul University's International Human Rights Law Institute is a good example of the first kind of connection—one that was international from the start. DePaul bills itself as Chicago's largest private school and the largest Catholic university in the country. Founded by the Vincentians in 1898, DePaul has programs in international studies, international business, and other fields.

But one of its strongest forays into internationalism lies with its International Human Rights Law Institute, begun in 1990. Now faculty and students from the institute offer legal assistance in a number of regions but with a significant focus on Latin America; work to create an international criminal court; document international crimes in the former Yugoslavia (see chapter 5); study the trafficking of women and children for sexual exploitation; work on the legal aspects of weapons control; and organize lectures and seminars for many prominent visitors.

"The international work of this university, aided by the Vincentian mission, is taken seriously even by the many of us who aren't Catholic," said Andrew Michels, then adjunct professor of law at DePaul and executive director of the Human Rights Law Institute. That commitment propels the international fieldwork of the institute, work that puts law students in impoverished communities in such places as Chiapas, Mexico, to learn what they can never truly understand from inside an American classroom.

A second type of global connection is one that has grown up with a program or a university. One example of this is the Institute for Science, Law, and Technology at the Illinois Institute of Technology. IIT is "the only technological university in the United States with a law school. That gives both Chicago-Kent and other units of IIT a unique capacity to understand the relationships between law and technology," said Henry Perritt, then dean of the school, in a written statement on Chicago-Kent's Web site.

The institute has always had an outward focus. But as its interests—including the impact of technological innovation, assisted reproductive technologies, and genetics—have become more global, so too has the institute.

Through Chicago-Kent (the IIT law school) and its Center for Law and Financial Markets, IIT has been actively involved in nation-building activities in Bosnia, Macedonia, and Kosovo. IIT students, staff, and faculty have connected the International Media Center in Banja Luka, Bosnia, to the Internet; developed a database that is used by the International Red Cross, the American Bar Association, and other international organizations for keeping track of war crimes evidence; established an externship program in Kosovo for Kosovar law students at the University of Pristina; and provided technical assistance to local governmental institutions and to would-be entrepreneurs in Kosovo to assist in establishing small and medium-sized enterprises as part of an economic development strategy for Kosovo.

The New Discoveries

The third broad type of connection is found at less well known schools. These schools may be a blip on the global radar screen, but they have a program, a presence, or a person (or sometimes all three) to help them dip a toe into international waters. Many of these schools educate nontraditional students, including adults who will go on to build careers in this region.

One example is National Louis University, with its main campus in Evanston. National Louis began in 1886, the first independent college for teacher preparation in the country. The school touted the virtues of compulsory kindergarten in this country and for decades concentrated on its core mission of teacher training. In recent years, however, it began to branch out, establishing, for example, a well-regarded business school in Nowy Sacz, Poland, that has an enrollment of about three thousand students.

Such a link may seem, on the one hand, a dilution of the school's strength. But seen another way it is an adaptation, and a shrewd one at that. Chicago has a Polish population to rival that of Warsaw. A program such as this one creates a host of international connections that grow from the Chicago area and its Polish community to Poland and beyond, as the adoption of the euro makes Europe's business borders more porous.

There are a number of similar examples. Harold Washington College, part of the City College system, holds a major federal government contract to provide distance learning to the military overseas. Roosevelt University, with a campus in downtown Chicago and one in the western suburbs, has pioneered the delivery of graduate business education to young Chinese professionals.

None of the city colleges—indeed none of the twenty community colleges in the region—has been considered a hub of international activity. Yet, each has an interesting and significant—though not comprehensive—global reach. Harper College in Palatine offers an international business certificate. Oakton Community College touts its semester abroad in Austria or England and has summer programs in about a half-dozen other countries.

The College of DuPage runs "Global Flicks 2002: A Festival of International Films." A faculty-led discussion follows the viewing of films from China, Italy, Iran, Brazil, and other countries.

Nongovernmental Organizations

Numerous nongovernmental organizations (NGOs) are located in the Chicago area. "Numerous" is an imprecise word acknowledging the difficulties in accurately reporting the number of such organizations because the count depends on how they are defined.

To include all organizations that are nonprofit, typically categorized by the U.S. Internal Revenue Service as the 501c(3) and c(4) organizations, would result in a tally in the hundreds. To include only the fifteen or so organizations that the United Nations counts would be to focus on groups engaged in the important work of building a more civil, just, and equitable society. But it would leave out the many important church groups and small, targeted groups, some of which have never bothered to incorporate. These groups are often marginalized and not connected to other organizations, which limits their effectiveness.

"They can be very difficult even to find because they generally operate in highly localized settings," said Thomas Derdak, executive director of a small NGO—Global Alliance for Africa—that focuses on the health care infrastructure on that continent. "You have to be part of the community to know what is going on in them and they are geared to their own country's interest or welfare. There's not a lot of connection even among the Nigerians. And they don't talk a lot to the Kenyans and the Kenyans don't talk all that much to the South Africans and the South Africans don't talk that much to the Nigerians."

Still, these groups may be important to particular ethnic enclaves in Chicago and vital to particular underdeveloped communities in other countries. Many of these groups—large and small—have ties to academics, but they may be weak, tenuous, or narrow.

"Traditionally there are not a lot of collaborations in the international sector between universities and NGOs because there hasn't been a lot of overlap," said Derdak, who also teaches philosophy at Loyola University in Chicago. "Universities and people in universities are doing their own thing and are concerned with their own research and the dissertations of students, which is very different from the more practical focus of NGOs, concentrating on the alleviation of poverty or food security."

The pool of scholars who actively seek to forge ties with NGOs—or indeed with any kind of entity outside of the university—may be constrained by the demands of a research career. Marshall M. Bouton, president of the Chicago Council on Foreign Relations, put it this way: "There is a generic problem which is that individual scholars, and especially younger scholars, have an agenda that is dominated by the need to do research and publish. They are reviewed and evaluated by their peers in the scholarly community and the incentives for involvement with an organization like ours or involvement in non-scholarly discourse on the issues are not particularly great."

Founded in 1922 to counter the prevailing isolationist attitudes of the times, the Chicago Council on Foreign Relations has been revitalized since September 11, 2001. Prime ministers and presidents, from Pervez Musharraf of Pakistan to Jiang Zemin of China and Jean Chrétien of Canada, spoke to council members in 2002–3. A debate about the wisdom of war on Iraq attracted overflow crowds, and subjects such as AIDS and human rights are now a part of the council's purview. The council has a national reach. Every four years it conducts a poll that tracks how Americans view U.S. foreign policy and international issues, and in 2002 it joined forces with the German Marshall Fund to collect comparable data from Europe. National conferences on trade (2003), the United States and the world (2002), and Mexico (2003) are now held in Chicago, thanks to the council. Through its Mid-America Committee it reaches out to business, and through Global Chicago it connects with the city's diverse population.

A number of prominent larger nongovernmental organizations that may broadly be considered civil society groups have their headquarters here. They include World Relief, Lions Club International, and the Rotary Foundation.

Rotary International was created in Chicago on February 23, 1905. In addition to advancing a spectrum of other social agenda items, it has played a seminal role in the attack on the polio virus worldwide. Paul Harris was a Chicago lawyer in 1905 when he decided to invite other businessmen to lunch in his office building where they could talk about themselves, their business, their community, and the world. They enjoyed it so much that they began to "rotate" their meetings to other offices and finally formed the Rotary Club of Chicago, which still meets every Tuesday at noon at the Chicago Athletic Club.

Rotary's top priority remains the eradication of polio. The organization has mobilized hundreds of thousands of volunteers and committed more than $500 million since 1998 to this effort.

Other civil society groups also are important here. They include organizations such as Amnesty International, which has a large office in Chicago.

When NGOs are examined through the lens of intellectual capital, another cluster of them must be considered: museums and zoos. While all of the city's large museums and zoos have international connections, the Brookfield Zoo and the Field Museum stand out.

George Rabb, the Brookfield Zoo's former director and the current president of the Chicago Zoological Society, turned the zoo into an international institution. Rabb formerly served as chairman of the Species Survival Commission of the World Conservation Union. The Brookfield Zoo hosted the International Ape Conference in 2001. With significant support from the Chicago Board of Trade Endangered Species Fund, Brookfield Zoo scientists have discovered a new species of marsupial in Australia and a new species of lemur in Madagascar. They are tracking lions in Namibia, working with a zoo in Thailand to improve leopard breeding protocols, and have joined the debate about the impact of navy sonar signals on dolphins.

The Field Museum was an international creature from its birth in 1893 as the Columbian Museum of Chicago (its name was changed in 1905 to honor its first major benefactor, Marshall Field). It was created to house the mass of stuff, the biological and anthropological collections, pulled together for the World's Columbian Exposition of 1893. That collection has grown to almost twenty-two million specimens today.

"We have seventy-five people here with Ph.D.'s, the full-time faculty plus research associates," said John McCarter, the Field's president and chief executive officer. "They are all over the world all the time."

The Field is probably best known for its collections and its research. But Field scientists sometimes work in partnership with researchers in other countries, as well as governments seeking to do such things as preserve habitat. One example, McCarter said, was the creation of a five-million-acre national park in Medidi, Bolivia. In some cases, the partnerships are more narrowly focused. The Field is training people from the National Museums of Kenya in Nairobi in fossil preparation. Another ongoing project is to take a color slide of every plant in the New World. Slipped into waterproof coverings, the slides could be used by botanists in the field.

The museum is also making some less-traditional forays into international cooperation as well. One example is the Center for Cultural Understanding and Change. The CCUC is working with Field Museum scientists and villagers in Peru to figure out how villagers can support themselves without damaging their ecosystem. And the relatively new Cultural Connections program links the Field to about eighteen smaller local museums and cultural centers to work together on programs and exhibits.

"We use the collection to open the world of cultural differences and similarities," said Madeleine Tudor, the center's special projects coordinator. "We try to develop some poignant comparisons."

The John D. and Catherine T. MacArthur Foundation of Chicago is the eleventh-largest U.S. foundation, with assets of $4.2 billion. About half of the grants totaling $175 million that the MacArthur Foundation makes each year have a global purpose. Many of Chicago's global enterprises and organizations, from the *Bulletin of the Atomic Scientists* to the Chicago Council on Foreign Relations, the Field Museum, and the Brookfield Zoo, use MacArthur grants to extend their reach around the world.

The MacArthur Foundation funds work in over eighty-five countries and has offices in India, Nigeria, and Mexico, as well as in Russia, where it was the first international foundation to open a local office after the collapse of the Soviet Union. Its grants help protect forests in the Himalayas and the coral reefs that line Australia's coasts, strengthen beleaguered women's organizations trying to reduce maternal mortality, pay for science laboratories in universities in Nigeria, and promote international human rights standards in Mexican law and institutions.

Strategically placed MacArthur grantees led the successful effort to put women's reproductive health at the center of the international community's population agenda in Cairo in 1994. The groups that successfully concluded the Landmine Treaty and the establishment of the International Criminal Court received key funding from the foundation. Today, the MacArthur Foundation is arguably the most important source of support for organizations engaged in efforts to reduce the threat posed by weapons of mass destruction.

Paper, Ink, and Internet Links

However it is read—from newsprint, a computer screen, or a glossy magazine—the written word is a font of intellectual capital. Chicago has many such sources. The two largest daily newspapers, the *Chicago Tribune* and the *Chicago Sun-Times,* both publish international news. The *Tribune* has a larger presence overseas, with bureaus from China to South America, Africa to Europe and the Middle East. In March 2001, the *Chicago Tribune*'s parent company, the Tribune Company, opened a news bureau in Havana. It was one of only two American newspaper companies to be invited to run a news bureau out of Cuba, and the *Tribune* has been reporting from there ever since.

The Chicago-based American Medical Association (AMA) publishes the *Journal of the American Medical Association,* one of the world's premier medical journals. As diseases cross international boundaries, so too do some of the papers in *JAMA.* The May 7, 2003, issue included an article on the clinical features of SARS in Toronto-area patients. Recent issues of *JAMA* have carried articles on polio eradication, developments in the treatment of HIV/AIDS, and the sequencing of the genome for the deadliest form of malaria, which kills more than one million people annually. Every August, it publishes an issue on violence and human rights to commemorate the bombing of Hiroshima. *JAMA* has a circulation of 360,000 worldwide and its seventeen international editions reprint articles in fifteen languages. The international editions have a combined circulation of 300,000. Some of the numerous medical specialty groups that have grown up around the AMA in Chicago, such as the American Academy of Pediatrics, also publish journals whose range of topics is frequently global, for example, the health of international adoptees.

The American Bar Association is headquartered in Chicago, and publishes the *ABA Journal,* with a circulation in excess of 376,000. The bar association sponsors the Central and East European Law Initiative (CEELI), which places rule-of-law liaisons and law-reform liaisons in developing countries for periods ranging from six months to two years. The ABA also involves hundreds of practicing lawyers as volunteers through its International Law Section.

Perhaps the most famous homegrown periodical that is—and always has been—international in outlook is the *Bulletin of the Atomic Scientists.* Born of the cold war from a group of scientists who opposed dropping atomic bombs on Japan, it is probably most famous for its "doomsday clock." The closer the clock's hands are to midnight, the more unstable international security is considered to be. The magazine's primary focus is global security. But in recent years topics under this rubric have included "everything from the landless movement in Brazil and the global trade in small arms to the detrimental impact of excessive government secrecy on policy-making and the global effort to stem the use of land mines," said Michael Flynn, associate editor.

The National Labs

The *Bulletin of the Atomic Scientists,* housed at the University of Chicago, has informal ties to some individual scientists at Argonne National Laboratory, which also has its roots at the University of Chicago. Argonne is one of the nation's first national laboratories, chartered in 1946. It grew out of the University of Chicago's Metallurgic Laboratory, which in turn was part of the Manhattan Project of World War II. The University of Chicago now operates Argonne for the U.S. Department of Energy. The laboratory is located about twenty-five miles southwest of the Loop.

Argonne is one of two national laboratories in the area, the other being the Fermi National Accelerator Laboratory. Both institutions bring in scholars from around the world and in recent years have stepped up outreach efforts, running teacher education programs, science career fairs, an Ask-a-Scientist service, and other programs.

Indeed, Fermi is particularly international, run by a consortium of eighty-nine universities, including several from overseas. Scientists at Fermi study high-energy physics because the lab houses the world's most powerful particle accelerator.

Crossing Borders, Pushing Boundaries

Try this experiment: find one Chicago-area college or university that lacks some kind of global tie. Can't do it? How about this: stroll the Chicago Loop gazing only at notable buildings by American architects. Missed some important sites? Then try this: walk through a farmer's market and look at the heirloom vegetables overflowing the bins, but bring home only those foods native to North America. And put down those nifty-looking purple potatoes. Potatoes originated in South America, in the Andes.

Behind what is visible—the campuses, historic buildings, magnificent museum collections, cutting-edge technological equipment, and the bounty of a midwestern harvest—are people. They are the real repositories of intellectual capital, and they have been moving across international borders real and imagined for thousands of years. They are everywhere, in every profession, in every community. What follows are thumbnail sketches of six such people. There could have been six thousand, but space does not allow.

Each of the six people spotlighted here fosters the growth of a certain kind of intellectual capital imperative to the maintenance of a global city. Some, like Peter Baugher, an attorney, are creating new frameworks within existing structures. Others, such as the art historian Sarah Fraser, are spanning disciplines to craft new approaches to learning.

The Attorney: Peter Baugher

While in the Bahamas in January 2002 for a securities fraud case that involved a Bahamian bank, Peter V. Baugher was tapped for help by a Nova Scotia company that manufactures surgical gloves and was being sued in Chicago. On his desk back home sat pending work on the case of an Italian oil manufacturer. And then there was his work, more than a decade of it, for a Texas bank entangled in Iraq.

Baugher, a partner in the Chicago firm of Schopf and Weiss, observed: "These days you don't have to be a Motorola or a Boeing in order to be involved in international commerce."

With enhanced global trade and investment comes greater opportunity for transnational legal conflict. To smooth growing global connections, Baugher said, a legal structure must exist to reduce the risk of such ties by resolving disputes. Baugher is a member of the International and Foreign Law Committee of the Chicago Bar Association and founder and president of the Chicago International Dispute Resolution Association (CIDRA). That group prodded the Illinois General Assembly in 1998 to pass a statute facilitating international commercial arbitration, called the Illinois International Commercial Arbitration Act. Though there is a federal act, Illinois is one of only about a dozen states to have an international arbitration statute.

"Part of the intellectual capital is to make sure that you have the legal infrastructure in place, which is laws and people conversant with them and international practice," he added.

The Art Historian: Sarah Fraser

Dunhuang, China, is as it has always been, a crossroads community. Skirting the Gobi and Takla Makan (sometimes given as Taklamakan) deserts, the town is touched by ancient trade routes that linked the Chinese empire to the rest of Asia and, ultimately, Europe.

Buddhist temples, known as cave-shrines, have been carved into cliff facades there. The interiors of the cave-shrines are covered with huge, intricate paintings that date from the fifth to the thirteenth centuries.

Now a community once frequented by men on camels carrying silks and spices is home to a new kind of interchange, that between art history and digital technology. Sarah E. Fraser, an art historian at Northwestern University, is working with engineers and technology specialists to create 3-D models and images from inside forty-two of the Dunhuang cave-shrines, digitize them, and put them online.

A revolution in database technology is revealing the evolution of medieval Chinese society. "This fits into a much broader interest in digitizing collections and having them online," said Fraser. That interest is growing.

"Art historians used to deal just with other art historians," she said. "Now there is a greater interest in visual material by people doing history as well as literature, for example. But the real fun part is when engineering and the sciences get connected to the humanities."

Dunhuang also is home to an ancient library of forty-two thousand scrolls, fragments, prayer books, financial records, and other texts. These manuscripts were hidden early in the eleventh century and not rediscovered until 1900. About ten thousand of the manuscripts will be included in the online database.

Online databases have created an explosion in intellectual capital, a veritable Big Bang of ideas. The available information is evolving from streams of straight text, records, and statistics to the kinds of things that Fraser is doing. As that happens, other questions arise. How will the information be gathered and presented? How will it be accessed, and by whom and at what cost?

"Permission to distribute photos, the copyright issues, are going to be at the forefront," said Fraser. Her work has been funded by grants and money from foundations, entities that are helping her deal with the legal issues and, on some level, set a precedent for how such matters can be resolved. "Everyone wants to have the technology for their teaching. . . . It will revolutionize the way that art history is taught."

What else can the technology do? A project such as Fraser's, called Merit, Opulence, and the Buddhist Network of Wealth, clearly is of interest to other scholars. It also is accessible, and interesting, to a general audience including schoolchildren. How would these groups of people know it is there, waiting to be accessed, unless they stumble across it? "I don't know where this will go," said Fraser, "but I have a feeling I should continue down this road."

The Scientist: Paul Sereno

Paul Sereno is that relatively rare species of scientist: the kind who wants the public, not just his colleagues, to be in on his discoveries. Sereno, an explorer-in-residence for the *National Geographic* and a professor at the University of Chicago, has discovered new species of dinosaurs on several continents.

But he is just as interested in helping kids discover science and the cultural context in which it thrives.

To that end, he and his wife, Gabrielle Lyon, an educator, founded Project Exploration, an organization that makes that connection in numerous ways. Project Exploration literally takes students along on some digs within the United States. During the months-long international expeditions, however, Sereno and his team file online dispatches from the field, explaining what they are doing, what they are finding, and what they are discovering. Children— and adults—worldwide write back with messages and questions.

"Scientists are coming to meet you," said Sereno. "You can go to a lot of paleontology Web sites and they're flat as a board. The actual people doing [the paleontology] are not engaging themselves and the people doing the Web sites are back here and are not trained educators," he added. "What we're trying to do with Project Exploration is narrow the distance between the effectors of science and the people who don't have access to it." Sereno's international expeditions have been featured in several documentaries, including one filmed by National Geographic Explorer on a trip to Niger, where he and his team discovered two new dinosaur species.

Using Chicago's Sister Cities program, Sereno helped found Morocco's first natural history museum, converting a small theater in a park in Casablanca.

The Farmer: Henry Brockman

At "The Land," an organic farm in Congerville, Illinois, Silver Queen sweet corn shares the fields with Shanghai bok choi. Tending these crops, along with scores of others, is Henry Brockman. Some of the seeds he uses have come from Japan and Italy. He and his Japanese-born wife, Hiroko Kinoshita, speak only Japanese to their three children, the language of choice as they work the fields.

Multilingual, multicultural, and outspoken about agricultural practices and consequences, he and his family have created the Land Connection. The nonprofit organization, incorporated in 2001, is trying to match organic farmers with land that would otherwise be developed for housing or linked with huge agribusinesses.

The Land Connection dreams big, hoping to foster the growth of organic farmers who grow everything from grapes for wine to goats for milk and cheese. On another level, Brockman seeks nothing less than a reevaluation of the way we farm, eat, and sustain life. Statistics gathered by the Land Connection show that in the last fifteen years, the number of farms across the state that were more than two thousand acres in size increased by 300 percent while more than 30 percent of small farms were lost.

"We see the food in the grocery store and we never think about the farmer in the field—what kind of seed he's using, how he controls pests," Brockman said. "We are increasingly divorced from our farmers."

The Activist: Maricela Garcia

In 1982, as war devastated her native Guatemala, Maricela Garcia fled to Chicago. Garcia feared for her life because of her work as a student activist at the University of San Carlos, the largest university in Guatemala. She created a new home in Chicago while she continued to work for change in her birthplace.

"If you are safe or quasi-safe someplace else, you carry the responsibility of that war with you," said Garcia, the former executive director of the Illinois Coalition for Immigrant and Refugee Rights. "You can't leave your family, friends, and community in danger and start fresh and not care about that life anymore," she said. "It's not possible."

Garcia carried more than her memories across the border. She also brought to Chicago political organizing skills honed by the life-and-death struggle of war. She and other Central American refugees pooled these skills and linked up with local churches that offered refugees sanctuary, part of the "Sanctuary Movement" of the 1980s that pushed for political asylum and human rights in Central America.

"Our numbers were growing in Chicago and we needed to make sure people understood why we were here," Garcia recalled. "Understanding that, people also questioned the effectiveness of U.S. foreign policy."

Now that the war in Guatemala has ended, Garcia's work is part of a broader Latino agenda that includes such issues as education and health. To carry out that agenda, Garcia taps her political skills, which helped the rights coalition partner with more than ninety public and private organizations to promote social justice. But her activism has yielded fewer ties to university scholars, something Garcia finds an unfortunate missed connection for both sides.

"A lot of the time, information from the university is disconnected from the issues, the trends, and the needs of public policy," she said. "I think universities need to become realistic about what studies are important. It's not what can be funded. Ask the communities and then work in real partnership."

Garcia said she is not suggesting that universities do advocacy work, a role she said would be inappropriate and lead to tainted research. But, she said, "A partnership needs to happen and a partnership is missing."

Some of the most highly educated immigrants now living in Chicago studied at universities in small countries that directly felt the effects of U.S. foreign policy. As a result, these individuals experienced global connectedness in ways that American students never do.

"We hardly see any other place in the world because our country [America] is so powerful," Garcia said. "But because of how powerful we are we make a tremendous impact on the lives and decisions of the rest of the world.

"We really need to tie our experience here [in America] to the rest of the world. Otherwise our policies will be shortsighted always."

The Educator: Barbara Radner

More than 48,000 students in the Chicago Public Schools are studying a foreign language—from American Sign Language and Arabic to Urdu and Vietnamese. About 14 percent of the more than 431,000 students who attend the city's schools do not speak English well enough to be considered fluent. The 25,000 teachers in the schools hail from nineteen countries.

Chicago public school students live global connections. Yet many still have very little understanding of world cultures and affairs, and they are poorly prepared to enter a global economy, said Barbara Radner, director of the Center for Urban Education at DePaul University. The center works in the public schools to improve instruction. "I'm in schools where they have no social studies stuff," Radner said. "I'm in one school where they have no nonfiction books in the whole school."

Some schools deepen their curriculum by tapping the resources of area museums and cultural centers. For more than ninety years the Field Museum, for example, has run the Harris Loan Program, sending animal skulls and skins, artifacts and cultural objects, and educational materials into classrooms. It is one of the oldest and biggest such outreach efforts in the region, but by no means the only one. About 2,500 area educators take advantage of the Harris program, just a fraction of the pool. More than 25,000 teachers work for the Chicago Public Schools, and tens of thousands more toil in the suburbs.

"Teachers know about these things, but it takes energy," Radner said. "There are little pockets of knowledge, a teacher or two, doing a nice job making a culture three-dimensional, and everybody else is flipping through their textbooks."

In the rush to raise reading and math scores, Radner fears, much else has been needlessly excluded. "They haven't dumbed down the curriculum in Chicago, they have narrowed it," she said. "I have schools where they just teach math and reading. My point to them is if you read the myths of ancient Japan you are learning to read as well as learning about the people of a different time."

Is the exclusion of teaching about the world dispiriting? "No," Radner said emphatically. "But it is annoying because it is so simple to fix."

Connections That Bind, Fray, and Choke

Even as ties increase among people nurturing Chicago's intellectual capital, tensions and barriers to cooperation exist and sometimes even grow. There are many reasons, but four are especially important: a lack of time; a competition for resources; a lack of knowledge about the work of others; and an immutable geographic fact—Chicago is not New York, Washington, D.C., or Los Angeles.

The first issue—and in some ways the most difficult to fix—is a lack of time. Simply to maintain its place as a global city, Chicago must work to make new connections among its centers of intellectual capital so that knowledge can grow. The task is frustrating.

"We need to be aware of opportunities for synergy and strengthening Chicago's international work and image. There is a de facto competition going on among global cities, as Saskia Sassen has written," said Douglass W. Cassel, director of the Center for International Human Rights at Northwestern. "I think if we want to be regarded as a significant player on the global scene in any field, we have to do everything we can to maximize our strengths and that would include more familiarity among those of us who work in an area."

That requires formal events—forums, conferences, and the like—that draw people from a range of sectors and disciplines. As a leading convention city, Chicago has the infrastructure to court those events. From those formal meetings grow the even more important informal connections that lead to new projects and directions.

"The informal connections are what make global cities work," said Dennis Judd, of UIC. "Informal connections can be more valuable than formal connections because they are flexible and innovative and virtually define the new economy."

Above all, cultivating formal and informal connections requires time, money, energy, and interest among those who create intellectual capital—

many of whom are extremely busy and not infrequently out of town. Personally meeting with others who are on similar but not exactly the same tracks takes time away from other things. The Internet offers opportunities to create bridges, in particular the online connections provided by the Chicago Council on Foreign Relations and Global Chicago. As Web sites and other online resources become more detailed, more easily searchable, and more widely known, they will be somewhat effective. But the pressures of time will always impede some possible connections, as the Chicago attorney Peter Baugher knows all too well.

In 1992, a group of lawyers from Illinois went to Moscow for a week to give mock trial demonstrations and to lecture. On May 1, the first May Day after the collapse of the Soviet Union, Baugher gave a speech in Red Square in what is now Moscow, Russia (as opposed to Moscow, Soviet Union). With the approach of the tenth anniversary of that occasion, Baugher wanted to write an essay in which he reflected on what has been learned since then and on the significance of law.

"If I had time it would be great to have lunch with Doug Cassel and other academics to kick some ideas around," Baugher said. "I'd learn from them. They'd learn from me. It would be a delight. But I don't know if that will happen. I don't even know if the essay will happen."

A second impediment to enhancing connections is that many of the Chicago region's knowledge centers must compete for funding, prestige, students, employees, and other resources. One obvious example of this is in the area of international human rights law. A half-dozen schools offer institutes, programs, certificates, or some type of training or regular seminars in international law. But these schools are more competitive than cooperative, a stance that keeps them from combining resources to become a stronger and more well known force.

There are many reasons for this. International work takes international human rights lawyers out of the country, often for long periods, making it difficult to coordinate schedules. Different universities specialize in different regions of the globe or emphasize different things, like local seminars as opposed to fieldwork. Individual egos play a role. Universities try to distinguish themselves through special programs like those in international law because such assets help during the furious competition for donors and students.

Would a cooperative venture for international human rights law ever work? "If you manage to settle the egos of people it would work," said M. Cherif Bassiouni, professor and director of the most well known of the programs, the DePaul International Human Rights Law Institute.

"The problem is, everyone wants to get a greater share of the credit," he added. "There are only two ways you can pursue something. If you've got enough resources and capacity, go on your own. If not, team up with others, develop a strategic alliance, and look at complementary areas. If you have overlapping areas, you synergize. But if you have complementary areas, you can have as many as you want."

The third significant obstacle to increasing Chicago's international ties is a simple lack of knowledge about the work of others. In some cases, this deficiency occurs because people have all that they can do to stay abreast of developments in their own narrow fields of focus. In other cases, it may happen because the established, well-regarded people whom the city attracts are already part of more intellectual networks than they can maintain as it is. In a sense, they do not need to know any more people. Indeed, if they did, they may become less effective because cultivating new or tangential professional relationships takes time away from maintaining the contacts that helped them become renowned in the first place. The University of Chicago social scientist Saskia Sassen, who studies global cities, had that experience.

"Here is my story. I lived in New York for twenty years," Sassen said in 2001. "I just came to Chicago three years ago. My life is already so crowded with opportunities and networks, I can't tell you. . . . I assume Chicago is great, but I came with an enormous set of connections to networks."

That is not to say Sassen has avoided making new connections in Chicago. She did, even though she really did not need to. "As soon as I came to Chicago, projects began to incorporate me," she said, adding that Chicago seems interested in aligning itself with people seen as internationalists.

The final issue works as both a blessing and a problem for Chicago; the city is not New York; it is not D.C.; it is not L.A. And the complicated challenge is to make that a blessing more often than a curse. "Being in Chicago—or in L.A., because I don't think it is just Chicago—adds another dimension because you are just a bit de-centered," said Sassen.

Computer technology is to some degree lowering all four of these barriers. But even high-speed modems and video conferencing cannot fully replace what is lost when people are unable to "bump into" many of the major policy makers, heads of state, international financiers, and others whose paths may be more easily crossed in New York City, Washington, D.C., and, to some extent, Los Angeles. Many globally connected people working in Chicago have expressed frustration with sometimes being out of the mainstream when decisions are made.

"By not being in the headquarters city of the United Nations in New York or the World Bank, the IMF, Organization of American States, Inter-American Development Bank, and other organizations in Washington, you've got one hand tied behind your back because when critical meetings are being held, consultations, the guys in Washington and New York are right there. Frequently they attend meetings I don't even find out about until they're over," said Northwestern's Cassel. "It's more difficult to have as expanded a range of contacts on as broad a range of issues as you would in New York or Washington."

Charles Lipson, a University of Chicago political scientist, said of the city: "It still doesn't have a really critical mass of business people who have a kind of sophisticated international interest. And it has almost no policy makers, so there is just not that ongoing discussion, even though some of the policy makers are former Chicagoans like [U.S. Defense Secretary Donald] Rumsfeld and [Rep.] Henry Hyde."

Connections Missed and Made: A Case Study

In the abstract, all four of these problems can be overcome to some degree or, in the case of Chicago's being Chicago, sometimes turned into an advantage. The messy world of reality demonstrates just how difficult the task is, as Northwestern's Andrew Wachtel learned.

Wachtel, a Slavic scholar, spent years listening to his colleagues tout the many benefits that would flow from closer cooperation and bemoan the many obstacles preventing the same. He did a little bemoaning of his own. Finally, Wachtel took action: "It seemed to me there wasn't a good way to work with like-minded colleagues, students, and organizations unless I organized it."

And so he did. In June 2001 the Institute for the Study of Southeast Europe was born. Among Chicago's centers of intellectual capital it is that rare creature, the cross-disciplinary, cross-town, cross-school venture.

Four separate schools at Northwestern are involved: Weinberg College of Arts and Sciences, the School of Law, the School of Music, and the Kellogg Graduate School of Management. Scholars from five other universities—University of Chicago, DePaul, University of Illinois at Chicago, Loyola, and IIT's Chicago-Kent College of Law—also are a part of it.

Six months after the birth of the institute studying a volatile region of the globe, Wachtel expressed frustration over the effort it takes to achieve cooperation among local schools. "Working with other universities is among the

most frustrating tasks you can have mostly because they still perceive themselves as worlds unto themselves," said Wachtel. Why? "I think they perceive
that if it's a great idea they should be doing it," he said. "To participate would
be to admit there was a great idea they didn't have."

Such cooperation is especially elusive in that smart but staid breed, the
humanities scholar. "If they all worked at Argonne, no problem, because
Argonne has a seven godmillion-dollar atom smasher and no one will build
one on their own," Wachtel said. "In the humanities, you don't have that."

In 2002 Wachtel staged a conference on security in Eastern Europe, in-
viting a raft of scholars from area universities along with people working for
nongovernmental organizations and other institutions. To increase the turnout, he even held the forum downtown, not on Northwestern's suburban
Evanston campus. The result?

"One person, a professor at UIC, came and otherwise it was an all-North-
western audience," he said. "A few people who work downtown came. But I
didn't get my colleagues from other universities to come." This experience,
Wachtel said, highlighted the need to connect with people who are not affili-
ated with universities, a form of outreach that he conceded may make some
academics squirm.

"If you bring in people who are interested, not strictly academics, you
have a better chance of doing things and that is clearly going to be the way
to go. But that includes being willing to include people on your speaking
program who wouldn't normally be considered academic by my colleagues,"
he said. "You have to get people who are clearly qualified, not just someone
who says 'I know something.' But I think you can do it."

In the Wake of 9/11

On October 4, 1957, Soviet scientists launched the first artificial satellite to successfully orbit Earth. Sputnik pierced American hearts with a fear of failure,
of being second place and second rate. The resulting scientific brawl between
the United States and the former Soviet Union is often described by the phrase
"space race." More accurately, the "space race" was an all-hands-on-deck intellectual competition that propelled numerous fields forward and helped lay
the foundation for America's late-twentieth-century prosperity.

On September 11, 2001, terrorists flew airplanes into the World Trade Center and the Pentagon, symbols of American capitalism and politics. The initial shock has become somewhat less raw, though perhaps the grief no less

painful. In the immediate aftermath, universities displayed their most thoughtful specialists in public forums that actually attracted the public. Schools reported a surge in interest in courses in Islam and related fields. Bookstores crafted displays featuring tomes on the Middle East—and sold them. Specialists in world politics, religion, current events, and other fields were invited to speak to service clubs and schoolchildren, business executives and politicians.

Viewed from a certain angle, the events of 9/11 may be seen as a Sputnik-like challenge to American knowledge, understanding, and education. In short, it is a summons to cultivate more fully, more carefully, intellectual capital in a process that must extend from cradle to grave. That challenge once again involves science and technology, certainly, but it also encompasses as equal partners those disciplines that may seem, if not dowdy, at least old-fashioned. These include philosophy, geography, religion, languages and literature, foreign policy, and ancient history. Chicago is poised to accept the challenge. It has the intellectual resources that, if pushed to cross-pollinate, can lead to new insights and understanding that will benefit all.

Indeed, Chicago must accept the challenge if it wants to be a global city for, as vast as its intellectual capital seems now, that knowledge must grow and grow well. Perhaps the mathematician-philosopher Alfred North Whitehead summed it up best when he said this: "Knowledge doesn't keep any better than fish."

7   The World's Art and Chicago's

MAGDA KRANCE

OF COURSE Chicago is a global city. It always has been. The city's cultural story since its beginning has been told in the voices of different cultures speaking first to themselves, then to their own communities, and, in time, to people in other communities. Globalization has now opened multiple pathways to and from the rest of the world. The global reach of the Internet, satellite communications, and cable TV enables you to see and sample the world and communicate with anyone out there without leaving home, without changing out of your pajamas.

Even a cursory look at Chicago's cultural life reveals the rich mix of indigenous, imported, and intermingled creative expression. There are franchised entertainments that are part of the local landscape—but only a part. They do not eclipse or supplant the multitudinous and multiethnic facets of the arts and performance scene in Chicago. The multimixing happens in Chicago as a matter of course. Global influences are so much a part of Chicagoans' daily lives that it's a challenge to filter them out for examination and discussion.

So, where to begin? With some glimpses at key moments in Chicago's history, perhaps, at a few of the circumstances, individuals, and institutions that have contributed to Chicago's evolution as a culturally global city.

Visual Arts

Architecture

Daniel Burnham envisioned Chicago as a "Paris on the Prairie" and crafted an urban plan that fostered the boulevards, parks, plazas, transportation corridors, and lakefront development that mark the city to this day. Theodore Dreiser called Chicago "This Florence of the West," likening it to the Renaissance capital of Tuscany that flourished as both a commercial and cultural center. Fifteenth-century Florence, as Donald L. Miller notes in his 1996 work *City of the Century: The Epic of Chicago and the Making of America,* was

> a great arts capital, [and] also a lusty, aggressive city. . . . One of Florence's greatest glories was its architecture. The Florentine elite had a passion for building, and their best buildings were constructed, like Chicago's, with rational clarity. . . . This is not to say that Chicago produced a culture as sinuous and enduring as Florence's or even that Chicago and Florence were similar types of cities. . . . [T]he real point of these parallels is to emphasize that in great cities crudity and commerce have often been accompanied by memorable advances in the arts. . . . [T]he architecture of both places mirrors what went on in them, as these cities built their biographies in the buildings they created.

The evolution of Chicago's built environment in the late nineteenth century was fostered more by the relentless demands of commerce than by any widely accepted aesthetic. Indeed, the transformation of the Loop into the prototype of the modern city center was marked by the dynamic between developers and speculators on one hand and architects on the other. The developers and speculators viewed buildings as "machines to make the land pay" and wanted to put them up as quickly and cheaply as possible; young architects migrated to the city to take advantage of the opportunities offered by an unprecedented building boom and were intent on creating an original American architectural vocabulary. No one knew what "skyscrapers" should look like. Inspired by classical precedent and natural forms, these men, among them Louis Sullivan, John Wellborn Root, William Holabird, and Martin Roche, went on to design buildings incorporating the tripartite elements of columns—base, shaft, and capital—with an emphasis on verticality and a greatly reduced reliance on applied decorative ornament. The result was buildings that, with the advent of new construction materials and technology, ushered in the first of the distinctive architectural styles for which the city is internationally renowned—that of the Chicago school.

The evocation of two cities where commerce and art keep company is apt, and, in Chicago, as in Florence, there is no better place to start than with its architecture. The great fire of 1871, which wiped out much of Chicago's first draft of itself, ultimately made possible a wondrous physical reinvention that began in the 1880s, after a hasty initial reconstruction that essentially replicated what the fire had destroyed. The groundbreaking new buildings featured iron and steel skeleton frames clad with terra cotta and were therefore fireproof, hence insurable. Among the best known of the architects were:

—William Le Baron Jenney: the "father" of the skyscraper, for the city's first full steel skeleton building, the Home Insurance Building, constructed 1884–86, no longer standing; the Ludington; the Leiter II Building; and the Manhattan Building;

—Daniel Hudson Burnham: also one of the earliest city planners, responsible for the World's Columbian Exposition in 1893 and for the Plan of Chicago, a reenvisioning of Chicago focused on the south lakefront, drawn up for the Commercial Club in 1909;

—John Wellborn Root, with his partner Burnham: the original Art Institute building (1887); the Rand McNally Building; the Rookery (1888); the sixteen-story Monadnock Building (1891); and the Montauk Block (1882), the city's first tall building, now demolished;

—Louis H. Sullivan: the Auditorium Building (1889); the Stock Exchange Building (now demolished, though the magnificent entry arch was saved and reassembled on the grounds of the Art Institute and the splendid trading room was reassembled inside the Art Institute); and the Carson Pirie Scott store.

A little later, Frank Lloyd Wright and his Prairie style architecture was widely influential throughout the Midwest, the nation, and the world. Other notable later contributors to the Chicago architectural scene include the German Mies van der Rohe, who for twenty years headed the School of Architecture at the Illinois Institute of Technology and was the father of American modernism—in effect the second Chicago school—through the influence of his teachings and work (the Lake Shore Drive Apartments, the Federal Center, the campus of the Illinois Institute of Technology—more than thirty buildings in the Chicago area), and his student Helmut Jahn (the United Airlines Terminal at O'Hare, 1985–88, and the State of Illinois Center, 1979–83).

With its physical plant, Chicago has always been the site of urban innovation, combining, as Dreiser noted, the best of commerce and art, as its businessmen have been supporters of advances in the arts. It is, we should remember, the world's first skyscraper city, singularly audacious and beautiful, and a global inspiration.

The Art Institute

Chicago has long been an internationally recognized center for the fine arts— painting, drawing, sculpture. The Art Institute of Chicago is the mighty anchor and the point of reference for the city's high art—albeit principally European—ranging from the ancient to the relatively contemporary. The Art Institute, founded in 1882, moved into a new building designed by Burnham and Root in 1887 and then into the grand downtown headquarters of the Columbian Exposition on Michigan Avenue after the fair ended in the 1890s, where it remains. The move was an expeditious way for the Art Institute's founder and president, Charles L. Hutchinson, to ensure that Chicago's cultural life would be boosted, immediately and permanently, by hosting the fair.

Hutchinson and his best friend, the civic-minded lumber and real-estate magnate Martin A. Ryerson, helped finance the expansion of the rather modest original collection. With their wives, the pair traveled the world from Europe to Asia in search of rarities. They acquired many of the museum's old-master paintings from a financially strapped princess who was poised to sell the lot at a Parisian auction. As Hutchinson said at the time, "We have made our money in pigs, but is that any reason we should not spend it on paintings?" Those shopping expeditions formed the foundation of the Art Institute's famous and influential collection.

To ensure that the Art Institute did not serve only the "carriage class," Hutchinson insisted on free admission three days a week, including Sundays, making its wonders accessible to immigrant laborers as well as the upper crust. The ploy paid off. Twenty-five years after it opened, Chicago's Art Institute attracted almost 250,000 more visitors annually than Boston's Museum of Fine Arts, and 150,000 more than New York's Metropolitan Museum of Art.

Contemporary Art

The Museum of Contemporary Art may be better regarded internationally than it is locally. Relocated in 1996 from a relatively low-ceilinged space on East Ontario Street to a grandiose but stark, boxlike $50 million building located east of Michigan Avenue's "Magnificent Mile," just south of Water

Tower Place, it has yet to connect fully with the city. But in April 2002, its senior curator, Francesco Bonami, was named artistic director of the prestigious Venice Biennale, among the most important international art expositions, enhancing the MCA's international prestige. In a 2003 profile, *Chicago* magazine noted that Bonami is "particularly well regarded for his ability to find interesting new artists from previously ignored corners of the world—that is, artists with the temerity to be neither American nor European—thus helping to advance a globalism that is by far the most significant trend in contemporary art of the past two decades."

The Renaissance Society has focused on "the forefront of the visual arts" since its founding at the University of Chicago in 1915. As it has aged, it has maintained its international reputation as one of the finest resources for contemporary art. In the 1920s and 1930s, the society was the first place west of New York to present works by Picasso, Brancusi, Mondrian, Noguchi, Miró, Moholy-Nagy, and Arp—works often brought to Chicago directly from the artists' studios. Its exhibition of Alexander Calder's mobiles in 1934 and its 1936 survey of paintings and drawings by Fernand Léger were the first solo exhibitions of these artists in the United States. Subsequent exhibitions and events presented work of Mies van der Rohe, Marc Chagall, Sergei Prokofiev, and Gertrude Stein. The society continues today its mission of bold and early commitment to the most challenging and provocative art.

Then there is Art Chicago, the descendant of the annual convention of international art galleries and dealers that has put Chicago in the global art spotlight since its first outing in 1980, when John Wilson of the Lakeside Group audaciously invited gallery owners from around the world to participate in the first-ever Chicago International Art Exposition. "Most people didn't believe it could happen in Chicago, especially around the world, even though Chicago had a fabulous tradition in the arts," recalls Thomas P. Blackman, president of Art Chicago. In its first year the Chicago International Art Exposition occupied only the rotunda of Navy Pier, only about sixty-five dealers participated, and only a few were from overseas. "But it was incredible the way it was embraced," Blackman recalls. "It was a mob scene. [Chicago gallery owner] Richard Gray sold his one painting, a Dubuffet, the first day. [New York gallery owner] Leo Castelli was there, André Emmerich was there, Robert Elkahn, Holly Solomon. The crowds were great, and sales were better than anyone expected. It was just at the time when the art market was about to go crazy—it was like the Internet craze of its time."

Each year Art Expo saw increased dealer participation, bigger crowds, and burgeoning sales. In 1983, about one hundred twenty-five galleries participated and the expo expanded into the sheds on the pier, the then-undeveloped stretch of building that extends five-eighths of a mile between the entrance and the rotunda. The number of participating galleries grew annually, with more international dealers and visitors each year.

But in 1991, the bottom began to fall out of the art market and the economy in general, and Lakeside atrophied and disappeared. Blackman was left as director of Art Chicago, whose first show in 1993 had about 65 dealers—just like Chicago's first International Art Expo thirteen years earlier. It eventually expanded again, to about 225 dealers, and has remained at about that level since 1996. "Chicago is one of the major shows now, and has been for some time," says Blackman (the others are in Basel, Paris, Madrid, New York, and Miami Beach).

Chicago's Writers

Early on, the city attracted young midwestern small-towners such as Carl Sandburg, Theodore Dreiser, and Upton Sinclair, and their journalistic and fictional accounts of the energetic and burgeoning young city shaped the world's view and expectations of Chicago. Upton Sinclair's investigative reporting informed his horrifying novel about Chicago's meat-packing industry, *The Jungle,* published in 1906. And Carl Sandburg's *Chicago Poems* (1916) forever identified this as the "city of big shoulders . . . hog butcher to the world." Sandburg later won two Pulitzer Prizes for his biographies of Abraham Lincoln (1940, 1951). Sandburg's deskmate at the *Chicago Daily News,* Ben Hecht, cowrote a play about Chicago's brawling daily newspapers, *The Front Page,* that became a major hit. It has been made into a movie three times and continues to be produced as a play today.

James T. Farrell, a Chicagoan, authored the *Studs Lonigan Trilogy* in the 1930s, about the tragic life of an Irish American Chicagoan. It inspired a transplanted Chicagoan, Louis Terkel, to change his first name. In 1956, as Studs Terkel, he wrote his first book, *Giants of Jazz,* and he has written eleven oral histories since, including, in late 2003, *Hope Dies Last.* Studs is unique in Chicago, one of the city's best known and most enduring global cultural emissaries. His global reach owes absolutely nothing to high-tech communications or multinational corporations: Studs writes in longhand and can hardly bring himself to use an answering machine. But he talks—oh, once you get him going, can he talk. He asks just the right questions. And he listens. His oral histories are a sort of literary cottage industry gone global, without his ever having particularly sought to do so. His books, he says with some bemusement, are "in Chinese, Russian, Japanese, Bulgarian, Swedish, Danish, Italian, French, German, also Portuguese, but no Spanish, for some reason."

Richard Wright's *Native Son* (1940) and Nelson Algren's *Man with a Golden Arm* (1950) remain seminal Chicago works. Gwendolyn Brooks, who published her first collection of poetry in 1945, was the first African American to win a Pulitzer Prize (in 1949) and was named Illinois Poet Laureate in 1968.

Saul Bellow, born in Canada but raised in Chicago and a resident of the city and professor at the University of Chicago until 1993, published his first novel, *Dangling Man,* in 1944. He followed it with more than a dozen others, including *The Adventures of Augie March, Henderson the Rain King,* and *Humboldt's Gift,* which won the Pulitzer Prize in 1975. The next year, he received the Nobel Prize for literature.

The careers of many of the past half-century's best local, national, and international writers of fiction and journalism were launched or established or confirmed in the pages of *Playboy,* the men's magazine launched in 1953 by a scrawny Chicagoan with a vision named Hugh Hefner. Hefner put photos of naked women in his magazine, interspersed with thoughtful, provocative, and outrageous articles and fiction by the best writers of the day. The new formula clicked beyond anyone's wildest imagination, and the magazine became the flagship of a global sexual revolution. With serious articles and equally serious centerfolds, plus wonderfully bawdy cartoons, it initiated and defined a change in the global culture.

Of the relatively current crop of widely read Chicago writers, Scott Turow, Sara Paretsky, and the Reverend Andrew Greeley have all written international bestselling mysteries, as did Eugene Izzi, whose career was cut short tragically by his suicide. Bill Brashler topped the charts with his 1973 novel about the Negro Baseball League, *Bingo Long Traveling All-Stars and Motor Kings.* The novelist Ana Castillo still lives in Chicago; Sandra Cisneros has moved to San Antonio, but Chicago continues to be her fiction's principal setting. The novelists Jane Hamilton and Carol Shields both grew up in Oak Park and decamped for Wisconsin and Canada, respectively. Elizabeth Berg, a relatively recent arrival to Oak Park from the East Coast, has written at least six bestselling novels and her work has been translated into ten foreign languages. Luis Rodriguez, who also recently moved to Chicago, has received several prestigious prizes for his poetry collections.

A rising star among newly arrived Chicagoans is the novelist Aleksandar Hemon, a native of Sarajevo who moved to Chicago in 1992, barely speaking English. His collection of short stories, *The Question of Bruno,* was named by both the *Los Angeles Times* and the *New York Times* as one of the best books of 2000.

Cultural Museums

Besides the Field Museum (see chapter 6), there are a number of museums in Chicago devoted to specific cultural traditions. A vibrant example is the Mexican Fine Arts Center Museum (MFACM), founded in 1987. It has grown into the largest Latino cultural institution in the United States, with an annual budget of $3.6 million. It lies in the heart of Pilsen, southwest of Chicago's Loop, which together with Little Village comprises the largest Mexican community in the Midwest. Over the past three decades, several Mexican artists and young community artists have created more than thirty colorful Mexican-themed murals throughout Pilsen. Francisco Mendoza, for example, designed mosaic murals for both the old and new Orozco Community Academy; his work can also be seen at the Eighteenth Street elevated train station. Other murals enliven the exterior walls of churches, schools, playgrounds, warehouses, and other available surfaces.

Perhaps the wealth of murals in the community predisposes its residents to support their neighborhood museum. Carlos Tortolero, MFACM's founder and executive director, notes that his institution has "already clearly demonstrated that not only can an art museum exist in the community, it can thrive by being in the community. . . . We have also demonstrated that a culturally grounded institution can draw a diverse audience."

A 2003 exhibition, Frida Kahlo, Diego Rivera, and Twentieth-Century Mexican Art: The Jacques and Natasha Gelman Collection, at the MFACM featured fifteen works by Kahlo—the largest collection of the Mexican artist's work outside Mexico. A longer-term exhibition at the MFACM is *Mexicanidad: Our Past Is Present,* which traces the development of Mexican art, culture, religion, history, and politics. On display until 2008, it consists of works from the museum's permanent collection plus other artwork from Mexican and U.S. art museums—about two hundred objects in all. It is the first permanent exhibition anywhere that includes Mexican artists from both sides of the border, present and past, and acknowledges the legitimacy of the popular arts as a vital form of artistic expression. The exhibition's—and indeed the museum's—underlying proposition is that being Mexican is an important cultural identity *sin fronteras* (without borders)—understandably, as nearly 50 percent of Mexico became U.S. territory in 1848.

The DuSable Museum of African American History is dedicated to the history and culture of Americans of African descent and Africans through the diaspora. It is the first and oldest black American museum in the United States. Founded in 1961, it was named for Jean Baptiste Point Du Sable, the fur trader of African descent who built the first permanent settlement in the area in 1779, near the mouth of the Chicago River.

Chicago Sound

In *City of the Century,* Donald Miller calls the construction of Chicago's Auditorium Theatre (in 1889) a "cultural coming of age. . . . The Auditorium was built because the city had a burgeoning cultural life, a strong theatrical tradition, and a record of supporting both serious and light music, especially operas, oratorios, and concerts by German-American orchestras and choruses." What it lacked was a building to house and encourage its new cultural activities. The success of the 1885 Chicago Opera Festival, which attracted an audience of more than one hundred thousand people to twelve operas presented by a touring company at the "ungainly barnlike" Inter-State Exposition Building, convinced the festival sponsor, Ferdinand W. Peck, a wealthy civic leader, that Chicago deserved a permanent music hall "larger and finer" than New York's old Metropolitan Opera House. Thus was the home of Chicago's music tradition conceived with a global eye, to be the largest, grandest, and costliest.

Classical

The Chicago Orchestra was formed in late 1891 and performed its inaugural concert at the Auditorium Theatre. It started touring almost immediately around the Midwest. The orchestra performed several times during the Columbian Exposition in 1893, with appearances by the pianist Ignace Paderewski and the composer/conductor Antonín Dvořák. Each year until 1913, a new work received its American premiere in Chicago: Tchaikovsky's *Nutcracker Suite* in 1892, Strauss's *Till Eulenspiegel* in 1895, and his *Also Sprach Zarathustra* in 1897, to name a few. When Orchestra Hall opened in 1904, the ensemble took up residence there—when it wasn't touring the United States or abroad or playing at Ravinia Park during the summer. Renamed the Chicago Symphony Orchestra in 1913, it has served throughout its history as a haven and prestigious destination for émigré musicians and as a cultural emissary for

Chicago abroad, through both award-winning recordings and overseas trips. The foreign concert tours began in 1971 under Sir Georg Solti; they have remained a key element in maintaining the CSO's international stature since the Argentinian-born Israeli conductor Daniel Barenboim was named music director in 1991.

Lyric Opera of Chicago

The internationally heralded success of *A View from the Bridge,* William Bolcom's opera based on Arthur Miller's play, first at Lyric in 1999 and then at the Metropolitan Opera, where it was revived in late 2002, reconfirmed Lyric's well-established global reputation for taking chances with new operas as well as older works outside the standard operatic repertoire. Lyric's home, the Civic Opera House, which seats 3,563, is a relative newcomer on Chicago's cultural landscape. Unlike the 1890s edifices along Michigan Avenue, it was completed in late 1929—unfortunately coinciding with the stock-market crash. From its opening, it was home to the Chicago Civic Opera, Chicago Grand Opera Company, Chicago City Opera Company, and Chicago Opera Company.

The Lyric Theatre (later renamed Lyric Opera of Chicago) was founded in 1954. In its early years, it was known as "La Scala West." The company positioned itself during its first season as a force to be reckoned with by prominently featuring the soprano Maria Callas in her American debut (Lyric trumped New York's Metropolitan Opera for that honor by offering the diva higher fees). As popular as a modern-day pop star, Callas drew sellout crowds for her title roles in *Norma, Lucia di Lammermoor, La Traviata,* and *Madama Butterfly.* Crowds lined the sidewalks, and the lines wrapped around the opera house. In Lyric's early years, opera fans were attracted by international stars such as Boris Christoff, Tito Gobbi, Marilyn Horne, Birgit Nilsson, Leontyne Price, Joan Sutherland, and Jon Vickers, among many others. Luciano Pavarotti was in his prime when he joined Lyric's roster; when Lyric's general director, Ardis Krainik, fired him in 1989 because of his habit of canceling as many performances as he actually sang, it made headlines around the world.

The company's repertory now includes at least one twentieth-century and/or one American work each season. A new Bolcom opera, *A Wedding* (based on the Robert Altman film), premiers in 2004, and another Bolcom opera is scheduled for 2010. The peripatetic English conductor Sir Andrew Davis became Lyric's music director and principal conductor in 2000, balancing performances in Chicago with orchestral and operatic conducting engagements around the world. When Lyric presented its first full *Ring* cycle, in 1996, the Wagner tetralogy attracted audience members from nearly every state in the union and twenty-two foreign countries. The Golden Jubilee season in 2004–5 and the *Ring* cycle that follows are expected to draw international performers and international crowds—as, indeed, every season does at Lyric.

Chicago Dance and Music Alliance

All manner of classical-music-making takes place in and around Chicago beyond the "big two" of Lyric and the CSO. The Chicago Dance and Music Alliance has more than one hundred fifty member organizations, from the aforementioned behemoths to upstart companies with shoestring budgets, including dozens of professional choirs, chamber ensembles, ethnic performing troupes, and the like, many of which record and tour professionally. All together, they put on more than two thousand professional performances and in-school outreach presentations each year, reaching nearly four million people in the Chicago area.

Jazz Chicago Style

Chicago's civic image suffered during the mobster years of the early twentieth century, and "Al Capone—bang, bang!" still remains an all-too-common response to Chicagoans traveling abroad. Fortunately, a more positive association also attached itself to the city in the years following World War I. Jazz may have originated in New Orleans, but it spread to Chicago and elsewhere. It took root here, as southern musicians headed due north looking for work after the Storyville brothels of New Orleans, where so many had played, were closed by the U.S. Navy in 1918 (in an effort to curtail the spread of venereal disease among sailors stationed in that city).

As the Chicago-based jazz journalist and broadcaster Neil Tesser recounts in his 1998 book, *The Playboy Guide to Jazz,* jazz took hold in Chicago by the early 1920s. One of the first and best ensembles, the Creole Jazz Band, was led by Joe "King" Oliver and employed a young cornet player also from New Orleans called Louis Armstrong, who quickly revolutionized the form.

Armstrong's musical pyrotechnics attracted the attention of some young white musicians in Chicago who were about to graduate from Austin High School, including Jimmy McPartland, a cornetist, and Frank Teschemacher and Bud Freeman, two saxophone players. They were joined by other teenaged musicians, including a North Side clarinetist named Benny Goodman (who would be playing with the short-lived but legendary Bix Beiderbecke by the time he was fourteen). Initially playing as copycats of the Creole Jazz Band's New Orleans style, the "Austin High Gang" soon followed Armstrong's lead in emphasizing solos over group improvisation. "Their efforts . . . earned the label 'Chicago Style,' [which] served as the second wave of early jazz, and it would exert an important influence on the nation's jazz musicians for the next decade," Tesser writes. By the end of the 1920s, though, Armstrong and his Austin High Gang followers had moved east to New York, and Armstrong was touring Europe, as well.

The envelope-pushing European composers of the early 1900s, including Ravel, Debussy, and Stravinsky, found inspiration in New Orleans- and Chicago-style jazz and incorporated its brash textures and audacious rhythms into their orchestral works. Recordings brought the exciting new music, with its groundbreaking syncopation and improvisation, to a broader audience abroad and sealed Chicago's global reputation as a premier jazz capital. Over the next two decades, Tesser notes, Chicago jazz took a detour into swing (and, to a lesser degree, bebop) with the erstwhile Chicagoan Benny Goodman ("King of Swing") one of the primary exponents.

"It wasn't until the '60s, with the advent of 'free jazz,' that a new Chicago style emerged that was more avant-garde, with greater influence in Europe than in the U.S. because the Europeans were more receptive to it," says Tesser. The radical musicianship of the saxophonist Ornette Coleman and the pianist Cecil Taylor "stirred up a number of young musicians centered in Chicago. . . . These artists constituted the 'second wave' of the avant-garde, building upon Coleman's innovation to create a thunderous cornucopia of new music. Working with Chicago's Association for the Advancement of Creative Musicians . . . they nourished the concepts of free jazz and explored its implications; the results ranged from bleak or tender interludes of intimacy to the cacophonous joy of polyphonic improvisation." A number of young artists carried the AACM concept into the 1970s and 1980s, Tesser writes, "but none of these musicians had as much impact as those who formed the Art Ensemble of Chicago, which in 1969 took up residence in Paris and proceeded to spread the AACM gospel. Combining music, costumery (including African face paint), and performance art, the AEC became an overnight sensation; their first recordings, made in Europe, ping-ponged their reputation back across the Atlantic. The band comprised trumpeter Lester Bowie, saxophonists Roscoe Mitchell and Joseph Jarman, bassist Malachi Favors, and drummer Famoudou Don Moye—five of the most accomplished and inno-

vative musicians the avant-garde has produced. . . . They still appear on a
semi-regular basis 30+ years after the AEC's formation, making it one of the
longest-running acts in jazz history. From their Parisian base, the Art Ensemble—along with the remarkable saxophonist and composer Anthony Brax-
ton, who had traveled with them—built a strong and long-lasting European
audience for the avant-garde. Never again would audiences automatically
conjure the images of Louis Armstrong and the Austin High Gang when they
heard the words 'Chicago jazz'—at least, not without such unlikely musical
heirs as Bowie and Jarman hovering behind them."

Some global influences have emerged in Chicago jazz in recent years, with
foreign-born musicians incorporating their native Indian, Chilean, Pakistani,
Polish, or other influences, and certainly the city's annual Jazz Festival and
World Music Festival deliver a multicultural range of jazz styles. More significantly, though, "Chicago jazz" continues to be a significant cultural export
and expression of the city's global cultural influence. As Tesser notes, the
artistry of the Chicago jazz percussionist Kahil El'Zabar "has been the subject of weeklong concert series devoted to his work in France and Africa. . . .
[H]e has regularly brought his strongly African-influenced music to Africa
on tours." The jazz pianist and singer Patricia Barber performs regularly in
France and Canada. Kurt Elling, a jazz vocalist, has toured Australia, Canada, and France and has performed at the Montreux, North Sea, Nice, and
Israel jazz festivals, among others.

The Chicago-based saxophonist and composer Ken Vandermark won a
MacArthur Foundation "genius grant" in 1999; he tours and records prolifically, specializing in jazz improvisation. For many years, Judy Roberts, a
Chicago jazz singer, performed in Singapore three months a year. And Von
Freeman, an octogenarian saxman and lifelong Chicagoan, was the headlin-
er at the Berlin Jazz Festival in the autumn of 2002; the festival was pro-
grammed by the 2002 artistic director, John Corbett, a Chicago jazzman associated with the Empty Bottle club and the School of the Art Institute.

Chicago Blues

The migration of African Americans from the Mississippi Delta (where
acoustic blues reigned) to Chicago after World War II gave rise to the amplified Chicago-style "blues" beginning in the late 1940s and 1950s. You could
hear bluesmen like Robert Nighthawk or Big John Wrencher with their hard-
driving combos on Maxwell Street during the Sunday morning market, no
doubt startling the klezmer-loving Eastern Europeans who originally estab-

lished the market, or you could slip into the jam-packed blues clubs of the city's north and west sides to hear the likes of the now-legendary Muddy Waters, Howlin' Wolf, Luther Allison, Willie Dixon, Little Walter, Elmore James, Buddy Guy, Junior Wells, Otis Rush, Hound Dog Taylor, Koko Taylor, and many more.

Over the years, Chicago blues artists have recorded prolifically and toured extensively. The platters put out first by Cobra and Chess Records (and a dozen other tiny labels) and later by Delmark and Alligator Records helped make the Chicago blues the first of its genre to reach a mass audience nationally and internationally. For decades, Chicago blues artists have gone abroad for concert and club gigs that electrified European audiences, and foreigners visiting Chicago continue to seek out the original and the upstart blues clubs on the south, west, and north sides. Type in "Chicago blues clubs" on an Internet search engine, and the first listing is a write-up, in French, with a detailed map, of "Les clubs de blues de Chicago."

As Muddy Waters sang, "The blues had a baby, and they named it rock and roll." But, happily, the birth and ascendancy of rock and roll hasn't meant the death of the blues in Chicago. Far from it—Chicago-style blues can now be heard routinely in blues festivals, clubs, and concert halls all over the world.

Political Chicago and World Culture

The midcentury reign of Richard J. Daley scarcely enhanced the city's global image in the arts. Mayor Daley the First was famously xenophobic, wary of the world outside the city limits, and wary of much within, as well. The riots surrounding the 1968 Democratic National Convention during his watch particularly scalded the city's image. Daley's immediate successor, Michael Bilandic, while famous mostly for being snowed out of office by Chicago's worst winter, in 1978–79, can be credited with promoting neighborhood cultural celebrations and with launching Chicago Fest, which attracted a half-million visitors to Navy Pier for an outstanding pop music lineup, and great food, in 1978.

Chicago's maverick mayor Jane Byrne was perhaps the first to declare Chicago a world-class city after she was elected in 1979 and to demand it receive commensurate recognition. She launched Taste of Chicago in 1981 as an offshoot of Chicago Fest. Two decades later, it attracts more than three million visitors to Grant Park to sample Chicago music and the multiethnic fare of more than a hundred restaurants over a three-week period each summer.

The city's well-established program of free music events downtown also enables visitors from abroad to sample with ease the best of what Chicago has to offer culturally. Jazz, blues, gospel, and other music festivals in the city, and much more, have evolved under the seemingly casual watch of Lois Weisberg, the commissioner of the Chicago Department of Cultural Affairs. Initially director of the mayor's office of special events under Harold Washington in 1983, and commissioner under Mayor Richard M. Daley since 1989, Weisberg has helped ignite and carry the multicultural torch that casts a new light on the city. While serving as assistant to the mayor for special projects, Weisberg mobilized Chicago's sister-city relationships, which became a municipal government program in 1990. Chicago now has twenty-three sister cities internationally and engages in cultural exchange with each.

Weisberg's most important contribution to Chicago's multicultural life, however, is the launching of the Chicago Cultural Center in 1991. The Cultural Center has a truly global reach and grasp and a genuinely small-"d" democratic mission. The only institution of its sort in the nation that charges no admission fee, the center occupies a mighty edifice on North Michigan Avenue that was the original home of the Chicago Public Library. Its interior is styled after that of a Florentine palazzo and is full of Carrara marble and wrought iron. Its centerpiece is a Tiffany-designed mosaic domed ceiling. The Cultural Center organizes exhibitions that explore the breadth and depth of a culture, using the visual arts as a core and then expanding outward to explore other aspects of that culture. For example, in the late 1990s an exhibition of two hundred photos titled Fifty Years of Indian Independence documented life in India from 1946 on. The photo exhibition was the core event, and a committee of Indian natives living in Chicago helped to explore contemporary Indian culture and to program a two-month-long series of events that encompassed film, contemporary and traditional dance, theater, political discussions, cooking classes, henna hand-painting, and more.

Appropriately, the Chicago Cultural Center also actively exports native Chicago culture. Funded by the U.S. State Department's Cultural and Educational Programs division, a 150-photograph exhibition excerpted from the massive photographic documentation project, Chicago in the Year 2000 (CITY 2000 for short), has gone to Paris, Aleppo, Alexandria, Amsterdam, New Delhi, Casablanca, São Paulo, and Durban so far.

The Department of Cultural Affairs has mounted a ten-day World Music Festival in late summer for the past few years. The festival is an outgrowth

of the Cultural Center's long tradition of presenting world music performances and offers a fresh infusion of global culture, from Eastern-European
klezmer music to Caribbean/African/African American jazz to Turkish gypsy
music to flamenco to the ancient traditions of Lapland. While world music
can be heard in other venues, from ethnic clubs to the Field Museum or the
Symphony Center (which in late 2002 hosted Yo Yo Ma's acclaimed multicultural musical collective, the Silk Road Ensemble), what makes the Cultural
Center different is that everything it presents is free, so that it can attract and
reach a broad demographic audience.

Perhaps the most famous recent initiative by the Department of Cultural Affairs was the wildly successful Cows on Parade summer public art exhibition of 1999. Chicago shoe-store owner Peter Hanig visited Zurich the pre-
vious summer and was enchanted by an outdoor exhibition of eight hundred
life-sized sculptures of standing and reclining cows, conceived by Beat See-
berger-Quin and designed by Peter Knapp. Hanig brought the idea home,
where dozens of Chicago artists, architects, and designers were engaged to
apply fanciful decorations to more than three hundred sculptures of charm-
ing horned cows in grazing, walking, and reclining poses, which were then
installed outdoors all over the city. The exhibition attracted more than a
million visitors to Chicago, had an estimated economic impact of more than
$200 million, and inspired other cities and countries to adopt the idea.

The Chicago Humanities Festival

Eileen Mackevich oversees the Chicago Humanities Festival, launched in 1990
as a subset of the Illinois Humanities Council (it has been an independent
organization since 1997). Its opening featured the playwright Arthur Miller
as the keynote speaker at Orchestra Hall and included among its eight events
at the Art Institute a presentation by the German scholar Rainer Rumold; a
discussion of freedom movements in Latin America, Eastern Europe, and
Africa; and performances of works by Bertolt Brecht, Kurt Weill, and Paul
Hindemith. Four thousand people attended.

By 2002 the festival had spread across 16 days and included a Children's
Humanities Festival. It encompassed over 150 programs at more than 20 sites,
with 200 presenters from around the globe. As if to mark its own arrival at
maturity, the 2002 festival again featured Arthur Miller as keynote speaker.

The Chicago International Film Festival

Founded by Michael Kutza in 1964, the Chicago International Film Festival is North America's oldest competitive film fest, intended to discover and present new filmmakers and acknowledge and reward their artistry in addition to honoring the living legends of cinema. Among the festival's discoveries over the years have been the now internationally renowned directors Martin Scorsese, Wim Wenders, Rainer Werner Fassbinder, Peter Weir, Alan Parker, Michael Apted, Krzysztof Kieslowski, Krzysztof Zanussi, and many others. Directors and actors in attendance field questions following most of the festival screenings; audiences have been able to interact with artists such as Geoffrey Rush, Liv Ullmann, Spike Lee, Billy Bob Thornton, and many others.

Each year, the festival features programs highlighting films from a specific part of the world, to raise awareness of the various voices and perspectives that exist within one country. Past festivals have focused on films from Mexico, Cuba, Japan, and the Philippines, among other countries. In 2002, one hundred feature films were screened, along with fifty shorts and documentaries, over a two-week period.

"Michael"

It is hard to argue with the proposition that the single person who connects world culture to Chicago and Chicago to world culture—meaning the largest number of people and cultures around the globe—is Michael Jordan. Visitors to remote rural villages in Africa have reported seeing children there wearing red shirts with "Jordan," "23" and "Chicago Bulls" written on them. Via satellite, unimaginable numbers of people everywhere have seen Air Jordan play and have marveled at his miraculous "hang time," his gravity-defying array of spontaneously invented dunks, his uncanny shots—and his shoes. The Washington Wizards coda might as well not have existed. Where once it might have been Al Capone who stood for Chicago, today, hands down, to millions across the globe it is Michael Jordan.

Performing Arts

Theater

One of Chicago's best-known cultural assets is its vibrant theater community, many offshoots of which have spread out to the wider world. There are more than two hundred theater companies of all descriptions at work and play here, in quarters ranging from tiny storefronts to expansive well-funded facilities, doing just about everything. Some preserve the classics faithfully, some reexamine them audaciously, some excavate lesser-known gems of various vintages, and some premier brave new works, an impressive number of which go on to find permanent life on stages around the world. Chicago's remarkable theater scene has consistently attracted national and international press coverage and has firmly placed the city on the map of the theater world. One of the strengths of Chicago theater is that the majority of its talent pool tends to remain here rather than decamp for New York or Los Angeles. The result is a discernible "Chicago style" of acting that attracts and intrigues visitors, and in turn inspires them in their own communities.

Many Chicago-based actors, directors, and playwrights have, however, gone global through the media of film and television. The actors John Malkovich (twenty-six films) and John Mahoney (television's *Frasier,* ten films) are both members of the Steppenwolf Theatre ensemble; David Schwimmer (*Friends*) is a cofounder of the Lookingglass Theater Company; William Petersen (*CSI: Crime Scene Investigation, To Live and Die in LA, Manhunter,* and several other films) cofounded Remains Theatre. The playwright-screenwriter David Mamet turned the gritty, profanity-laden patter of street Chicago into theatrical poetry with his Pulitzer Prize–winning play (and film adaptation) *Glengarry Glen Ross,* his Obie Award–winning *American Buffalo,* and others. Mamet, whose plays are staged internationally, has been compared to Samuel Beckett, Harold Pinter, and Arthur Miller.

Among the Chicago theater people whose work has attracted national and international attention are the actors Mike Nussbaum, Gary Sinise, Hollis Resnik, Joan Allen, Amy Morton, and dozens of Second City veterans. The Goodman Theatre has sent its artistic director Robert Falls's production of Eugene O'Neill's *The Iceman Cometh* to Dublin's Abbey Theatre, and his productions of O'Neill's *Long Day's Journey into Night,* Tennessee Williams's *The Night of the Iguana,* and Arthur Miller's *Death of a Salesman* to Broadway all are unqualified triumphs that shed a fresh Chicago-style light on established masterpieces.

Steppenwolf Theatre's Tony Award–winning production of *The Grapes of Wrath*, directed by Frank Galati, traveled to Broadway, London, and California; the company's South African epic, *The Song of Jacob Zulu*, directed by Eric Simonson with Ladysmith Black Mambazo, traveled to Broadway and Australia, and its recent revival of *Glengarry Glen Ross*, directed by a company member, Amy Morton, traveled to the Dublin International Theater Festival. Remains Theatre's *In the Belly of the Beast*, starring William Petersen, traveled to Washington's Kennedy Center and to London. A recent Tony Award winner for best director of a play was Mary Zimmerman, whose 2002 Broadway production of *Metamorphoses* originated at Chicago's Lookingglass Theater Company.

"Chicago is not only sending out productions; Chicago attracts world-class theater for engagements here," notes the recently retired *Chicago Tribune* theater critic Richard Christiansen. "The Goodman presented world premieres of a new August Wilson play, *Gem of the Ocean*, and a new Stephen Sondheim musical, *Bounce*, directed by Harold Prince. Add to that the commercial tryouts of *The Producers*, *The Sweet Smell of Success*, Twyla Tharp and Billy Joel's *Movin' Out*, and *Hollywood Arms*, and you see that Chicago is recognized as a place with a valid and vibrant theater scene. It's a good place to let a [commercial] show breathe a little bit before taking it on to the next step."

Christiansen attributes the vitality of Chicago's theater community "on every level, from the smallest to the largest, to the fact that it's not a television- or movie-oriented town—it's a town where people do theater. It's also a very youthful community, very vibrant. It's a big city with a lot of educational institutions churning out graduates in theater work. Many decide to stake their flags here and see what they can do. Through the years Chicago has developed a justified reputation of being a very bustling and active theater town."

Chicago Shakespeare Theater (formerly Shakespeare Repertory Theater) has made the Bard a household name in the city under Barbara Gaines's artistic direction. Her (mostly) locally cast, lively productions have earned the attention and admiration of critics and directors from around the world. The ensuing relationships have in turn led the company to bring in some outstanding directors, and sometimes productions, from abroad. The 2002–3 season, for instance, included *The Winter's Tale* directed by Michael Bogdanov, founder of the English Shakespeare Company, in his third guest-directing engagement with CST.

The World's Stage initiative was launched in Chicago in November 2000. Through this initiative, international theater companies and guest artists bring their finest work to Chicago's Shakespeare Theater—"embracing our stage as The World's Stage." Recent works produced through the World's Stage initiative include the U.S. premiere of the British actor Simon Callow's one-man show, *The Mystery of Charles Dickens; The School for Scandal* and *The Molière Comedies* (directed by and featuring Brian Bedford from the Stratford Festival of Canada); *The Tragedy of Hamlet* (adapted and directed by the expatriate Briton Peter Brook, whose theater company is based in Paris); *La Dernière Lettre* (featuring Catherine Samie of the Comédie-Française); and *Le Costume,* an adaptation of a short story by the South African writer Can Themba, performed in French and again directed by Peter Brook at CST in its only U.S. engagement. In June 2003, CST remounted it in English as *The Suit,* and then took it to London. In late 2003, Shakespeare's Globe Theatre brought its all-male original-practices production of *Twelfth Night,* featuring Mark Rylance as artistic director, from London to CST; it overlapped with *Rose Rage,* an adaptation of the *Henry VI* plays, also with an all-male cast, directed by Edward Hall (son of the legendary director Sir Peter Hall). In 2004 the Comédie-Française will bring its production of Molière's *Imaginary Invalid* to CST. And now the company is exporting, as well; its critically and popularly acclaimed 2001 studio production of Stephen Sondheim's *Pacific Overtures,* conceived and directed by the associate artistic director, Gary Griffin, traveled to London's prestigious Donmar Playhouse, in Covent Garden, in June 2003, garnering eight Olivier Award nominations.

At least some of the foundation for the current internationalism of Chicago's theater community was laid by the late International Theater Festival of Chicago, conceived and created by Bernie and Jane Nicholls Sahlins in 1984. There were five International Theater Festivals held in Chicago between 1986 and 1994, importing a wide range of startling and stimulating productions from all over the world. "For the first one, we brought in the National Theatre of Great Britain, the Haifa Municipal Theatre, the Market Theater of South Africa, and some French company," Jane Sahlins recalls. "What's important about what we did . . . is that we opened the eyes of the audience and the local theaters to what was out there. One of the reasons we were successful is that we required that every foreign company do workshops and lectures with the local community, not merely perform." In addition to setting up lectures and workshops to benefit members of the Chicago theater community, the ITF was determined to have members of the local theaters see everything the festival presented. "At first we let them in for free, then $5, then a top price of $7.50. Actors, designers, and directors all took advantage of it, which was great. I think it did catalyze a change in Chicago theater."

Of course, before the Sahlinses launched the International Theater Festival, Bernie had his hands full with another venture that distinguished Chicago internationally as a breeding ground for unconventional comedy and hyperenergized actors. Second City still thrives as an improvisation-based cabaret theater and operates theaters in Toronto and several U.S. cities, including Los Angeles and Las Vegas. In its first few decades it launched the acting careers of John and Jim Belushi, Dan Aykroyd, Joan Rivers, Harold Ramis, Gilda Radner, Shelley Long, and Alan Arkin, among others.

Dance

Although the Chicago Dance and Music Alliance has more than 150 member organizations, dance companies have tended to spring up and disappear in Chicago over the years. There are a couple of noteworthy exceptions. One is Mordine and Company Dance Theatre, founded in 1968, which focuses on contemporary dance and has toured to Yugoslavia, Israel, Australia, and Mexico. Another is the Hubbard Street Dance Company, founded in 1977. Its troupe of 21 culturally diverse dancers performs innovative contemporary works year-round; to date the company has performed in 16 foreign countries and 42 states. Another company recently relocated to Chicago—the Chicago dance world's Boeing. The Joffrey Ballet, founded in 1956 as a touring ensemble, moved in 1995 from New York to Chicago, where it has built a loyal audience over the years.

The Dance Center of Columbia College in Chicago's Loop is the city's leading presenter of national and international contemporary dance performers. One of its burgeoning programs is DanceAfrica Chicago, which highlights dance traditions of the African diaspora with performing groups from the African continent, the Caribbean, and South America.

Radio and Television

Many television shows, such as *ER, Chicago Hope,* and *Hill Street Blues,* have been shot in Chicago. The first two of those shows have a Chicago setting and have represented the city around the world in syndication or via cable. Oprah Winfrey's long-running, touchy-feely television talk show also connects Chicago to the world—international tourists are often as keen to gain a seat in her audience as they are to visit the top of the Sears Tower or the city's museums. And back before World War II, when television was a fledgling medium, Burr Tillstrom's *Kukla, Fran, and Ollie* was one of the first regularly scheduled programs available. It originated in Chicago and stayed in Chicago for the length of its successful life.

For decades, WFMT-FM, Chicago's fine-arts radio station, aired live broadcasts of Chicago Symphony Orchestra concerts and Lyric Opera of Chicago opening nights to its local audience and would then rebroadcast to a national and international audience. Those global broadcasts served a vital outreach function for both organizations and enabled substantial international audiences to enjoy the artistry of both. Alas, the funding to air the Chicago Symphony dried up in 2001, and the same thing happened to Lyric Opera in 2002. A long tradition has been suspended until further notice.

Movies

Chicago played a key role in the early history of motion pictures. Essanay Studios on Argyle Street was founded in 1907 and churned out hundreds of silent movies before moving to California with the rest of the industry. The original studio is now a Chicago landmark and is still in use, mostly for producing TV commercials. Essanay's early productions brought rising stars to the north side of town, including Charlie Chaplin, Gloria Swanson, and the studio's cofounder, "Bronco Billy" Anderson, the first cinematic cowboy hero. At that time, the Uptown Theatre, an extravagantly rococo movie palace, was the area's defining landmark.

The success and international visibility of the Chicago International Film Festival has begotten many spinoffs over the years, including the Chicago Lesbian and Gay International Film Festival (the second-largest of its kind in the world), the Chicago Underground Film Festival, the Black Harvest International Festival of Film and Video (focusing on recent African and African American independent films), Festival of Films from Iran, the Polish Film Festival in America (the world's largest screening of Polish films, with more than forty features and documentaries shown), the Hong Kong Film Festival, the Israel Film Festival, the International Children's Film Festival, the New French Cinema Film Festival, the Irish Film Festival, the Chicago Latino Film Festival, the Asian American Showcase, Women in the Director's Chair International Film and Video, the Silver Images Film Festival (the only one of it kind in the United States, showcasing films that celebrate older adults), and even a Festival of Cinema for the Deaf.

Several films shot in and around Chicago have represented the city to the world—for better and for worse. *Ferris Bueller's Day Off, Ordinary People, A Wedding, The Blues Brothers, The Untouchables, The Fugitive, When Harry Met Sally, The Sting, Harry and Tonto, Looking for Mr. Goodbar, My Bodyguard, Bullitt, Medium Cool, Risky Business, Sixteen Candles, Punky Brewster, About Last Night, The Color of Money, Personal Foul, She's Having a Baby, High Fidelity, While You Were Sleeping, My Best Friend's Wedding, Hudsucker Proxy, Uncle Buck, Home Alone (I, II, and III), Meet the Parents, Dennis the Menace, Road to Perdition, Ali, Ocean's Eleven*—all were made in or around Chicago, along with many others. Several of these movies were written, directed, and/or produced by two longtime Chicago suburbanites, John Hughes and Harold Ramis.

Conclusion

As extensive as is this catalogue of Chicago's rich cultural life and the ways in which it influences and has been influenced by the near and far corners of the world, there is more—much more. There is no slow season in Chicago's cultural and multicultural life, no time when the city retreats to low-key localism. Performing companies or presenters have their down times, but one company's off season is another's peak, and touring productions and performers add to the mix to saturate the culture market with more choices than one could ever exercise given a bottomless budget and no time conflicts. The offerings run the gamut from free to breathtakingly high-priced, from big familiar shows and concerts at the downtown venues to brave forays into the cultural unknown in little storefront clubs and theaters. There is *always* something enticing to see, to hear, to sample in Chicago, and whatever cultural diversion one chooses, it is likely to have strands of one kind or another, apparent or unseen, that connect it to the global community. It almost goes without saying.

8 Shaping Global Chicago

MICHAEL H. MOSKOW

THE CHICAGO metropolitan area has transformed itself from an industrial metropolis, anchor of the Rust Belt, into a global business capital. Its still significant manufacturing sector now coexists with a burgeoning set of globally prominent corporate headquarters and financial, transportation, and business-service establishments. In 2001, the metropolitan area had a gross product of $320 billion, ranking it eighteenth in the world, ahead of Russia and Switzerland. Its economy is increasingly global, with $23 billion in international exports in 2001. And the Chicago area is becoming increasingly cosmopolitan; immigrants from over two hundred countries now make up 17 percent of its population.

The transformation has not come easily. During the 1970s and early 1980s, the combination of worldwide oil price shocks and emerging foreign manufacturing competition made it clear that the city's industrial structure was outmoded, no longer competitive in attracting investment and workers. Largely as a result of a decline in the manufacturing sector, the region's per-capita income fell sharply in comparison to national averages. Employment growth slowed significantly.

But during the mid-1980s, Chicago-area businesses and workers began to reinvigorate the region's economy. Manufacturing companies adopted new technologies and business practices, while investment in service industries expanded rapidly, particularly in the financial, travel, and business-service sectors. By the 1990s, the Midwest was regaining its share of the nation's manufacturing, and those manufacturing businesses were looking to Chicago for services and finance. More important for Chicago, its own industrial composition—led especially by business-service growth—had been restructured sufficiently to re-ignite its economy. The business-service growth was boosted by the development of world-class air travel and business-meeting facilities and by a revival in the attraction of the central city as a place to live. Per-capita income climbed as a result, and in the 1990s, the central city's population grew for the first time since the 1940s.

It is not, however, a done deal. If such progress is to continue, Chicago and its surrounding metropolitan area must redouble their efforts. For metropolitan economies, the world only continues to become more competitive. Chicago will have to fight hard to win a proportionate share of the world's talented people and business investment. Essential to this fight will be two things: (1) providing opportunities for all Chicagoans to develop the skills that the workforce needs, and (2) creating an environment of openness, access, fairness, and mobility in which Chicagoans can advance their careers and found new businesses.

Chicago's performance in pursuit of these goals will depend not only on the quality and extent of its global connections, but also on its local—or "inside"—performance, that is, how well the region provides its citizens with opportunities for work, learning, and recreation. Chicago can't attract global talent—and it won't be able to keep homegrown experts either—if it fails to deliver an appealing quality of life, a well-functioning economy, and a business climate of openness and opportunity for all. Yes, to be sure, a global city needs extensive international air transport facilities, well-developed personal and institutional connections throughout the world, and an extensive fiber-optic infrastructure—but it also needs safe streets, good schools, smart land-use, diversified culture, ample recreation facilities, efficient surface transportation, and a supportive environment and culture for new business investment.

Inside Performance: Does Chicago Stack Up?

What a region does on the "inside" will determine its global fortunes just as surely as its connections to the world economy. From a city's performance in shaping its "built" environment and providing appropriate public services spring the possibilities for individual well-being and the growth that will attract residents and businesses.

How, then, can we conceptualize whether a city is up to world-class standards? One schematic has been offered by Edward Glaeser of Harvard University, the preeminent urban economist of our day. He divides a city's basic functions—what it is that makes a city productive internally—into three categories: (1) transportation of goods and people; (2) delivery of public services to residents; (3) transmission of ideas and information.

Transportation

In moving physical goods, proximity can boost productivity for industries ranging from manufacturing to construction, from retail to wholesale. For manufacturers, proximity means that parts and components are accessible more cheaply and faster from cross-town suppliers, and there is a close analog for retailers, construction, and wholesalers. It is not just transportation costs that are improved by proximity, but repair, servicing, and replacement of complicated machinery and parts are smoother, and the negotiations that accompany the setting of specifications is made easier by face-to-face communication.

According to Geoff Hewings of the Regional Economics Applications Laboratory, Chicago's manufacturing productivity was once demonstrated by the visible interdependence of the suppliers and manufacturers within the metropolitan area. Steel companies fed machinery makers, machinery fed production plants, and production plants were often linked with nearby plants through their purchases of components and parts from each other.

Although Chicago's manufacturing complex has since "hollowed out," with much of its supplier trade and interdependence now having moved outward to the greater Midwest and beyond, overland transportation remains very important to the city's productivity. The greater ease of "intermodal shipment"—packing in standardized containers that can be readily transferred, especially between truck and rail—has sharpened Chicago's transportation advantage in this regard. The current challenge to this development, however, is traffic congestion. Local roadway congestion slows truck transportation (and, it might be added, vice versa). Similarly, Chicago's freight yards, and especially the connections between railroad lines, have become outdated and slow. In the central city and near suburbs in particular, many highway underpasses and other elements of infrastructure are outdated, unusable for modern trucks and trailers.

While manufacturing and distribution remain a sizable part of Chicago's economy, service activities are inexorably displacing heavy industry. As Chicago moves further toward a service economy, the transportation of people to and from their place of work becomes more vital. As congestion increases, travel times continue to climb in Chicago. This will only intensify strain and lower productivity for the workers commuting to office buildings throughout the metropolitan area. Continued planning and construction of roadways and timely maintenance are needed to keep Chicago moving well in this regard. It makes sense that this should be supported in part by strategic pricing of roadway use on tollways.

Individual decisions by households to live nearer to job centers can also be helpful in easing congestion and promoting access to job opportunities, but only to a limited extent because so many households now have more than one worker—often working in disparate locations. However, there is one respect in which closer coincidence of job and housing location may be helpful. It may be that residential land-use restrictions erected by suburban municipalities are aggravating commuting distances and times by precluding the construction of affordable housing near jobs. In this, the challenge is not one of transportation, but of a different public service, that being land-use control and management.

Delivery of Public Services

Cities provide their residents with access to economic opportunities through public services. Aside from transportation, the most important are education and land-use management. Ideally, public transportation systems and roadways bring job opportunities within reach of low- and middle-income families. But as job creation in the Chicago area continues to shift to locations further from the central city while the affordable housing stock for low- and middle-income workers remains behind, access to job opportunities by lower-income households becomes more difficult. Central-city residents may find it difficult to commute to jobs on the periphery, and information about job vacancies may be more difficult to acquire. As the work world moves further away, children in the central city—and some in low-income suburban neighborhoods—may become culturally isolated from the norms of workplace behavior and procedures, thereby adding challenges to employment more difficult than transportation alone.

One possible solution would be for economic growth and attendant job opportunities to return to the central city. Housing would be cheaper to provide there because of the presence of depreciated or older housing stock for rehabilitation. At the same time, public transportation by bus and light rail is cheaper where population density is high, as in the central city.

While this sounds ideal, there often seems to be little that municipal governments can do about job loss when the causes lie rooted in external forces such as technological change and profound shifting of industries. For example, the central city of Chicago has been losing manufacturing at a torrid pace in recent decades, but this owes more to technological changes in manufacturing processes than to public policy.

But in spite of such headwinds against preservation of jobs in the city center, the great potential benefit to city residents compels the effort. At the very least, local government can listen carefully to the needs of business for appropriate regulation and services. Meanwhile, sensible reassembly of land parcels, even-handed taxation, education of a motivated young workforce, and planning and provision of transportation infrastructure on an appropriately wide geographic scale fall squarely within the purview of state and local government.

However, a fragmented and locally autonomous governance structure has contributed to slow progress on regionwide land-use and public-service issues. According to the Chicago Metropolis 2020 project, the six-county region has more than 1,200 units of local government, including 267 municipalities, 113 townships, 303 school districts, and hundreds of other special districts addressing issues such as mosquito abatement, sanitation, and parks. This translates to one unit of government for every 6,000 people—five times the ratio for greater Los Angeles and seven times the ratio in New York City. As a result, the Chicago area faces significant challenges in devising regionwide strategies.

There have, however, been some recent initiatives that are promising in this regard. In 1997, suburban mayors and Chicago's Mayor Daley formed the Metropolitan Mayors Caucus. The 270-odd mayors or their representatives now meet on a regular basis to address regionwide issues and opportunities.

In some respects, the City of Chicago and its business-sector partners are also doing their part for rational land-use planning. The 2002 Central Area Plan lays out a vision for the Loop—the central district—that will guide development for decades to come. In this way, competing land uses for residential, commercial, and public purposes will be prioritized so as to maximize the value of Chicago's most desirable and intensively used real estate.

On a wider regional basis, in February 2003, Chicago Metropolis 2020 released *The Metropolis Plan: Choices for the Chicago Region,* focusing on growth and transportation. The plan demonstrates how thoughtful planning can address issues of competing land use and development at lower cost than the business-as-usual scenarios now on the drawing boards. Using "scenario planning" techniques, Metropolis 2020 sought out ideas from over a thousand regional leaders, tested different policies on sophisticated computer models, and then developed prescriptions for healthier growth. Its plan shows that it is possible to reduce the amount of time the average resident of the region will spend in the car in 2030 by eighty hours annually relative to what can be expected if growth continues in its present patterns. The region can protect more than three hundred square miles from overdevelopment and spend more than $5 billion less for infrastructure than now projected.

Education Spending on education has grown to be the largest state and local public expenditure by far. Local governments in the form of school districts fashion and deliver education, but in large cities like Chicago, municipal governments are increasingly taking back responsibility for elementary and secondary education in an attempt to raise the performance of schools serving low-income populations. The City of Chicago's sweeping experiment in this regard—with the mayor directly appointing a CEO and school board—has brought it national if not worldwide attention. So far, as reflected in standardized test scores, the improvements realized in bringing up the levels of the lowest performing students and schools have been positive but inadequate, although great improvements can be seen in capital spending, purchasing, and administrative activities. There have, in fact, been some heartening recent signs that many Chicago city schools are getting better under the renewed leadership commitment and redesign of school organization. But certainly much remains to be done.

Suburban schools perform no better with low-income students, suggesting that the problem is not unique to the city system per se, but is a widespread challenge. The paramount importance of education for everyone if they are to participate in our great economy means the improvement of schools must be a top goal for the region. The substantial per-student resources being spent suggest that funding alone is not the problem. We must find better procedures and systems to bring along children from disadvantaged households. It must be said that Illinois has been extremely timid about facilitating experiments to see if choice and competition might work to improve educational delivery in public schools. The charter-school program, for instance, has been capped at sixty throughout the entire state, with only thirty allowed in Chicago.

Transmission of Ideas and Information

Face-to-face interactions of workers in an urban economy are a primary underpinning of high productivity, ranging from office meetings, retail-wholesale negotiations, trade shows, and conventions to the transfer of ideas and technology among trendsetters, engineers, scientists—also between company scientists and corporate boardrooms. Chicago's burgeoning business-service sector suggests that its economy has been highly successful in this more mundane—though lucrative—market for ideas and information. Nor has the digital age left Chicago behind as its infrastructure comprises a primary interchange of fiber-optic communications.

But despite its robust overall economy, Chicago's performance in the so-called high-tech industries—computing, biotechnology, and the like—provokes widespread dissatisfaction. In addition to its rich array of business services and telecommunications facilities, the Chicago area produces enormous scientific and research output. The region houses several of the nation's strongest research universities, including Northwestern University, the University of Chicago, the Illinois Institute of Technology, and the University of Illinois at Chicago, and two large federal laboratories—Argonne National Energy Laboratory and Fermi Lab (high-energy physics)—along with large technology companies that would seem ripe for public lab–private firm collaborations. Given all this, Chicago's production of high-technology start-up firms is very disappointing. For example, a recent Brookings Institution report on the growth of biotechnology centers in the United States classified Chicago as a "biotechnology research center," while the city failed to make the grade as a "biotechnology center." And across all industries, the Chicago region's economy cannot point to many so-called gazelles, or rapidly growing firms that derive their strength from emerging technologies. In 1994–98, Chicago ranked twenty-eighth out of fifty large U.S. metropolitan areas in job growth from rapidly growing firms.

Recognizing that there is much greater potential here than is being realized, the Illinois Coalition, Mayor Daley's Technology Council, and other initiatives have gotten under way to examine and prepare the institutions and infrastructure that can create new industries, such as the technology transfer policies of local universities and the existence of informal networks by which fledgling companies can interact and find venture capital. Such efforts should most emphatically be continued and supported.

Outside Performance: Do We Connect?

Are Chicago's connections to the global exchange well chosen and well developed for participation in the global economy? Almost since it was founded, Chicago has been a city with extensive global connections. These connections followed directly from its role as "nature's metropolis," the nineteenth-century gathering point for the enormous natural bounty of the midcontinent. Chicago gathered the lumber, grain, and livestock, which found their way to markets around the world, principally in Europe. In the process, it became the hub of an extensive railroad structure.

With its advantage as a port city to both the Great Lakes system and the Mississippi River basin, Chicago was favorably positioned to become a superstar during the age of mass production. As this manufacturing stardom came to pass, shipments of steel, machinery, processed foods, and all types of manufactured goods found their way from Chicago to the markets of the world. In turn, dispossessed or adventuresome peoples of the world—Irish, Germans, Jews, Poles, African Americans, Italians, Slovaks, Greeks, Scandinavians, and others—found their way to Chicago's neighborhoods to work in its factories and to found its businesses.

Such external connections remain important today for Chicago's economic vibrancy, and indeed, many of the region's policy efforts are directed toward their support and revival.

Cargo Hub A case in point is the city's extensive railroad system, which connects the nation's major railroad lines. The rise of "containerization" of cargo and intermodal shipment by sea, truck, and rail has breathed new life into overland cargo transport, especially through Chicago. Appropriately, under the organizational guidance of civic groups, the major players in Chicago's rail transit industry are now working to make it more efficient and more competitive and to expand its capacity.

Workforce Training and Land Assembly Similarly, the importance of a globally competitive manufacturing sector to Chicago's economy is not going unrecognized. A training system to produce workers with the skills to meet tomorrow's manufacturing needs was considered and addressed in a recent report by Chicago's Federation of Labor. The report set out a series of proposals to further a well-organized system of workforce preparation and skills certification for tomorrow's manufacturing workforce.

Chicago continues to work on land-assembly and infrastructure to retain and encourage manufacturing investment, including efforts to fashion and negotiate zoning and land-use arrangements that encourage continued and expanded manufacturing activity in the city. For example, the city has invested in a joint venture with the state of Illinois on a "supplier park" and worker-training facility that will be built adjacent to Chicago's Torrence Avenue Ford auto-assembly plant. That facility will be producing Ford's upcoming "crossover" vehicle, a hybrid station wagon/SUV. In some instances, such as Goose Island on the city's North Side, robust gentrifying neighborhoods are arising adjacent to existing manufacturing facilities, so that competing land uses must be mediated.

Exports Many local organizations have emerged to provide technical and information assistance to firms in exporting Chicago-area products. While such programs and connections have strengthened the region's prowess in trading manufactured goods and commodities, the nature of Chicago's global connections has changed and is changing as the economy evolves. That economy is moving away from commodities and manufacturing activity and toward services, invention, entrepreneurship, and information.

A Business Center While Chicago has always been the center of services and finance for business in the Midwest, these activities have now become its primary function, with job numbers in business services and finance alone easily displacing those related to manufacturing. As recently as thirty years ago, manufacturing jobs easily outnumbered business service and finance jobs. Today, the count is close to one million for these service jobs, versus 650,000 in manufacturing.

A Travel and Convention Center Personal intercity air travel has been the bedrock underlying Chicago's rising service economy. Face-to-face communication among customers, clients, and colleagues has remained an essential factor in value creation for emerging business-service activities, and in the broader geographic context of global commerce, this has come to require frequent and long-distance travel. Chicago was fortunate, perhaps prescient, in developing its air travel facilities so extensively early on. The "hubbing" of two major airlines at O'Hare—United and American—along with O'Hare's new international terminal with its extensive international flights have helped make Chicago a major nexus for business-service industries.

The city's great stature as a meeting and convention center has been fostered by the wide scope of its air travel connections and high frequency of flights. Its location at midcontinent—at least with respect to the distribution of U.S. population—helped to build Chicago as a meeting center, and the growth of business travel led to the growth of airport capacity. It is equally true, however, that Chicago could have ended up an also-ran in air travel and business meetings had it not started the initiatives and invested heavily in airport infrastructure and in unparalleled meeting facilities in a bold and timely manner.

Recently, Chicago's global air connections have blossomed with the rise of international flights and the opening of the international terminal at O'Hare. In comparison with large coastal cities, midcontinental Chicago is surely less visible to potential foreign visitors; nonetheless, the numbers of foreign visitors to Chicago—business visitors, government delegations, and tourists alike—have climbed steadily over the long term. Such visits present a great opportunity for Chicago to imprint overseas visitors with favorable impressions of the city and to deepen Chicago's business linkages and capacities.

Visitor Services Once visitors are on the ground, however, Chicago must play catch-up in one respect. Some cities are well organized to receive requests from foreign delegations and channel their requests to those who can best address their needs and establish longer-term connections. To date, Chicago's performance in ensuring that foreign visitors and delegations are received and well directed has been subpar—though this is changing. The major organizations that receive such visiting delegations are now working to set the Chicago "receiving line" at or above world-class standards.

Increasingly, it is more than the impressions of passing visitors that are important to global business connections. The productivity of large world cities has come to depend on their ability to attract the world's most talented people to live and work there. Indeed, some skilled and creative workers are so highly mobile that the distinction between visitor and resident quickly blurs. At any given time, the Chicago workforce is comprised of, for instance, world-class scientists here on temporary assignment, symphony conductors and performers who shuttle among the large cities of the world, and streams of workers from Mexico and points south, many of whom return home annually. Travel connections are important to these workers, as are the diverse and abundant business opportunities in Chicago. And to a rising extent, the culture and recreation of the city are also big draws.

Recreation The high incomes of workers in world cities, along with the pressing and varied demands of two-worker families, make time a most precious commodity. Recreational opportunities that are close at hand—whether restaurants, clubs, sports arenas, theaters, or museums—are highly valued in the job and business-location decisions of working households.

To anyone who has lived in Chicago for even a few weeks, many of its cultural and recreational assets are obvious: twenty-nine miles of lakefront and beach; thirty-four orchestras (one among the best in the world); an opera company that is one of the top three in the nation; museums with stunning collections and inspired new exhibits; a vibrant blues, jazz, and folk scene; stunning architecture old and new. The mayor's drive to beautify the city, including planting more than one hundred thousand trees and uncounted flowers on street corners and median strips, stuns Chicagoans who return after a few years' absence.

One feature of such achievements that is particularly worth noting is a locally committed, highly active group of corporate leaders. The city has been experiencing a vigorous cycle of business growth, which, unlike the case in many other cities, has spawned a local leadership whose members are highly committed and generous of their time and money in supporting the arts and recreation. In reaching out to the global arts community, they have helped to bring Chicago to the world, and the world to Chicago.

These cultural and recreational assets generate all sorts of tangible and intangible benefits. For one, they bring in tourist dollars. The Cows on Parade public art show in the summer of 1999 generated an estimated $16 million in sales of exhibit-related merchandise. More broadly, such events make the city attractive to the global professional elite and put Chicago on the radar screens of foreign investors.

Letting the World Know

Of course, none of what Chicago offers to the world will be known to outsiders without informational and promotional programs to present them. Chicago now has several vehicles to present itself to the world. On the commercial front, World Business Chicago is a public-private partnership whose mission is to expand the Chicago regional economy through the growth of the private sector and its connections to the world. Similarly, a partnership of state and local governments has set up the Chicago Convention and Tourism Bureau to promote and facilitate tourism and meetings.

Even more important, Chicago's current generation of civic leaders has a "can-do" attitude and openness to foreign ideas, high culture, and the importance of amenities to attract people to our city. Culture and recreation matter, and the leaders of the region have always known it. Why else has the city of Chicago moved an eight-lane freeway to create a thirty-six-acre museum campus? Why else is it celebrating the new millennium by adding one million square feet of green space, a new theater, and a band shell designed by Frank Gehry to the lakefront park envisioned by Daniel Burnham a century ago? Why else is it setting aside 19,165 acres on the site of the former Joliet Arsenal to be managed as open space, clearing the way for creation of a tallgrass prairie ecosystem? This new vigor and receptivity have gone a long way toward easing foreigners' qualms about investing in a city that some still think of for its bygone era of organized crime and corruption.

A Vibrant Business Economy But public art, culture, and beautification are not enough. Other cities—some of which have better weather—can also boast of rich cultural and recreational assets. Public amenities and services are themselves derivative from a strong and vibrant economy. This means that the region's highest priority should always be those efforts and policies that build and are conducive to a vibrant economy, which can then, in turn, finance amenities and public-service needs. Even at the upper end of the talent spectrum, for example, amenities cannot contribute as much to attracting mobile young business and professional people as the underlying business and career opportunities.

Today, professional workers are continually learning, training, and moving among jobs in fashioning custom-made careers. Most workers, often their spouses, too, must always be looking ahead to their next job or business opportunity. Being plugged in to the knowledge and information necessary for such career paths comes largely through personal contacts at one's present job. Accordingly, the location of one's job must have the depth and diversity of exposure to the business world that only a large and vibrant city can provide. In this, the decision to live and work in Chicago cannot be assessed by amenities and salary alone. There is value in having the deep concentration of active, successful, and diverse companies and associated workforce opportunities in a single metropolitan area. Chicago remains second nationally as a corporate headquarters domicile to companies with global reach. In addition, Chicago's universities and professional schools—especially its excellent business schools—mean that fledgling careers can be further developed here. And the active residential neighborhoods adjacent to the city center facilitate a lively social scene for many workers. Here, the recreational scene often serves a dual purpose—to entertain, but also to tune into career and business opportunities.

Civic Organizations Looking Outward Part of what also makes business learning and career mobility a feature of a successful city are connections to and awareness of global events and developments. Chicago's vibrancy in business and career growth will depend on how intelligently and intensively Chicagoans tune in to events, developments, issues, and technologies that are unfolding on the world stage.

In recent years, Chicagoans have been looking globally with clearer sightlines than in the past. City and state government leaders are fashioning Chicago with world-class benchmarks in mind and promoting its strengths accordingly. The city, like most, has long had its established membership organizations to discuss foreign policy or host world business leaders as they relay the latest wisdom from global business practice. These organizations are now joining forces, working more cooperatively to connect Chicagoans to the world. The Global Chicago Center of the Chicago Council on Foreign Relations (this book's sponsor) is a case in point. Global Chicago merged into the council during 2002, as did the MidAmerica Committee, a group noted for its program of international speakers serving the business community. Perhaps for the first time, these organizations—Global Chicago included— are now looking to Chicago's recent immigrants, drawing on newly arrived residents and businesses from around the world to help inform Chicagoans of the issues and developments in other countries, to develop cultural and business ties with them and to bring them, into the mainstream.

Turning Chicago Inside Out

Globalization and technological change have sharpened Chicago's competition. In the United States, midsized cities such as Nashville, Atlanta, and Denver are maturing into viable places for world commerce and culture. From the other end of the size spectrum, mega-cities such as London and New York have reemerged as centers of the highest order in finance and commerce. Chicago has done well to hold its own as a premier national center of commerce, and as a significant global city. It remains host to many important corporate headquarters and a highly developed set of business-service activities. Chicago's prodigious air-travel infrastructure has been helpful—essential, really—and it will be important to keep building on this asset as O'Hare's physical capacity becomes strained in the near future. There are a number of other important areas where Chicago must focus in the effort to measure up as a global city.

Attracting Talent

Business-service firms rely on the ability to recruit the best and brightest from throughout the world. Chicago's world-class business and professional schools are helpful in this regard, and Chicago is fortunate, even unique among its peers, in having a strong and vibrant central city at its core, one that is now experiencing a revival in its culture and entertainment. As a complement and alternative to placid green suburban communities, central city neighborhoods—with their liveliness and diversity—are a helpful draw in attracting the world's most talented people, especially among the young.

Education

The challenges of educating children from low-income and recently immigrated households also figure into the equation of access to opportunity and regionwide economic growth. These challenges are not easy to address, but the alternative is unthinkable. The intractability of this problem to date suggests that experimentation with new procedures and delivery systems may be needed. As with markets, the incentives to innovate and to serve customers that flow from choice and competition may well lead us to better educational solutions.

Transportation

Despite its successes in traversing the recent wave of global upheaval and competition, Chicago will need to surpass those efforts and accomplishments. Looking to its connections to the world, it will need to redevelop its outward-looking, large-scale infrastructure, especially the airports and surface transportation systems. Innovative mega-projects such as the O'Hare expansion and the rechanneling of the waterways have fashioned Chicago and allowed it to restructure its basic industries into today's global service entities. Unfortunately, it is far more difficult to redevelop and rebuild infrastructure after settlement has taken place. Less tractable problems of governance, displacement, and agreement have replaced the technical problems of earlier eras such as engineering, finance, and design.

With regard to long-haul, overland transportation, Chicago's rich legacy and good fortune now invite its policy makers to act on the opportunities. While Chicago finds itself, at midcontinent, located away from the coastal cities where overseas commerce is naturally active, the new intermodal transportation technology has brought east-west transcontinental commerce through the city, by way of containerized truck-rail shipment. And the coming of NAFTA has opened up directions of trade that are conveniently north-south rather than east-west.

Unfortunately, Chicago's very legacy as the major rail-lines hub means that it is now a chokepoint as well as a crossroads. Competition will find and choose ways to bypass the region unless the city's problems of aging rail yards and truck terminals are solved.

Communications

Curiously enough, Chicago's long-established railroad right-of-way system is playing a part in the building of the infrastructure of the new economic age. Thanks in part to the land easements created by yesteryear's railroads, Chicago finds itself with a promising communications backbone for industries supported by high-volume data transmission, and also with a high concentration of telecommunications equipment producers. Chicago is a global telecommunications center, perhaps even the world's largest Internet exchange point. However, it will need more than the simple strategy of "build it and they will come" if Chicago is to find itself with the companies and professionals to occupy this communications infrastructure for the future. We will need to create new businesses that will "light up," or activate, the partly inactive telecommunications infrastructure that now serves the metropolitan economy, adding value and job growth here at the crossroads of the network.

High Tech

Chicago's great research promise in biotechnology and nanotechnology must not be allowed to die on the vine. The entrepreneurial drive of Chicagoans across all business sectors must be encouraged through complementary private-public partnerships and initiatives, while regulation is thoughtfully crafted to avoid strangulation.

Governance

A vibrant and growing economy is the single most necessary condition for individual growth and well-being, but well-crafted public policy and governance is also necessary. Chicago will need to push forward on the basics of urban living, including schools, safety, environment, amenities, and transportation, if it is to keep up with the rising standards of other great cities of the world. A great feature of the city has always been its active and civic-minded citizens and business community. However, the ability of these policy leaders to act concertedly and cohesively is now challenged by the sometimes narrow focus of local government policy, and by the ongoing dispersal of organizations and business headquarters across the broadening landscape of metropolitan Chicago.

Whereas once the lion's share of large corporate headquarters could be found in the central business district, or at least within the 588-square-kilometer area of the city of Chicago, the primary metropolitan region now covers twenty times this area; over 60 percent of the region's large corporate headquarters are now located in suburban Chicago. While suburbanization has helped the Chicago economy to prosper, this same spatial deconcentration requires greater efforts to effectively govern. What is needed for the greater good of the whole region is renewed regionwide cooperation and thinking. It is this need that gave birth to the ambitious efforts of Chicago Metropolis 2020, which has recently begun to fashion more effective regionwide policies and planning for transportation and land use.

Chicago's People

Looking broadly at the foundations of Chicago's economic success, the key elements are the same as those of global cities everywhere: a high density of people who have managed to fashion the governance structures, mutual understanding and trust, and physical infrastructure that allow them to work together in a highly productive fashion, with abundant access to opportunity.

Fifty years ago, a handful of people meeting with the mayor of the City of Chicago made decisions for the region. Today that group of decision makers has expanded considerably. Large-scale projects ranging from Millennium Park to the Central Area Plan for the Loop have been launched by the mayor's office but given life by civic leaders and their organizations. Business and community leaders serve on the boards of the region's cultural, educational, and social institutions. And civic and community organizations composed of many individuals of diverse backgrounds now help shape the policy agenda for the city. Empowered citizens and their organizational leaders have championed school reform, the expansion of O'Hare Airport, neighborhood economic development, the remake of public housing, and the development of an agenda for the region for the twenty-first century.

Despite the talents and efforts of these empowered citizen activists, a bright future for the Midwest's global city is by no means assured. Entrenched bureaucracies are hard to move. Special-interest groups often prevail. Urban problems are deep rooted and persistent, often in need of multiple approaches applied simultaneously before any sign of daylight appears. Chicago will have to work hard to maintain the momentum of the past decade. Global investors look for stability—economic, political, and social. Chicago has it now, but it cannot rest on its laurels.

For this reason, the city is looking outward, looking globally, looking for its performance and standard of living to measure up against worldwide standards, and even to set the standard once again.

CONTRIBUTORS

Stephen Franklin, a reporter for the *Chicago Tribune,* has written about human rights in the Middle East as well as in Central and Latin America. He is a former U.S. Peace Corps volunteer in Turkey and has a master's degree in international politics and development from American University, Washington, D.C.

Ron Grossman is a staff reporter for the *Chicago Tribune,* covering the city's ethnic neighborhoods, among other subjects. Before turning to journalism twenty years ago, he was a professor of history at Lake Forest College, Michigan State University, and the University of Nebraska. His 1982 map of ethnic groups in Chicago was widely adopted by universities and government agencies and remains the definitive survey of the city's neighborhoods.

Magda Krance is manager of media relations for Lyric Opera of Chicago and has been with the company since 1992. As a freelance journalist, she has covered many aspects of Chicago's cultural life for more than two decades and has developed an extensive network of contacts within the cultural community. She has lived in Chicago's Uptown neighborhood since 1977; as a child, she made frequent trips from Oshkosh, Wisconsin, with her parents to visit the city's cultural attractions.

Richard C. Longworth is executive director of the Global Chicago Center of the Chicago Council on Foreign Relations. He was senior correspondent for the *Chicago Tribune,* specializing in economic and international news. Longworth is a veteran foreign correspondent, a former business editor and columnist, and an adjunct professor of international relations at Northwestern University. He is the author of *Global Squeeze,* one of the first books on globalization for a general audience, and of "Global Chicago," the MacArthur Foundation report that led to the founding of Global Chicago.

Charles Madigan is coauthor of *Dangerous Company: Management Consultants and the Companies They Save and Ruin.* He collaborated with Arthur Martinez on *The Hard Road to the Softer Side of Sears* and Jerry Greenwald on *Lessons from the Heart of American Business.* He edited the Economic Club of Chicago's *History's Witnesses.* A veteran national and foreign correspondent, he is Perspective editor and senior correspondent at the *Chicago Tribune.* Madigan is currently writing a history of his family's sixty years in the coal fields of Pennsylvania.

Michael H. Moskow has been president and chief executive officer of the Federal Reserve Bank of Chicago since 1994. He has fourteen years' experience in senior management positions at three Chicago corporations and has been confirmed by the Senate for five U.S. government positions, including Deputy U.S. Trade Representative with the rank of ambassador from 1991 to 1993. He has also been active in academia, having taught at Northwestern University most recently. Moskow chairs the National Bureau of Economic Research and the Economic Club of Chicago and serves on the board of the Chicago Council on Foreign Relations.

Saskia Sassen is the Ralph Lewis Professor of Sociology at the University of Chicago and the Centennial Visiting Professor at the London School of Economics. Her forthcoming book *Denationalization: Territory, Authority, and Rights in a Global Digital Age* is based on her five-year project on governance and accountability in a global economy. Her most recent books are *Guests and Aliens* and her edited collection *Global Networks, Linked Cities.* Her volume *The Global City* came out in a new, fully updated edition in 2001. Her books have been translated into twelve languages. She is a member of the National Academy of Sciences Panel on Urban Data Sets and chair of the newly formed Information Technology, International Cooperation, and Global Security Committee of the Social Science Research Council.

Cindy Schreuder is a former reporter for the *Chicago Tribune.* She has written about science, medicine, the environment, and education for a variety of publications for twenty years.

Adele Simmons is vice chair and senior executive of Chicago Metropolis 2020. She is a founder of the Global Chicago Center, president of the Global Philanthropy Partnership, and a senior adviser to the World Economic Forum. From 1989 to 1999 she served as president of the John D. and Catherine T. MacArthur Foundation, which works in Chicago and more than sixty countries. She serves on a number of boards including the those of the Field Museum, the Mexican Fine Arts Center Museum, and the Chicago Council on Foreign Relations.

William A. Testa is vice president and director of regional programs in the Research Department at the Federal Reserve Bank of Chicago. He has written widely in the areas of economic development policy, the structure and growth of regional economies, and state-local public finance. He chairs the Illinois Council on Economic Education and serves as adviser to various midwestern initiatives and organizations.

INDEX

The University of Illinois Press
is a founding member of the
Association of American University Presses.

Composed in 10.5/13 Adobe Minion
with Minion display
by Jim Proefrock
at the University of Illinois Press
Designed by Paula Newcomb
Manufactured by Thomson-Shore, Inc.

University of Illinois Press
1325 South Oak Street
Champaign, IL 61820-6903
www.press.uillinois.edu